14,125

629.13 Titler, Dale M.
T 619w
　　　　Wings of
　　　　　adventure

DATE			
3-16-73			
NOV 27			
OCT 10			
MAR 28 79			
MAY 5			

14,125

**LEWIS CENTRAL
HIGH SCHOOL LIBRARY**

© THE BAKER & TAYLOR CO.

WINGS OF ADVENTURE

Also by Dale M. Titler

WINGS OF MYSTERY

THE DAY THE RED BARON DIED

WINGS OF ADVENTURE

By Dale M. Titler

ILLUSTRATED WITH PHOTOGRAPHS AND MAPS

DODD, MEAD & COMPANY

NEW YORK

Copyright © 1972 by Dale M. Titler

All rights reserved

No part of this book may be reproduced in any form without permission in writing from the publisher

ISBN: 0-396-06469-8
Library of Congress Catalog Card Number: 78-175309

Printed in the United States of America
by The Cornwall Press, Inc., Cornwall, N. Y.

This book is for Dale M. Titler, Jr.
  A fine young man with wings in his future.
    ... Adventure will take care of itself.

Acknowledgments

When I wrote my first aviation book several years ago, I learned that no writer can accomplish the task alone, and I said so. Since that time I've put two more nonfiction books behind me, each of which has strengthened my conviction as to the culmination of every sustained writing effort. It depends on the generosity of strangers who are sufficiently interested to offer their help and encouragement. For this, I am most grateful.

Writers meet many interesting people in their research. Here are those persons and organizations who helped me put *Wings of Adventure* together.

In writing the accounts of Jimmie Angel's South American flying adventures, I am indebted to Mrs. James Crawford Angel, Sr., who personally related the details of his quest for the gold atop fearsome Auyántepuí.

For much of the material that went into the "Greater Rockford" account, a special note of thanks is due Colonel Bert R. J. Hassell, USAF (Retired), and his resourceful daughter, Mary Hassell Lyons, who patiently worked with me to assure an accurate recording of the flight and the return of the long-distance flyer. Recognition is also given to His

Excellency, A. C. Normann, Minister for Greenland Affairs; Count Egil von Rosen, Scandinavian Airlines System Public Relations Director; V. Lauritsen, President, Greenlandaire; Colonel Willie Knudsen, USAF (Retired); Major Hans Halken, Danish Liaison Officer; Mr. Axel Olson and Mr. E. Bolvinkel. A valued friend who helped me put final touches to the book is also deserving of special recognition: Robert E. Carlin, an aviation illustrator and historian, was helpful in rounding out the chapters on the Hassell-Cramer flight and Jimmie Angel's search for the riches of Auyántepuí.

In telling the story of "The Man on Devils Tower" I am most grateful to George C. Hopkins and his long-time friend Earl Brockelsby, as well as to Mrs. Reta M. Maierhauser, Clyde W. Ice, Philip Potter of the Baltimore *Sun* and Elvin T. Aaberg, Acting Superintendent of Devils Tower National Monument.

Generous assistance was given to me for the "Mad Trapper" episode by Inspector W. R. Pilkey, Liaison Officer, Royal Canadian Mounted Police, Ottawa. Three of the men actually involved in the chase were also most helpful with their personal accounts of the grueling case: Inspector Alfred W. King, RCMP (Retired); Major Robert Francis Riddell, Royal Canadian Signals (Retired); and Major Earl Franklin Hersey, Royal Canadian Signals (Retired). Recognition is also given the Ryerson Press, Toronto, and the Toronto Star Syndicate for permission to quote from an article which appeared in the Toronto *Star* of November 3, 1937, on the rescue and mercy flights of W. R. May; reprinted with the permission of the Toronto *Daily Star*.

I was fortunate in obtaining the personal assistance of those two intrepid pioneer airmen who established the official endurance record of 1937: Algene Key and his brother Fred. I am also grateful to one of the men foremost in the ground crew who kept the *Ole Miss* flying, A. D. Hunter. Journalist-photographer A. G. Weems and Gene Brady of the Memphis *Commercial-Appeal* also gave me a helping hand.

In presenting the England to Australia flight of Parer and McIntosh I was assisted most ably by Mrs. Mary W. (Parer) Shiel of Brisbane and Mr. H. F. Hollier of the Australian News and Information Bureau, Canberra, A.C.T.

Those who helped me to clarify the details of Lieutenant Pat O'Brien's remarkable escape from wartime Germany include: Mr. Jack O'Brien of Alhambra, California; Mr. Jack M. O'Brien of Momence, Illinois; Mrs. G. A. Lascelles of Toronto; Mr. Emerson A. L. F. Smith, Victoria, British Columbia; Mr. N. G. Hoskins, Air Historical Branch, Ministry of Defence, London; Mrs. Sue Blake; Mrs. Mary Jane Goude of the Kankakee *Daily Journal;* and Harper and Row, publisher of *Outwitting the Hun* by Pat O'Brien.

My thanks go to Lieutenant Colonel Ira N. Sussky, USAF (Retired), for his exacting help with information on the phenomenal Burma rescue of Lieutenant Melvin Kimball. Group Captain Thomas P. McGarry, R.A.F., has my sincere appreciation for his personal account which appears in "Two Miles Down." In recording the story of "The Girl Who Rode the Buzz Bomb" I am especially grateful to Fraulein Hanna Reitsch for taking the time from a busy schedule to clarify the account. Chester P. Klier graciously and painstakingly provided the vivid details that recorded the thoughts and actions of a combat aircrewman in a Marauder squadron of World War Two. In helping me collect data for "War Flying for the Films" I am grateful to Ivan Unger, a contemporary of the famed Black Cats, and to Jimmy Barton, Sr., a flying companion of the late Dick Grace in the film *Wings,* for the use of his photograph collection. Also, for giving me a candid insight to the thrills and excitement of the great days of Hollywood stunt flying, I am indebted to my close friend

O. C. LeBoutillier, a former motion picture pilot and World War One fighter ace.

Although he admits to being a "one-foot-on-the-ground sort of bloke," my long-time Australian friend, Frank Baker, has been a source of information and encouragement to me on several of my aviation books. He came through once again —this time on the story of the Parer-McIntosh flight—for which I am most grateful.

I wish to thank my friend Grady Byrd for lending his artistic talents in drawing the maps for this book. My thanks to Hans Herlin, author of *Udet—A Man's Life,* for the use of an excerpt which appeared in the chapter "A Flier's Life—A Pilot's Luck," and also to Stephen St. Martin, who allowed me the use of his library of rare aviation volumes. Recognition is due G. P. Putnam's Sons for data contained in *Flying the Arctic* by George H. Wilkins. Others who made valued contributions to the book were: Colonel Roger C. Pryor, USAF (Retired); Robert E. Hare; Loretta Jean Gragg, Headquarters Secretary of the Ninety-Nines, Incorporated; and the editorial staff of the Sydney *Morning Herald.*

Preface

This book is about fliers who deliberately sought out challenges to their daring, skill, and imagination. Although none was contemptuous of death, and each took precautions against it, they considered the gamble well worth the risks involved.

These are accounts of man's venture into the unfamiliar, his challenge to the elements, and his personal battle with Fate, which in most cases he wins. The word for these stirring achievements is one we all know—adventure.

What drives men and women to seek flying adventures? Is it a desire for wealth? For fame? Recognition? A love of country? Perhaps for some, but long ago my own reflections, as I skimmed the cloudtops and looked far below, convinced me that the motives of great fliers spring first from a love of flight and adventure that outweighs all else. Flying is more than a profession or livelihood; it is a way of making life worth living.

There is something wonderful about the sensation of flight. As a young man of twenty, when flying was far more hazardous than it is now, Charles Lindbergh decided if he could fly for ten years before being killed in a crash, he would willingly trade an ordinary lifetime for those air experiences.

Such individuals were—and are—not ordinary fliers. Ordinary fliers do not tumble from a light plane wearing a single parachute and aim deliberately for a rocky platform raised a thousand feet in the sky. Who, but an extraordinary aviatrix, would dare to test-fly a guided missile? These are people eager to put their lives on the line, to explore unmapped deserts, frigid polar regions, and steaming jungles, and, in so doing, to cross new horizons in human achievement. The ordinary person hesitates, even withdraws, in the face of seemingly unsurmountable barriers to freedom and discovery. The unusual person does not. He becomes a different sort of pilot, and it is in this difference that achievement is savored.

Centuries ago the crude hull opened the seaways to travel; later the wheel revolutionized land travel. Within this century—within the past three generations—our mechanical wings have mastered the envelope of air around our planet. Now man looks for conquests beyond his tracks on the moon, in far distant space.

Recently Colonel Bert Hassell, the pilot of the *Greater Rockford* on its 1928 great circle flight that came to an untimely end on the Greenland ice cap, received warm letters from President Richard M. Nixon and astronaut Neil Armstrong. The occasion was Armstrong's acceptance of the Bert Hassell Award on behalf of the Apollo XI crew which had followed closely the old plane's return to Rockford after forty years in the frozen wilderness. The venerable airman reflected: "What an example of the progress of flight—when a man who holds Aeronautical License Number 20 can live in the same era as the first man to walk on the moon."

Man's curiosity stirs him to venture from the doorway he knows to the doorway unfamiliar. Then onward—across the threshold. The basic ingredient in every true adventurer is the desire to go, or be, somewhere else, and once there, to expose himself to the test of whatever awaits. Once begun, the bold undertakings which follow hang upon unforeseen events.

Wings of Adventure, then, reflects those characteristics of flying man that compel him to pit himself against the elements, the sky, the unexplored, and fear itself. Through personality, action, and the result of struggle, the central figure of each account in this book has defined adventure in an individual way. Across continents, to the high places of earth, over the jungles, against strange peoples, in bitter cold or sweltering heat, against forces and elements apparently created to crush them all. Adventure is a human need, present to some extent in all of us. It is fulfillment, the experience of a freedom never before known and therefore never to be lost. It is the mixture of the personality, and the place, and the challenge.

Because the human instinct is rooted in earth-bound existence, a flying man must summon resources of heart and mind. There is nothing inherent in the airman's physical being that has prepared him for mechanical flight. As I reflect again on my early flying experiences I am awed more by the expanse of man's intellectual and spiritual resources than by his accomplishments with the airplane. Adventure of any kind is a quality of the human spirit, and I am convinced that it is our human spirit that will lead the way as man reaches toward the stars.

DALE M. TITLER

Contents

Preface   xi

Part One: Exploration

1. "No Foxes Seen"   *3*
2. Down on the Greenland Ice Cap   *32*
3. Auyántepuí—and the Bush Pilot of Angel Falls   *54*
4. Hell's Airport—and the Lure of Lassetter's Reef   *71*

Part Two: World War I and II

5. O'Brien Outwits the Huns   *99*
6. A Hero's Life—A Flier's Luck   *129*
7. Burma Rescue   *163*
8. Two Miles Down   *178*
9. The Girl Who Rode the Buzz Bomb   *191*
10. Sixty-six Sorties in a Marauder   *213*

Part Three: Danger and Endurance

11. England to Australia—the Hard Way   *239*
12. "Get the Mad Trapper!"   *262*
13. War Flying for the Films   *292*
14. Four Weeks in the Air   *314*
15. The Man on Devils Tower   *336*

Index   359

Illustrations

Following page 142

The *Greater Rockford* in 1928
Helicopter lifting the bundled *Greater Rockford*
Marie Angel and her husband, James Crawford Angel
Lieutenant Pat O'Brien
Ernst Udet
Lieutenant Sussky, Lieutenant Kimball and Captain Colwell
Hanna Reitsch at a glider demonstration meet
Bursts of flak around a Martin B-26
A 20mm cannon shell hit the B-26
The DeHavilland 9, "P.D."
Scene of Albert Johnson's last stand
Death photo of Albert Johnson
Fred Key on catwalk of the Wright J-6-5

M A P S

Wilkins-Eielson Expedition   16–17
Lassetter's Reef   85
Parer-McIntosh Flight   248–249

Part One

Exploration

1

"No Foxes Seen"

THE American, a broad-shouldered Midwesterner with piercing gray eyes, loved the Far North and its colorful people. At thirty-one, he had the sober, determined look of an older man. Carl Ben Eielson was destined to become one of the best remembered of Arctic fliers.

The Australian, a scientist and explorer, was at home in the frigid North. At forty, George Hubert Wilkins had years of Arctic adventuring behind him.

Together, they blazed the first flight from Alaska to Europe across the Arctic.

Eielson was of Norwegian descent, and, despite his outdoor boyhood, he was unusually serious. He also had a restless spirit. In 1914 he entered the University of North Dakota and gained a reputation for logical thinking. He transferred to the University of Wisconsin to study law, unable to settle down for long.

The U. S. Air Service had thirty-five pilots in 1917 when Eielson enlisted. He knew at last he'd found his element—the sky and wind. He earned his wings, was commissioned a second lieutenant, but while under orders for France, the Armistice was signed. Back in his hometown of Hatton he talked several businessmen into buying a surplus Jenny. He flew the plane to college and barnstormed the Midwest during summer vacations. In 1920 he advertised: *"Time Flies; When Will You? . . . We Are Approaching an Aerial Age!"* It was a great life; he was at peace with the world.

Eielson's father heatedly opposed Ben's flying. Convinced his son would be killed, Ole Eielson threatened to burn the Jenny. But Fate was first. In a takeoff from a short Minnesota cow pasture, the wheels snagged a telephone line and over went the plane, smashed beyond repair. Eielson walked away unhurt and remarked, "Well . . . back to school." At Georgetown University in Washington, D.C., he met Dan Sutherland of the Alaska delegation, who told him of a teaching job in Fairbanks. The appeal of the North was strong in Ben's Norse blood and Ole Eielson encouraged his son to go to the still untamed land. To the rest of the family he winked broadly. "No planes in Alaska," he said.

So, ostensibly, Eielson arrived in Fairbanks in 1922 to teach school and put his gypsy air-adventuring behind him forever. He checked into the Alaska Hotel, where Mrs. Foster, the proprietor, approved of the polite, intellectual newcomer and gave him a modest room. In a few weeks he was teaching mathematics and general science, and coaching basketball. His friends found their soft-spoken pedagogue not at all bookish, although he read a lot. He was a fastidious dresser, attended dances, and enjoyed life. At parties people crowded around the tall figure and in the streets youngsters sometimes followed him like a pack of hounds.

Mrs. Foster remembered the occasional noisy parties Ben gave in his room. In later years, she reminisced over a worn box of snapshots. There was Ben in fur parka and helmet, leaning against an open-cockpit Jenny. Another showed the "flying professor" in a business suit, solemnly accepting a gold watch from the mayor.

Like a ghost, Ben Eielson's restlessness returned. He couldn't settle down in his new job. Often the day's lessons were forgotten as he talked for hours about airplanes. Wide-eyed youngsters listened to the science of flight, the challenge of the elements, and what aviation could mean to the people of a vast and virtually trackless Alaska. Ever a visionary, he told them how Alaska lay squarely on a Great Circle route. It connected the States with the Orient, and goods and mail would one day cross the Far North in transport planes—in hours instead of the weeks required by mid-Pacific boats. His students listened—and believed him. He wanted an airplane, and if the town would buy him one, he would show them how quickly the era could begin.

Fairbanks residents heard him out and wondered about this man's odd ambitions. Some said he was crazy, others said his ideas for flying in Alaska were simply impractical. Many agreed Eielson hardly fit the image of the rough, tough, dashing flier of that day. But despite his scholarly reputation, some saw in Eielson's eyes the look of a man of action and he hounded local merchants until he won his point. The following summer a crated Jenny with an OX-5 engine waited at the train depot. Eielson and a few mechanics assembled it and the local ball park became Fairbanks first airport.

On July 3, 1923, with banker Dick Wood, Eielson took off on Alaska's first commercial flight. Their destination was Nenana, a settlement only fifty miles from Fairbanks on the railroad line. It was an easy course—he had only to follow the track—but he decided to take a short cut, left the railroad and couldn't find it again. Below, wooded hills drifted past with dreary monotony. He headed toward a wisp of smoke—it was only an Indian village. Eielson circled, zigzagged, and backtracked until finally he recovered his bearings, found Nenana, and set the long-overdue Jenny down on the local ball park.

The Nenana flight nevertheless proved profitable. The

next day Eielson flew passengers and performed spectacular airshows with loops, rolls, and spins. The natives loved it and paid well for the exciting demonstration rides. When Eielson and Wood returned to Fairbanks the plane was more than half paid for.

The airplane gave the citizens of Fairbanks something else to puzzle over, for it caused an odd part of Eielson's nature to surface. Despite his outward calm, he was high-strung. He admitted to restless nights before each important flight. He was a sleepwalker. Once a friend found him struggling with the end of his bed. "I'm trying to set the tail," he shouted, "but the darned wind keeps shifting!" Sometimes he wandered through the streets and awoke pounding the side of his plane. When he tried to leap from the hotel window and resisted rescuers so furiously that he had to be knocked unconscious, Mrs. Foster moved him to a ground room. "It didn't keep us from worrying," she said, "and always before a big flight the boys watched him closely."

Paradoxically, and despite the fact that Ben Eielson—more than anyone—was the undisputed founder of aviation in the Far North, his beginnings as a pilot were anything but impressive. Close friends who flew with him were agreed on Ben's flying skill. He was not a "natural-born" airman. Although adept at aerobatics, he had to work at ordinary flying, and his landings and takeoffs were erratic. On cross-country flights, even short ones, his sense of direction was poor.

The Flying Professor gave an airshow when President Warren G. Harding visited Fairbanks, and he carried passengers and light freight on cross-country trips. He felt ready for bigger things. Wrong Font Thompson, editor of the Fairbanks *News-Miner,* knew what Eielson was trying to promote and late in November 1923 happily printed the historic headline: MAIL SERVICE FOR KUSKOKWIM THROUGH AIR. Eielson had won a contract with the Post Office Department for ten twice-monthly mail flights to McGrath, three hundred miles distant. He would use a Liberty-powered DeHavilland DH-9 and receive two dollars a mile—less than half the rate by dog sled. It was an adventure into the untried, but Eielson was jubilant and anxious to begin. "It's progress," he said. "Real progress!"

Until now, no winter flights had been made in Alaska. No one knew how an aircraft's engine would operate in the sub-zero Arctic midnight or whether a plane could survive icing hazards en route. This man who had lost his way on several short summer flights must now navigate alone over hundreds of miles of white wilderness, his only landmarks an occasional roadhouse or Indian camp scattered over the craggy frozen expanse. In clear weather he could follow the dog trail, but a blizzard or a forced landing could mean death even though he might land safely. Weeks would pass before ground parties could find him—if at all.

When the crated DH-9 arrived, Fairbanksians helped assemble it. A carpenter shaped a pair of ungainly, 300-pound flat-bottom hickory skis. Machinists argued over the Liberty engine until it was installed. Finally, on the bitter-crisp morning of February 21, 1924, the plane stood on the ball park loaded with five hundred pounds of mail for McGrath. Heavily bundled in furs, Eielson wedged himself into the cockpit and, with a wave, took off southwest, streaming a powdery fog of snow. He reached McGrath without incident, but a celebration in his honor delayed the immediate return he had planned. It was two thirty in the afternoon before his plane, refueled and loaded with Fairbanks-bound mail, got airborne.

The Arctic winter daylight was short so Eielson decided to leave the slightly longer dog trail to fly a straighter compass course. An hour and a half later he was completely lost —somewhere north of the Alaska Range. He picked up a winding river but was unable to identify it. The purple dusk blended into blackness and he knew he was skirting dangerously near the mountains. It was too late to land now. He flew blindly on and later recorded in a Post Office Department report:

The country looked flat in the pitch darkness. The sky was entirely overcast; not a star showing. I wandered around completely lost for almost an hour . . . I saw a light so I cut my altitude and went down to it. It must have been a trapper's cabin . . . I was tempted to set the ship down there and have a nice place to sleep but I knew I would wreck it if I did. I went back to the big river and after following it for some time I saw a light in the distance . . . It turned out to be my home field.

The patient home crowd had almost abandoned hope when someone heard the engine. Bonfires blazed and the low-flying DeHavilland droned into their glow. It sliced through the treetops and flipped over. The landing gear crumpled, a ski splintered, and the propeller shattered. Eielson had seriously misjudged on his first night landing, but unhurt, he was dragged from the plane by cheering friends and swept into the hangar, where he was presented with an engraved watch by the mayor.

The DeHavilland was repaired, and between the mail flights Eielson demonstrated the superiority of the airplane over the sled and husky. A bale of wire was carried to the telegraph station at Takotna. Newspapers hot from the press were dropped by small parachutes to roadhouses and camps. At McGrath the Indians took Eielson into their tribe with the title "Moose Ptarmigan Ben." He had—at last—a sense of accomplishment, of fulfillment.

But there were difficulties. Fog and snowstorms harassed him and the spring thaw added to his problems. As he landed on the river at McGrath, his skis were sheared off when the DH-9 broke through the shell ice. Ben changed to wheels and made future landings on the gravel bar. His Fairbanks base gave similar trouble. The ball park, fourteen hundred feet long with a woodpile and tree stumps at one end, was a poor field in the best of weather. Now it was a spongy bog. The DeHavilland flared out at sixty miles an hour, much faster than the Jenny, and in three out of eight landings, Eielson nosed over. On one of these he brought a sick passenger, Hosie Hummell, to the Fairbanks hospital. After the plane settled on its back, Ben slipped out to assist Hummell. He reached into the cockpit, released the passenger's safety belt, and the big Swede dropped on his head with a crunch.

"Yeezus yimminy, Ben!" he groaned. "You always land this way?"

Eielson shrugged and grinned sheepishly, "Not always, Hosie."

The last crackup demolished the plane. Its wheel sank into the mud on landing, it swerved sideways, wiped off the gear, propeller, and rudder, and damaged two wing panels. The local mechanics shook their heads; this time they needed new parts.

The Post Office Department refused to supply the items and ended the airmail venture. Eielson went to Washington for another mail contract but failed. He tried to arouse interest in a Polar exploration flight over the Arctic. The Army's 1924 globe-girdling flight didn't help his restless spirit. To Army Air Chiefs he proposed an air service from the States to China, by way of Alaska. No encouragement. Next he argued for military aircraft for Alaska. Another rebuff. He got all the way to Billy Mitchell but nothing materialized. Although he was now a full-time lobbyist, buttonholing congressmen to urge them to open Alaska to aviation, the year 1925 was worse. Again he bid for an Alaska air route, and lost to the dog teams. Ole Eielson, aware of his son's despondency, pleaded, "Go back to school, Ben."

He didn't. He worked as a bond salesman with his brother Oliver, and he was miserable.

In 1925 Hubert Wilkins arrived in Detroit, and with all the hoopla of an old-time political campaign he toured the city and made speeches. He appealed for funds to finance flights that would determine whether another land mass lay near the North Pole. The Detroit Aviation Society, the American Geographic Society, and the North American Newspaper Alliance backed him, along with eighty thousand contributors, many of whom were school children who gave their nickels and pennies. Wilkins bought two Fokkers and shipped them to Fairbanks.

Before he left Detroit, the explorer had a pilot in mind. His old comrade Vilhjalmur Stefansson, whom Wilkins had accompanied on a 1913 Arctic trip, knew the Australian was looking for a pilot. Stefansson suggested a man who was known to a tribe of Yukon Indians as "Brother-to-the-Eagle."

A despondent Eielson, sitting morosely in a barbershop in Langdon, North Dakota, was called to the telephone. His anxious father said Stefansson had wired to ask if he would fly for Wilkins' Arctic expedition. Blaze a new air trail over the boundless Northland? Eielson signed on without hesitation.

The two adventurers were friends immediately. Eielson was to fly and Wilkins, although a pilot, would handle all air navigation. Eielson recognized Wilkins as a capable and determined man with great knowledge of the raw Arctic. The Australian had distinguished himself in France as a combat photographer. As a contender in the 1919 London-to-Australia air race, engine trouble had forced him down on Crete. Soon afterward he tried—unsuccessfully—to obtain a dirigible for a flight across the great unknown Arctic Ocean. In 1921

Wilkins accompanied Sir Ernest Shackleton's last Antarctic expedition and now, at thirty-seven, he had trudged five thousand miles over the rough-hewn ice terrain of both polar continents. It convinced him that his future explorations would be by air. Tens of thousands of square miles of the Arctic ice ocean had been unseen by human eyes; no living man could say land did not lie where professional cartographers wrote "unexplored" across mysterious stretches. To Wilkins the challenge was near-maddening; he would not rest until he had transferred this region from the realm of conjecture to that of geographic fact. Short flights would come first—then the great one.

The most pretentious air expedition to visit the North assembled at Fairbanks in the spring of 1926. One Fokker was a Wright-powered trimotor, the *Detroiter*. The other, the *Alaskan*, was a single-engine, Liberty-powered monoplane with dual controls. With Eielson and Wilkins came other expedition pilots, among them Major Lanphier of the Army's First Pursuit Squadron, technicians, and newsmen. Fairbanks natives stared and shook their heads. They remembered Ben's flying luck on short trips with slower planes. But if Eielson looked forward with misgivings, he gave no sign.

At Point Barrow they would establish their jump-off point. No flight had ever been made there from Fairbanks. No telegraph connected these points; there were no maps. The air route lay over the least-known part of Alaska, across the jaggedest range of mountains on the continent, the unmapped Endicotts. Beyond them was a seemingly endless stretch of Arctic prairie that few men had seen.

The expedition got off badly. As Lanphier taxied the *Detroiter* for its first flight, disaster struck. Among the mechanics and onlookers standing nearby was correspondent Palmer Hutchinson. The men stepped forward and stamped down the snow in front of the trimotor's wheels to get it rolling.

The outboard propellers were directly in front of the wheels; to clear the snow there was a dangerous job. Wilkins told what happened.

> Hutchinson was one of the first to reach us . . . He carefully stamped down the snow. The sign "all clear" was given, and Lanphier thrust the throttles open. The machine had scarcely begun to move when we heard a dull, heartsickening thud. Lanphier, sensing trouble, throttled the engines down and shut them off. I looked over the side and saw Hutchinson lying beneath the propeller. In the excitement of the moment, when the machine began to move, he had stepped right into the propeller instead of away from it. He was killed instantly.

The next day Eielson test-flew the *Alaskan*. He misjudged his approach, stalled, crashed into a fence, broke the landing gear and bent the propeller. A short while later Lanphier took the *Detroiter* off. He too misjudged his glide, stalled and smashed it with even greater damage. The *Alaskan* was fitted with an old wooden club propeller until a new metal one could be shipped from the States.

In late March, Eielson and Wilkins left on the first flight to Point Barrow with a load of fuel and supplies for stockpiling. Fifty miles from Fairbanks they encountered fog and blustery weather. Near the Endicotts the fog cleared, giving them a view of the ground. It was fortunate, for they discovered the peaks shown at five thousand feet on their map were nearer ten thousand. With their load, they could not climb higher than nine thousand, but they could see between the peaks, and, carefully threading their way, they passed to the broad white plain beyond. Now their map was blank—and ahead lay soft, floating cloud masses with hazy-topped edges that obscured the horizon. The sunlit-topped clouds blended into the sky and covered the land below.

"It was a weird and uncanny sight," Wilkins said. "We seemed to be the only speck in a boundless world."

Surrounded by the unbroken monotonous gray mass, they

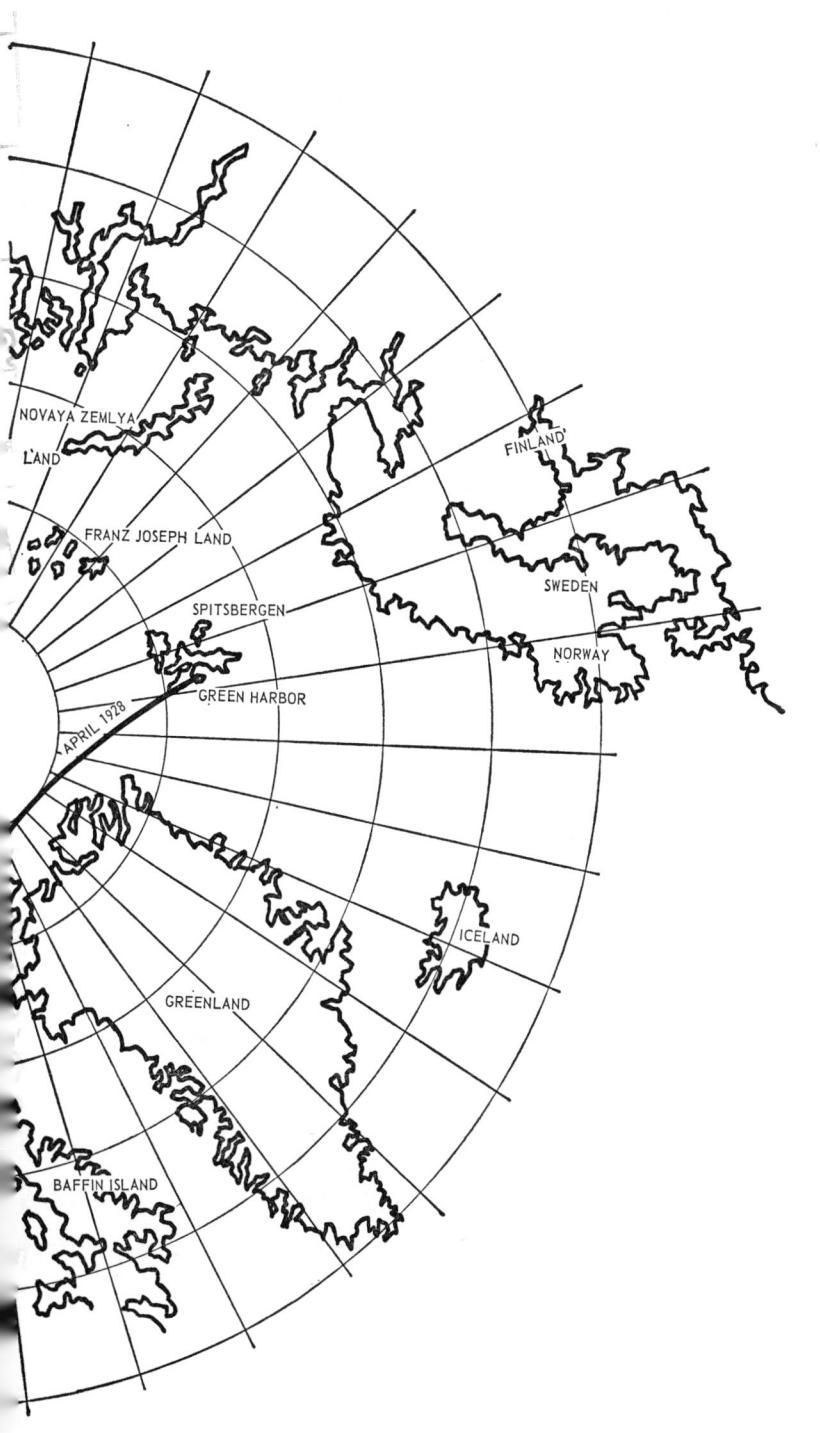

bent over the fuselage fuel tanks and, watching the compass, touched Eielson on the right or left arm to keep him on course. Then, at two minutes past nine:

> ... the engine cut out suddenly, as if the switch had been snapped. There was no splutter or gasp because of starved carburetor, but a sudden silence, except for the hum of the wires. We could feel the sag of the falling plane. With great coolness and skill Eielson steadied the machine, righting her to an even keel and an easy glide. His eyes were glued to the turn and bank indicator. My hands were ready to guide and keep the compass course. As we came within a few hundred feet of the ground the horizon neared and we could dimly see it serrated with ice ridges.
>
> Near the ground the air was rough. The plane swerved and pitched, but Eielson—still calm and cool—corrected each unsteady move. In a moment we were in the snowdrift. We could not see beyond the windows. I felt Eielson brace himself against the empty gas tank; I leaned with my back against the partition wall of the cabin and waited. The left wing and the skis struck simultaneously. We bounced and alighted as smartly as if on the best prepared landing field. I gripped Eielson's shoulder and slipped through the door of the machine to the ice. Wind and driving snow filled my eyes. Dimly I saw pressure ridges as high as the machine. We had, undoubtedly, struck one as we came down. Along the extreme edge of the lower wing the fabric was torn. The machine still rested on the skis, but they had turned on their sides, stanchions twisted and broken.
>
> It was too dark to see well and the snowdrift too thick for close examination of our machine or position. We climbed back into the cabin ...
>
> The intense strain of the past two hours over the Arctic through the blizzard after sunset had left us weak and tired. Eielson stretched out in a sleeping bag on top of the empty gas tank and I huddled in a corner of the cabin and we slept.

In the morning they discovered their luck in coming down on an ice island. Their blind landing set them on a smooth stretch of less than thirty by fifteen yards with high ice ridges on every side. Wilkins estimated they were less than seventy miles northwest of Barrow, but drifting almost due east at six miles an hour. The gale raged for the next five days as they huddled inside the plane.

The floe steadily drove along the coast until they were a hundred miles northeast of Barrow. Colder, clear weather came on the sixth morning and the air explorers were quick to prepare a dash for safety. They drained the remaining half gallon of fuel from the tanks and fashioned an oil burner from a gallon can. Two slats of wood from the cabin roof made a wick.

All that night and the next day the wind continued. We selected what we required for walking ashore and made improvised sleds—one from the lower part of the cowling and the other from the tail-ski—to which was attached a section of corrugated duralumin from the cabin wall.

After loading the sleds with concentrated foods they were again forced to await calmer weather. On April 3 they left the plane's shelter and set out across the frozen ice pack.

... we were on the trail by 8:15. A sharp wind blew and nipped our tender-skinned cheeks, chins, and noses. Hard, dry snow was dribbling over the ridges and pack ice and by 1 P.M. it was drifting as high as our waists. Five hours of steady, hard pulling was enough for our first day out, so we stopped and Eielson helped build the first snow house he had seen.

Day after day the fliers struggled across the ice, often sinking into soft drifts, crawling across broken ice ridges on hands and knees. Eielson's work on the engine had frozen four fingers of his right hand. They were blistered and blackened and so painful he was unable to use them. "He must have suffered excruciating pain which he bore heroically without a murmur," Wilkins recorded. Eielson never faltered, but carried supplies under his armpits as they trudged together mile after mile in silence.

Hard physical work, danger, uncertainty, and anxiety had stilled our tongues during the march shoreward. A little ruminating now and then; short discussions as to the accuracy of navigation; solicitous inquiry as to tender parts and condition after strains and falls that brought uncontrollable sharp cries of pain from one or the other as we tumbled or pinched our feet and ankles between the steel-like ice, was the extent of our conversation . . .

On the fourteenth they had to detour around young ice too thin to walk on. "Eielson looked at it with misgiving," Wilkins remembered, "but my heart was glad, for I recognized it as the edge of the shore ice; there would be no more rough ice to cross." Another day's journey proved Wilkins correct. They stumbled up to the fur-trading post at Beechey Point, 180 miles east of Barrow. Word was sent by dog sled and in a few days reserve expedition pilot Alger Graham flew them to Barrow. Wilkins wrote later:

Reaching there, Dr. Newhall confirmed my suspicions. Eielson's finger was in serious condition. It was necessary to amputate two joints from the little finger—and one of the best traveling companions I ever had will carry as long as he lives, a constant reminder of eighteen strenuous days.

The 1926 and 1927 expeditions had been, to Wilkins and some backers, disappointing. He resolved that his 1928—and final—venture would restore their waning faith in the practicality of northern air explorations. It would be a long nonstop flight from Alaska to Spitsbergen. He knew it would be difficult to get more financial aid and decided to fly it alone in a Stinson Detroiter, a proven distance airplane. What he really needed, he knew, was a faster plane, with adequate load-carrying ability for the long haul.

One afternoon, soon after his return to the States, he sat in his room at the St. Francis Hotel in San Francisco, gazing out the window when:

. . . across my distant vision flashed the most efficient-looking monoplane I have ever seen. The machine was broadside to me. I marked its beauty of streamline, angle of incidence, and attack of the wing in level flight. The speed and the angle gave me a first impression the machine was descending from a height, but its constant position above the horizon soon showed it to be flying level. As it turned towards me I realized the full beauty of its design. It apparently offered no head resistance except for the engine, leading edge, and a slim landing gear. It had no flying wires; no controls exposed—nothing but a flying wing. I sensed unmistakably in my own mind the transient glimpse of that machine was the beginning of the road to success.

He finally tracked down the machine at the Oakland Airport. It was a Lockheed Vega powered with the highly dependable 225-horsepower Wright J5 Whirlwind, the same model engine that carried Lindbergh to Paris the year before. The forty-one-foot wing held extra fuel tanks, and the plane was constructed entirely of wood, thus eliminating metal-magnetic interference with a compass. The fuselage was roomy enough for two men—and the plane had a top speed of 136 miles per hour. Wilkins sold the expedition's other planes and ordered a Vega. In the spring of 1928 he and Eielson were again ready to fly from Point Barrow. There was no similarity to the 1926 trans-Arctic flights of Byrd and Amundsen. Byrd, who flew a trimotor Ford from Spitsbergen to the Pole, had paralleled a meridian and changed direction only once— at the Pole. Amundsen and Nobile in the dirigible *Norge,* also followed a straight line, first north, then south, after they crossed the Pole. Eielson and Wilkins, to traverse its vast cross-section, proposed to fly a great circle course across twenty-two hundred miles of the polar sea, across meridians.

This would require more than fifty changes in their heading as they flew over the unmapped stretches. They would bypass the Pole completely to cross the ice ocean north of the Canadian Archipelago and Greenland. And they would fly the course in an untried airplane—with one engine. When the flight was ended, Wilkins hoped to have the answer to two questions. Did land lie there? Was the region suitable for a permanent weather station?

The odds were great. Their compass could not be relied upon across that area of extreme Arctic magnetic declination; solar navigation must be used as well. An extended overcast could mean off-course meandering that would end in a frigid death. They had no forewarning of the weather they would meet in this vast Arctic blind spot. Barrow had no radio station, nor could Spitsbergen radio them weather reports; the Vega carried no receiver. The fliers would transmit however —with a hand-cranked generator transmitter. They left a small receiver with Leon Vincent, a Barrow school teacher. If new land was found en route, its discovery was to be relayed to Dr. Isaiah Bowman, director of the American Geographical Society. Wilkins would transmit the coded message to Vincent: *Black Foxes Seen,* followed with an estimate in hundreds of square miles. The plans were these: they would leave Barrow in silence, unaware of what lay ahead and with barely enough fuel to reach Spitsbergen; they would make the elements work for them where they could, fight them when they had to, and trust to Providence for the rest.

The restless Eielson again walked in his sleep. During the day he sat in a big chair at Charles Brower's whaling station and stared into space or read. In 1944 Brower recalled: "I couldn't tell what he was thinking about . . . he wouldn't talk much. Once I mentioned another pilot's fatal crash. He said when his time came he hoped to go the same way."

Elson Lagoon, 10 A.M., April 15. The engine roared throatily and the steel propeller dissolved into a powerful whirling disc in the northern sunlight. Wilkins climbed aboard, Eielson gave the Wright full throttle, and the brilliant orange monoplane started down the hard-packed runway.

Eielson kept his nerve. I prayed. Sixty, seventy miles an hour. We lifted, swung sickeningly, touched the ice again—then soared smoothly into free air. Never has there been a more fervent prayer of thanksgiving than the one I uttered . . .

Favorable weather was forecast for the start of their journey, and for the first fifty miles the horizons east and north were clear. Below were drifting ice floes. Wilkins could see them slip slowly past the landing wheels. Eielson kept the Vega in a slow, steady climb to three thousand feet. As they passed the first hundred miles, Wilkins looked sharp. Was there land ahead?

Two hundred miles . . . three hundred . . . four. Nothing broke the monotonous ice pack except an occasional lead of open water. Eielson flew steadily on, rechecked his instruments, and faithfully made exacting course corrections according to Wilkins' directions. At 4 P.M., back at Barrow, an anxious Vincent heard this broken message: . . . *one hour . . . nowhere clouds . . . right over the mountains . . . skimming the tops* . . .

At seven hundred miles the clear skies and favorable winds steadily changed. Late in the afternoon the skies darkened threateningly. At 5 P.M. Vincent heard: . . . *KDZ . . . Above the clouds . . . now in latitude 80 . . . O.K. . . . KDZ.*

Soon they were in low clouds and although Eielson descended to find the clear, the next 120 miles passed without seeing the ice-bound surface. At 6 P.M. Vincent picked up: . . . *over . . . Clouds ahead KDZ* . . . Then, another message crackled across the bleak miles at 6:20. *KDZ . . . Clear now, but cold . . . but fog ahead KDZ . . .*

For the next seven hundred miles the view below was brilliantly clear, but still barren of land. Wilkins was pleased that fourteen hundred miles were now added to the mapping of the earth. At 7 P.M.: *. . . KDZ . . . Are O.K. so far. Three hundred miles from Grant Land.* Then, crisply at 9 P.M. came: *KDZ clear. We are O.K. KDZ Wilkins Arctic Expedition. One hundred miles from Grant Land.*

Another hour, and far on the southern horizon jagged peaks rose through towering cloud banks. Grant Land. Wilkins was reassured; they were squarely on course. Their destination lay only eight hundred miles farther. As the Australian tapped out a message at 10 P.M. the weary and faithful Vincent pressed the phones against his ear. The messages were fainter and static-ridden. *KDZ . . . Clear but clouds ahead . . . KDZ . . .*

Droning eastward over the barrens north of Greenland, Eielson saw a heavy storm ahead. Clouds rose to heights greater than the Lockheed's ceiling. Doggedly, he kept the plane climbing to eight thousand feet but the overcast blocked the path to Spitsbergen. The 11 P.M. message was: *KDZ . . . Clouds. Stormy here, but we are not far from coast . . . Can't see it . . . fog . . . storm . . . KDZ.*

After thirteen hours aloft, the men were tiring—and concerned about their fuel consumption. Eielson had been forced to weave about the cloud banks to find better flying weather. Four hours fuel remained—barely enough to reach land. At times they passed fleetingly through sunlit patches that allowed quick sun readings with the sextant. Although the sun at no time dipped below the horizon, there were problems in this difficult form of cross-longitude navigation; the great cloud canyons turned this final part of the flight into pure conjecture.

To keep our course we had to rely on our sense of direction, a study of the tilt of the cloud tops and occasional sights of the sun, rather than any reliance on the compass.

At 1:20 A.M. Vincent heard faintly: *KDZ . . . Wilkins Arctic Expedition . . . Greenland . . . storm . . .* Then, briefly, at 2 A.M. he caught only: *. . . our tanks . . .*

Their gasoline dwindled. The cloud layer was too thick for them to judge their position from the sun. Wilkins believed they were somewhere over northern Spitsbergen, but where? Time was running out and a decision had to be made, and quickly. Wilkins' message at 3:30 A.M. was heard only as a faint, indistinct buzz. The navigator passed a note to Eielson.

There are two courses open. We are above storm now. Down there we can land and wait until it's over. Can we get off again? If we go on we will meet storm at Spitsbergen and perhaps never find the land. Do you wish to land now?

Wilkins watched Eielson's back as the pilot pondered the message. Eielson wriggled in his seat. There was only a few inches of his shoulders visible above the tanks and his head was hidden by the wing. A minute later he passed back the paper.

I'm willing to go on and chance it.

Wilkins smiled. Somehow, he knew Eielson would say that.

The weather worsened and in the extreme cold of forty-eight degrees below zero the engine began to misfire. Several times Eielson had to increase power and climb steeply to warm the powerplant. More precious fuel was consumed. They dropped lower through the clouds, toward the mountainous coast of Spitsbergen.

The air was turbulent above the clouds; beneath them it was boisterous. Our now almost-empty plane was tossed like a cork on a stormy sea. Loose things in the cabin tumbled and rattled . . .

we came down to within a few feet of the ice-strewn water near the coast where the surface wind was furious and the salt spray, whipped from the sea, filled the air . . . A patch of smooth, snow-covered land was passed in an instant's flash and dead ahead loomed a mountain. With an adroit swerve Eielson avoided it by a narrow margin . . . We knew we were running short of gas. We had no choice but to relocate that one smooth patch of white . . .

The windshield before Eielson was almost totally obscured with snow and frozen oil. His vision was restricted to the little he could see through the small open windows and by looking first on one side and then the other.

We hawked this way and that. I passed note after note to Eielson as fast as I could write them . . . we were past the place almost as he saw it so he swung once more out to sea in a narrow circle and, heading into the wind, came low into the teeth of the snow drift. It was a right anxious moment for both of us. It was impossible for Eielson to see but with steady nerve he leveled the ship and lowered her gently until lost in the swirling snow.

We came smoothly to rest. Because of the high wind our ground speed was necessarily slow . . . twenty or thirty miles an hour . . . the machine moved scarcely thirty feet . . . we could see no more than a few feet to each side . . . I flung the engine covers and an empty oil can from the cabin and struggled forward to empty the oil tanks before the oil should freeze.

"Open the tap!" I shouted to Eielson, and held the can under the drain pipe—but nothing happened. Again I shouted, as loudly as possible. But Eielson was temporarily stone deaf as a result of the constant throb of the engine. He could not hear a word and by signs I made him understand, and the oil flowed. The wind continued with hurricane force and high drifts soon formed. We stamped the snow about the skis [to] freeze and prevent the ship from swinging or turning over. Promptly as we could we threw the covers over the engine . . .

We could convey our meaning to each other only by signs at first but, as had been the case last year when we had fallen through a dark, raging blizzard five thousand feet to the pack ice, there was nothing we needed to discuss immediately. Silently we climbed into the cabin and brushed the snow from our clothing. "Thank God the machine's safe," I screamed in Eielson's ear. He nodded solemnly. The hearts and minds of both of us were too full of thankfulness for conversation even if hearing had been easy.

The plane rocked and trembled in the gusty wind. I reached for the remainder of the lunch and we munched dry biscuit, chocolate, and pemmican. There was still in my Thermos bottle enough hot coffee for a swallow each. Ben had a few cigarettes in his pocket and after a smoke we settled down to rest. Neither of us, I think, was physically tired but the strain of the last two hours had told on our nervous systems. Sleep for a while was impossible.

On Spitsbergen, we had to fight [for the landing]. Fight every inch of the way, anxious, uncertain, never quite helpless but ever against tremendous odds. We had, as we sat in the plane, reached a position of safety.

They were not on the mainland of Spitsbergen. After twenty hours and twenty minutes in the air, they had come down on the barren coast of Dead Man's Island. Twenty gallons of gasoline remained—enough for an hour and a half in the air.

The storm marooned them for five days. On the sixth they tramped a runway in the snow and prepared to take off. Wilkins suspected they were not far from their destination at Green Harbor. With a canvas shroud around the engine they warmed it with a firepot. The engine started easily enough, but when Eielson opened the throttle the plane refused to move. Its skis were frozen to the ice. Wilkins jumped down and pushed. The plane broke free and lurched forward. Wilkins leaped for the step but missed it. Eielson, unaware, took off without him. Soon realizing he was alone, he circled, and saw Wilkins standing in the snow. He landed and they tried again. A second time Wilkins missed his footing as he broke the skis free. Again Eielson circled and landed.

An hour's fuel—more than half their remaining supply—had been used in trying to get off together. Wilkins told Eielson if the failed to get aboard on the third try, he was to drop a tent and supplies, then return for him by boat or dog sled. Eielson agreed.

Wilkins tried something different. He took a sturdy length of driftwood from the beach and, with one foot inside the fuselage, pushed the length of wood vigorously against the hard-packed snow, poling the plane along canoe-fashion as Eielson gave the Whirlwind full throttle. It worked. The Lockheed accelerated slowly and Wilkins, confident they would reach flying speed, tumbled sideways into the fuselage and slammed the hatch.

Eielson leveled off at three thousand feet and almost immediately sighted two tall radio towers and a cluster of houses. "Green Harbor," Wilkins scribbled to Eielson. The Vega crossed five miles of open water and landed beside the wireless station. Two Norwegian flags fluttered in the breeze. Five men on skis—personnel of the government radio station—swept down the slope to the plane. Said Wilkins: "There was a look of pleasant astonishment when Eielson, from the cockpit, greeted them in Norwegian..."

"This is Captain Wilkins," Eielson explained. "We've flown from Alaska."

"Impossible!" one man said. "The plane is too small—and besides, you're speaking Norwegian!"

But within the hour a celebration was in full swing as messages were flashed from the far northern station to the astonished world. To Dr. Bowan, Wilkins transmitted *No Foxes Seen*—they had found no new lands across the Arctic Ocean.

Eielson and Wilkins were honored by eight European

rulers. The Leif Ericson Memorial Medal was awarded to Eielson, praised as "the Transpolar Flier of Norwegian Ancestry, for Viking Deed and Daring." In England, Wilkins was knighted by King George V. An ovation followed in New York, and in Eielson's home town there was wild acclaim as their smiling son climbed from the cockpit of his plane on the hayfield in which he had landed his first Jenny. Reporters crowded around. He answered them sparingly. "Twenty and a half hours and two meals . . . that's about all there was to it." He became disturbed when asked to recount his hardships. "Hardships? It's a mockery to compare our flight in a well-warmed cabin airplane with the real hardships other explorers had to endure," he replied brusquely.

In December, Eielson and Wilkins were off again, this time to explore the Far South. They struck out from the South Shetlands a few days before Christmas, covered twelve hundred miles and discovered six previously unknown islands. They were the first men to fly into the Antarctic and the first to sight new land from the air.

Eielson was now among the foremost pilots in America. He was awarded the Distinguished Flying Cross and President Herbert Hoover presented him with the coveted Harmon Trophy in recognition of his 1928 Arctic flight. He changed his plans to accompany Sir Hubert on a second Antarctic expedition and returned to his first interest—Alaskan aviation. His prestige enabled him to get the financial backing to develop northern flying on an international scale. "Mrs. Foster," he told his long-time landlady at the Alaska Hotel, "we're really going to put Fairbanks on the map now!"

November 1929 brought Eielson the chance to show commercial air possibilities to his backers. The *Nanuck,* an American ship, was icebound off North Cape, Siberia, with a million dollars and furs and fifteen passengers. The Swenson Fur Company of Seattle offered Eielson fifty thousand dollars to rescue passengers and cargo. He made one trip to the stranded vessel, the first Alaska–Asian winter flight. On November 9, Eielson and young Earl Borland, a Fairbanks mechanic, readied their big Hamilton monoplane for the second trip. The weather along the Bering Strait was blustery and unsettled. Borland was strangely morose as the time neared. "I have a feeling," he said half in jest to Eielson, "we're not going to come back from this one." Eielson just chuckled. "Earl, we're going to have a real blowout when we get back."

At 11:15 A.M. they bumped off the sea ice at Teller and faded into the threatening snow squalls to the west, Asia-bound. Later that day, no one knows when, they crashed into a slope near the mouth of the Amguyema River, in Siberia, sixty miles from the ice-locked *Nanuck*. Air search parties could not find the wreckage until January 25, 1930, and the bodies, imbedded in the ice, were not freed until mid-February. On Eielson's casket, heaped high with wreaths, was one banner which read: *"Ben, Fairbanks, Alaska's Golden Heart—There's a Soft Spot in It for You."* It was true. He was their rugged kind, and no man was more admired in their land. Miner, trapper, trader, all liked this warm and friendly man of Scandinavian heritage, a man who, through all his confidence, never swaggered. Oddly, as Eielson's body was lowered into the family plot at Hatton, a sudden swirling blizzard swept across the gathering.

Sir Hubert continued his explorations with other polar flights, engaged in search and rescue operations and scientific research. In 1931, aboard the submarine *Nautilus*, he attempted to reach the North Pole by traveling under the ice pack, but failed. He married, and continued to lead an active life until his death in 1958 at age seventy. When the U.S. nuclear submarine *Skate* broke through the ice to surface at the North Pole on its historic 1959 voyage, Wilkins' ashes were scattered to the inclement winds of the continent he loved and knew so well.

Carl Ben Eielson did not live to see his vision of international air traffic through the Far North come into being, to see Alaska surpass the States in per capita flight volume. Near the site of the old Fairbanks ball park large airfields support military and commercial air traffic bound for all parts of the world today. During World War Two and the Korean conflict, Alaskan skies shook as thousands of bombers and fighters headed for Europe and Asia.

And there may be a long-time resident who can still remember seeing as a youngster the speck of Eielson's flimsy Jenny or lumbering DH-9.

2

Down on the Greenland Ice Cap

THE urge to fly the Atlantic captured the fancy of scores of daring pilots in the mid-twenties, and for several years this blustery stretch of dangerous water became a proving ground for men and flying machines.

Like many barnstormers and airmail fliers of the day, Bert Hassell aspired to fly from America to Europe—but he had his own ideas as to how it should be done. A far-seeing visionary as to the coming commercial prospects of the airplane, Hassell sought a route he knew would one day serve the air fleets of peace and war. That was over four decades ago, and today the route Hassell and his companion, Parker Cramer, pioneered is the great circle path used extensively by military aircraft and modern-day jet liners to connect Europe with the west coast of North America.

Bert was born in 1893 of Norwegian stock, and the cool determination of the Viking heritage was strong in him. The son of a clothing merchant, he went to school to study for the ministry, but he didn't stay. His interests turned to airplanes and engines. At twenty, he met air pioneer Glenn Curtiss and soloed in June 1914. Then he began a barnstorming tour in seaplanes that carried him from New York to Michigan. In a seaplane one blustery March day, two hundred feet over Lake Michigan, his engine quit. In minutes the plane was broken up in the water and sinking. Hassell had no choice but to swim for survival. When the Coast Guard finally reached him in the frigid water, he was still thrashing through the floating pieces of ice. Aghast, one of the rescuers exclaimed: "Anyone who can swim like that must be a fish!" The nickname Fish stuck. Hassell was so chilled from the ordeal it took hours of cold applications to free him from the cramped position.

During the Mexican border dispute Hassell served as a civilian pilot with the U. S. Army and, as World War One threatened, he became the chief instructor for the Curtiss Aviation School. When America entered the hostilities in 1917, he instructed for the Signal Corps as a civilian, then enlisted as a private. After flight school he was commissioned a second lieutenant and continued as a flight instructor.

Hassell foresaw the value of the airplane. Encouraged by his friend Eddie Stinson, who suggested that he should sell the public on flying, he experimented with several uses for the airplane during the postwar years. First he flew mail for the U. S. Postal System. He barnstormed across the Midwest. In a Curtiss Jenny, he delivered suits of clothing from Chicago to Midwest towns. Cheesemakers in Monroe, Wisconsin, anxious to use the advertising novelty of the airplane, sent Green County cheese back to Chicago. In his home town of Rockford, Illinois, Hassell used the JN-4 to deliver newspapers, drop ice cream certificates, and fly in machine parts for the local factory.

In 1926 Bert Hassell did some serious thinking about an air route to Europe. Not the usual air route plotted by Lindbergh, Berthaud, McDonald, and others, but a route that would have to cross only nineteen hundred miles of water before reaching Europe. Hassell plotted such a track, a great circle route that would take him safely over more land with smaller water jumps. Instead of originating on the northeast seaboard, the jumping-off place would be north-central United States. The route would cross over Canada, Greenland, Iceland, and the Scandinavian peninsula, or dip south to England.

From his airmail experience, Hassell realized that organization beforehand meant success. At strategic places along the course there must be ground facilities for service and refueling, plus a communications link. And the plane had to carry a great load of fuel with proven long-range performance.

Hassell knew precisely where to obtain such a plane and he went to his old friend Eddie Stinson. At the Stinson factory in Northville, near Detroit, he laid his plans before the brilliant, young aircraft designer. "Eddie," he said, "I'm going to fly from Rockford to Stockholm. I want you to build me a plane that will carry seven hundred gallons of gasoline." Both Hassell and Stinson knew the machine for the job; it was the SM-1. The first of this model that Stinson built won the 1927 Ford Air Tour and was flown by the manufacturer himself. This same plane was later modified for long-distance flying and carried Edward Schlee and William Brock across the Atlantic in the course of their thirteen-thousand-mile flight from Newfoundland to Tokyo which ended in September 1927. That year thirty-six Stinson SM-1s were built. Many established world records; a few ended disastrously.

The SM-1 was a comparatively large six-place monoplane. Bill Naylor, the chief engineer on the outstanding design, put together a plane that could be flown easily and landed in small fields. It had a cruise speed of 105 mph. Ben J. Jacobsen, who was involved in its construction, recalls those days at the Stinson factory:

> We had short-term ideas then. What we would like to have done was discourage the customers; everybody just wanted to break records. When we were building this ship, Hassell was always

Down on the Greenland Ice Cap

around. I always admired "Fish" and when I heard the *Greater Rockford* didn't reach Stockholm, I felt like crying. I think I did.

In modifying the Hassell plane, a large auxiliary tank was installed directly behind the pilots' seats. Eddie Stinson hired two Austrian specialists who came to the factory for this job. The tank was so large the pilots had to crawl over it to get into the cockpit. A hand pump was installed to draw the gasoline from the large tank into the main wing tanks from which it flowed by gravity to the carburetor. The tried and proven engine of the day, the Wright J-5 Whirlwind, powered the monoplane.

Hassell took delivery of the specially modified Stinson on May 1, 1928. He brought it to his home town and there it was named the *Greater Rockford*. Then he selected his co-pilot and navigator, Parker "Shorty" Cramer. The Burgess Battery Company installed a radio code transmitter—but no receiver —in the plane. Both men took a short course in its operation and on the test flight that followed they reported that it performed well.

The route and destination was firm. They would take off from Rockford's Machesney Airport—said today to be the oldest privately operated airport in the world, and still managed by Fred Machesney—and set a course for Stockholm. Short test flights around the Midwest convinced the pilots the plane would perform as they expected.

As the departure date of July 26 neared, there were parties, luncheons, and celebrations to give plane and pilots a rousing send-off. Meanwhile, arrangements had been made with Doctor William H. Hobbs, leader of the University of Michigan Greenland Meteorological Expedition. The expedition was based at Søndre Strømfjord in southwest Greenland, and would stockpile aviation fuel for their aircraft.

To give the loaded Stinson every margin for its difficult

takeoff, the final task of removing a few fence posts at Machesney Airport was completed shortly before the scheduled start. Just after daybreak the crowd cheered as the Wright engine burst full out with its 225 horsepower and the plane lumbered forward. It staggered sluggishly into the air after a long and tense ground-hugging run and inch by inch struggled for altitude.

"The *Greater Rockford* could hardly pull off the ground with the heavy fuel load," Hassell said. "The Stinson was staggering; we picked up airspeed but couldn't gain altitude. I knew I couldn't hold it long so I just let it stagger along. About a mile west of the Rock River I saw a cornfield coming up and decided to put it down. We landed heavily, the gear collapsed and the plane was damaged—propeller, fuselage, controls—but we were unhurt. And luckily, the fuel tanks held together."

The Stinson was repaired, but their sobering crash-landing caused the air pioneers to reconsider their flight plans. Major L. H. (Ky) Frederick, Bert's close friend and editor of the Rockford newspaper, did much planning for the flight by making arrangements for flight clearances, permissions, and fuel supplies. He suggested they make a refueling stop in Canada. A logical place along their great circle course was at Cochrane, Ontario. Shorty Cramer's brother, Bill, went to Cochrane and, with the help of Otto Thorning, enlisted the volunteer aid of a thousand townspeople to hack a 4400-foot runway out of the scrub oak. In two weeks it was ready.

On August 16, carrying only 250 gallons of fuel, Hassell and Cramer made a second—and successful—takeoff from Rockford and struck out north and east for Canada. They were escorted as far as Janesville, Wisconsin, by four Stinsons and a Fairchild. The flight went smoothly, but after landing in Cochrane seven hours later they were forced to await clear weather. In the early morning of the eighteenth they raced down the hard-packed runway, pulled the heavily laden plane off and headed for the Greenland base at Mount Evans on the Arctic Circle.

They remained precisely on course to Rupert House, Quebec, on the shore of James Bay. This they circled to confirm their exact location. From there they struck out northeast again where they sighted several sites suitable for commercial airfields. A storm en route caused them to swing off course so Cramer delayed sending their regular position report, which would have been erroneous. Nightfall reached them as they flew into the Ungava Bay area, but they knew daybreak would find them over Cape Chidley, Labrador. They reached this landmark on course and had an exact check of their position when they headed across the Davis Strait. Shorty pounded out a report that all was well and six hundred miles ahead lay their Greenland stop.

For the first fifty minutes the flight across the open water was in clear weather. Then, slowly, cloud formations built over and below them, and for almost three hours they were unable to make any drift calculations. They droned confidently on, cheered by the steady rhythmic beat of the J-5 engine. Passing between cloud layers, out of sight of the earth's surface, they were uncertain how the winds were altering their flight path. And both wondered how seriously their three compasses were being affected by the extreme northern magnetic variation.

Then ahead, they saw the lower cloud layer breaking up. Soon the faint outline of the Greenland shore stretched before them and a bright sun reflected on the great ice cap beyond. True to Professor Hobbs's prediction, they found the coastal interior free of fog, and a welcome sight. A check of their maps to pinpoint their position revealed two things: the high winds they encountered had slowed them greatly and depleted their fuel supply, and they had been carried far south of their intended crossing point on the coast. Later they learned they had crossed the coast at Fiskenaesset, where a broad arm of ice running to the coastline stopped.

In their search for Søndre Strømfjord they soon learned they were nowhere near the area that would lead them to the refueling base. With scarcely an hour's fuel remaining, Hassell and Cramer faced a decision that would mean their life or death. They decided not to try to reach the camp by flying along the forbidding coastline where there was no chance to land safely. If their fuel gave out somewhere along those "hideous ice crevasses," as Hassell described them, they would crash in mountainous terrain. Wisely, they agreed to use their remaining fuel to go by way of the inland ice, which appeared smooth and white. They flew over the beginning of the arm of ice that marked the Sukkertoppen District. Ahead was Lake Taserssuak, with its occasional sand flats that resembled to some extent what they expected to find at the University of Michigan expedition's landing site. They circled the lake several times looking for "a field under a mountain wall" which had been described to them as the appointed place. Both men were stiff and bone-weary, having been aloft for more than twenty hours. As they flew over the ice crevasses they tried to fix their characteristics firmly in their mind, hoping it would help them on their walk out. Later they realized the futility of trying to remember what they had seen from the air. They droned on, knowing any minute their faithful J-5 would be starved for fuel.

Meanwhile, at Søndre Strømfjord, there was mounting concern for the two fliers. Professor Hobbs was rapidly becoming suspicious that the fliers were lost and may already have perished. Weeks earlier he and his small party had selected and marked off a suitable landing place for the Rockford fliers and had wired them before their departure that all was ready. The waiting men posted themselves on the airfield shortly after noon on Saturday, long before Hassell and Cramer were scheduled to arrive the next morning. As soon as the dawn light permitted, the professor sent up a pilot balloon and was satisfied the wind conditions were favorable. The men grew anxious as the arrival time drew nearer. Tension increased as they watched and waited all Sunday morning. By ten o'clock they knew the *Greater Rockford*'s fuel supply was almost exhausted. Further, their radio operator had heard none of the plane's scheduled position signals. Inquiries to other stations brought the distressing news they too had heard nothing. In the afternoon their vigil ended and they made their way back to the main base, much disheartened. Hobbs, knowing what lay in store for two inexperienced men on the rugged ice cap —if indeed they even reached the great mass—believed it was highly possible they had perished. Still, he would not give up hope entirely. He sent a wireless report to Hassell's promoter in Rockford, Ky Fredericks. The journalist replied he believed the men had most likely come down south of Camp Lloyd, across the Søndre Strømfjord. He said that if the men were there, and aware of their location, they would probably try to work their way to a prominent headland on the south shore, opposite Hobbs's base.

Encouraged by the logic of this, Professor Hobbs instructed a party under Belknap to proceed in a motorboat and to take a canoe with fuel, food, and a lantern into that region. He also sent the party's most experienced hiker, Potter, to the edge of the inland ice. With an Eskimo, Potter scouted on a two-day journey into the rough region south of the fjord across from their base. None of the searchers found any trace of the men or their plane.

Hobbs was now convinced Cramer and Hassell must have been far off course when their fuel ran out—and were dead. He knew their Stinson was not equipped with pontoons, and if they had been forced down at sea or in one of the great fjords near Julianehaab, there was no hope for them.

The *Greater Rockford* droned on with its fuel very nearly exhausted and its long reel antenna trailing behind them. They signaled desperately to Hobbs or anyone who would hear them.

KHAH . . . KHAH . . . KHAH . . . Landing on the ice cap in the Sukkertoppen District!

Then their engine missed and began sputtering. Starved of gasoline, it choked to a stop and Hassell looked sharp for a level stretch. Skillfully, he glided the lightened machine onto a length of flat ice that was centuries old, and flared out for the touchdown. To their surprise they settled on ice that was firm and crusty with two inches of hoarfrost over it—an excellent landing strip.

As the Stinson crunched to a stop, the two fliers breathed a sigh of relief. They were down on the dreaded ice cap, safely. Lady Luck must have been perched on the empty gas tanks behind them. For several minutes they merely sat and rested their taut nerves and weary bodies. When they climbed down from the cabin, they found the cold air brisk and invigorating. The sun was shining brightly, and the coastal mountains appeared to be only a few short miles away. To them, their plight seemed a mild one. But they were mistaken, and ill prepared for the ordeal that lay ahead. When Bert Hassell stepped onto the ice, he was wearing a blue serge suit, a wool shirt, silk socks, and oxfords. "I wasn't even wearing an undershirt in that polar air," he recalls, "and Shorty was dressed in just about the same stateside fashion. He had a cloth cap and my only headgear was my old felt hat. Luckily we'd carried along two parkas, and two pairs of muk-luks—Eskimo boots—that my Rockford newspaper friend Ky Fredericks presented to us just before our takeoff. At first we didn't want to take them because of their additional weight, but it was good we did. They saved us; the trip out would have been impossible with our regular shoes. Unfortunately we didn't have gloves or fur caps. We didn't even have a canteen; just a small tin cup.

"We also failed to bring snowshoes and skis—which would have helped tremendously."

Elated about their safe landing, they predicted a quick return to the *Greater Rockford* with enough gasoline to continue their flight to Stockholm. They even relaxed their tight nerves with a short snowball battle beside the plane. Although they had the terrifying sensation of feeling the great ice cap tremble as though its surface were alive, neither fully realized their perilous predicament as they gathered the few food supplies and prepared to start across the ice. Their only food was some malted milk tablets and some evil-tasting pemmican—concentrated reindeer meat—wrapped in tallow. It had been left over from one of Byrd's expeditions and Hassell obtained it at Abercrombie & Fitch in New York when he purchased the other sparse survival gear. "In 1928," Hassel explains, "no one really knew what was needed to survive on the ice cap. Few people, in fact, knew anything about the Arctic. We had a small Very pistol to shoot colored flares for air-to-ground signals, a light 6.7-caliber Mannlicher rifle, a few boxes of cartridges, an axe, a hunting knife, and a few boxes of matches."

Before leaving the SM-1, they tied the radio antenna to an aileron and got the radio working for the last time. Hassell tapped out repeatedly: *Landed safe on ice cap* . . . but no one heard. He turned off the set and they began to walk.

They did not take any of the plane's compasses with them, which would have been cumbersome and undependable in those latitudes anyway, but they knew they would have to follow a reasonably accurate path of foot navigation to reach the shore. They navigated by the stars and headed north for Camp Lloyd, sixty miles distant. When they reached the first crevasse in the glacier, they realized what brutal hardships awaited them. The only way to cross was to walk along the crevasse until they found a narrow place. Then they would have to double back to keep their bearings. Maps were useless; the land was uncharted. Because of the great dangers that lay in the ever-shifting ice, Eskimos did not venture onto the ice cap, nor will they to this day. Aside from the crevasses, there were the fjords—rushing waters that had to be crossed. They knew they could not survive the walk in wet clothing so they removed their clothes and half-swam, half-waded across the ice-water stretches, holding all their clothes, gun, and food over their heads. Each time they crossed, the rushing waters forced them downstream. In all, they had to cross four bone-chilling fjords.

Their pemmican, though vile-tasting, gave them the strength and stamina to keep going. When they reached a mountainous area, they supplemented their rations by shooting wild arctic hare and ptarmigan, which they ate raw. The mountains, however, did not mean the end of the ice cap. They passed one mountain only to find the ice cap resume on the other side. They melted snow for water.

Their meager rest and shelter was under raw and bitter circumstances. They had no tarpaulin with which to erect a windbreak, and their only alternative was to sleep against one another for warmth. Their boots kept their feet dry, and the parkas protected them from the worst of the cold.

One factor, Hassell believes, may have enabled them to survive the ordeal on the ice. In 1927 Hassell had met Knud Rasmussen while the famed Danish explorer and author was visiting New York City. In an interview, Rasmussen told Hassell everything he had learned about the Greenland ice fields—the vanishing, treacherous rivers of ice, the crevasses, and the dangers that were unexpectedly found everywhere. The explorer gave Hassell tips on walking, how to observe and interpret landmarks, and where and how to find smooth ice.

"It's best to walk downwind," Rasmussen had advised Hassell. "The wind on the ice cap flows down from its great height in the center, moving like a great invisible stream to the coast. If you walk downwind, you will also be walking downhill and this will be the shortest distance to the shoreline." Unfortunately Hassell neglected to query Rasmussen about survival equipment. The fliers had no thoughts of failure, and besides, they did not wish to add extra gear to their already heavy fuel load.

The torturous, snail-like pace continued. They stopped only to eat their sparse rations, rest and sleep. Foot by weary foot they moved ahead in what seemed to be a hopeless ordeal. At one time Cramer was disoriented and became separated from Hassell. The sturdy airman turned back to find his friend and saw him seated dejectedly on the ice, head down, exhausted. Hassell looked at Shorty's haggard features. His co-pilot had lapsed into a stupor. Hassell realized if they stopped to rest now they would surely die of exposure. He shook Cramer to restore his circulation and snap him free of his dazed condition. Then together, they staggered on toward the coast.

Fifteen days after they had abandoned the *Greater Rockford,* Hassell, leading, came to the water's edge on the south shore of Søndre Strømfjord, proving their navigation to have been startlingly accurate. But they were far from safety. Ahead of them lay deep rough water and miles of rugged, inhospitable coastline. Cramer and Hassell rested and held council. They could not walk around the steep fjord to the north shore. Neither could they dig in here against Greenland's bitter winter months; they could not survive without food and shelter. The situation appeared hopeless unless they could somehow let the weather party on the opposite shore know where they were. And time was running out. Having kept account of their days of travel, they knew the expedition's date of scheduled departure was fast approaching.

"We prayed Professor Hobbs' expedition would stay as planned until the fourth or fifth of September," Hassell remembers. "That meant we had only three or four more days to contact them—or die. Shorty suggested building a fire and shooting off the rifle and signal pistol in hopes the noise might carry to other human ears in that ice and rock wilderness."

In the afternoon Cramer shouted that he had seen a sail briefly on the distant horizon, but neither man could see a boat. Cramer fired two shots from the rifle, but nothing appeared. They turned back to their small campfire, which had helped ward off the mosquito swarms, and piled on more wood. The blaze was the only hope they could cling to in order to stay alive in the creeping cold.

Unknown to both of them, Shorty really had sighted a sail. It belonged to a fishing party in a large Eskimo skin canoe.

On September 2, two weeks after the fliers had been reported lost, the men of the expedition were packing for their return to the States. In two days the power launch would arrive to take them down the coast. About three in the afternoon Professor Hobbs was carrying a pack to the observatory when he heard—carried on the blustery wind from across the fjord—the familiar buzz of an outboard motor. Hobbs realized that only some word about Hassell and Cramer could have induced his men to go out on the boisterous water under such extreme conditions. At the landing Hobbs found a group of Eskimos who had arrived about thirty minutes earlier in their large skin boat. They told how, before leaving the opposite shore, they saw "white man's smoke" rising near the shore and brought the news to Elmer Etes and Duncan Stewart. Eskimos make small campfires with very little smoke. This, then, was clearly a signal fire, as no one except Hassell and Cramer were believed to be across the Søndre Strømfjord. It must be they.

The Mullins boat cast off with great difficulty in the rough waters of the icy fjord. The swells rose and fell with such force that they threatened every moment to engulf the two struggling boatmen. After a churning, nightmarish passage between rolling walls of water, they approached the opposite shore; and Etes and Stewart, still in the bobbing boat, saw a rewarding sight. Stewart told about it.

We saw a figure coming down a slope. He was dressed in a fur parka and was followed by another man in a parka. I saw that one of them was wearing a helmet and I shouted it out to Etes. The first man began waving his arms and I knew darn well no Eskimo would exercise like that. It was Hassell and Cramer.

By sheer determination and the will to survive, they had struggled against massive odds and won.

"When Etes came ashore," Hassell remembers, "I almost collapsed in his arms. They fed us right away, then we climbed slowly and awkwardly into their motor boat, barely under our own strength."

It was well after dark when Hobbs and his men saw the flashlight signals moving toward them from the opposite shore. They peered into the blackness, and as the boat came ahead to grate on the beach they saw it held four persons. Eager men waded into the water and reached out to help the fliers ashore. "When we arrived at the camp, the men of Professor Hobbs' expedition greeted us with astonishment," Hassell recalls. "To them it was a miracle we could have made it through. Before them stood—rather weakly—two men inexperienced in Arctic travel who had been walking on the dreaded ice cap for two weeks and who had cheated an icy grave in the face of a thousand-to-one odds."

Painfully the fliers inched their way up the bank to the dining tent. There was hot soup, and caribou steaks, but because the men had been on a starvation diet for fifteen days, all that they could hold down was the soup.

Within the hour, the radio operator at the observation tower had tapped out the message: 2UO-URGENT, followed by: Hassell and Cramer safe. The following morning the story of the rescue was on the front page of the New York *Times*.

The season was too far advanced, the manpower too limited, and the ice hazards too great for the weather expedition members to try to take gasoline to the Stinson. Besides, Hassell and Cramer were to weak to accompany a party and then fly the plane off the ice. There was no alternative but to abandon the *Greater Rockford* to the elements.

The following day Cramer and Hassell boarded the motor sloop *Nakauk* for the voyage south down the fjord. During the night, the Captain fell asleep at the helm and the boat struck a reef. The ship went down but in the mad scramble all hands were able to reach land. They waited on the barren shore four days before a rescue ship arrived.

When the returning expedition finally reached Holstenborg on the coast, the fliers boarded a tramp freighter, the ore steamer *Wagland,* that took them to Copenhagen and a royal welcome. Knud Rasmussen and Peter Freuchen were at their sides when the Crown Prince of Denmark offered a toast to the intrepid fliers. After a short celebration in Stockholm, they returned to New York City and the traditional ticker tape parade, given for American heroes. In Washington they were greeted by President Calvin Coolidge and President-elect Herbert Hoover.

Parker Cramer later flew on to other Atlantic attempts. When the Chicago *Tribune* sponsored the Untin Bowler Chicago-to-Berlin dash, Cramer was the pilot and Bob Gast the co-pilot. The seaplane flight ended off Fox Harbor at Port Burwell, Labrador, where the machine was wrecked by ice floes as the men slept overnight. In August 1931, while on an unannounced survey flight for a transatlantic airmail route north of the Arctic Circle, Cramer and his Canadian wireless operator, Oliver Pacquette, were lost at sea without a trace somewhere east of the Orkney Islands. Thus, Cramer's third attempt to fly the Atlantic, like his two other attempts, failed.

Forty years passed, but the vivid memories of 1928 persisted in the minds of those who had engineered the ambitious flight. Bert Hassell worked with several aircraft companies and eventually became director of aircraft sales and engineering for Rockford Screw Products. In 1941 he returned to military service and became commander of air bases in Labrador and Greenland, both refueling points for American bombers and cargo planes that traveled along his great circle route to bomber bases in England.

While Colonel Hassell was commanding officer at Goose Bay, Labrador, a U. S. Navy air crew photographed his old bird from the air on one of their flights in Greenland. They flew into Goose Bay and asked Colonel Hassell for permission to use the dark room. A short time later they brought out some pictures that clearly puzzled them—the bare upturned skeleton of the *Greater Rockford*. Newsman Bob Considine was there along with other newsmen when the Navy men asked Hassell what he made of it. It was the first time he had seen his plane since it was abandoned on the ice cap sixteen years earlier, and the story came out. The excited newsmen asked if they could have a copy. Hassell, with a twinkle in his eye—realizing that fierce winds had turned the plane over —growled brusquely: "Hell, no! Do you think I want my friends to believe I landed her on her back?" Of course, the newsmen got their picture.

From 1942 to 1945 old NX 5408, frozen into the glacier, was sighted several times by bomber crews as they ferried their planes to England. When Hassell and Cramer abandoned it in 1928 it was undamaged and resting upright on its gear. The seasons of buffeting winds, which sometimes reach a hundred miles an hour, had tumbled the Stinson on its back and stripped most of the fabric from its metal framework. Oddly, during all of Hassell's military service in the North and his many search and rescue missions, none of these activities took him to that desolate and lonely expanse of ice sixty miles south of what is now Søndre Strøm Air Force Base. There was, after the war, some thinking about recovering the plane, but the difficult terrain was still formidable enough to discourage the undertaking. At one time a recovery effort by Roy Malm, D. S. Hart, and Hassell was planned, but this failed.

After the war Hassell returned to civilian life and directed the construction of the air base at Keflavik, Iceland. Then followed, during the Korean War, another tour with the Air Force in 1953 in England. He had served his country in four conflicts.

The flying Colonel retired from the military at sixty, and citizen Fish Hassell returned to Rockford. He promptly took on a new project, helping build the DEW line—the Distant Early Warning outposts that are America's network of radar stations stretching across Alaska, Canada, and Greenland. Eventually, for the airman who had flown for nearly half a century, the years ushered the Colonel into full retirement.

Then, in the summer of 1967, a former Rockford native and his wife returned for a visit to his home town. Bob Carlin, district manager in Houston for National Airlines and a talented aviation artist as well, was painting a series on historical flights and decided to get some authentic details on the *Greater Rockford* from Bert Hassell himself. Carlin was astonished to learn the old Stinson was not in a museum but still on the ice cap. "I became all unglued," said Carlin, "and suggested to Colonel Hassell we try to bring the bird home." But Fish Hassell shook his head. "It would be a very difficult undertaking," he warned. "There are almost insurmountable problems."

Carlin, a World War Two Liberator pilot who had won the D.F.C. flying in Italy, could not give up the idea. It haunted him. He believed it *could* be done, with enough determination—and he had plenty of that. Back in Houston, Carlin, with the Hassell family, sparked a crusade to bring the plane home to Rockford. It became a two-year campaign. To every aviation group that might be able to lend assistance, Carlin coaxed, argued, and pleaded the importance of rescuing the long-lost plane. In the next year he turned to the U. S. Air Force in Greenland for help. They had no recovery helicopters of the type needed to airlift the remains. "They also suggested I forget about it," Carlin said. "Too hazardous; abandon the idea."

But he wouldn't. He wrote to Gordon Langhorn, station manager for Scandinavian Airlines System at Sønder Strøm, who, although pessimistic about the chances, in turn contacted Greenlandaire, a commercial helicopter service. But after weeks of correspondence many of Carlin's associates began to have second thought about the undertaking.

Matters worsened. A B-52 crash in the region had sprinkled radioactive dust in the area. The would-be rescue team was stopped cold. Then Roy Malm of Rockford, who was to spearhead the recovery operation, died. Next, two disastrous airplane crashes on the ice cap brought up another matter—insurance. The coverage for the helicopter recovery was set at ten thousand dollars. The following week it skyrocketed to twenty thousand. But through it all, Carlin held fast to his sense of humor. "Gordon Langhorne was talking to everyone for help," he said. "By day to people, by night to polar bears!"

In April 1968, Carlin received word that the wreckage had once again been sighted by a U. S. Air Force plane. Gale-force winds had pushed it several miles from its original landing site. Then Greenlandaire sighted it. Months passed. The time would soon come again when the temperature would plunge to forty degrees below zero and the wild, howling, unchecked winds would careen down the ice slopes and whistle through the upturned steel skeleton. Still the twenty-thousand-dollar insurance requirement squarely blocked the path.

King Frederick IX took a surprising hand in the situation. While on a state visit to Greenland aboard the H.D.M.S. *Ingolf,* the King learned of the problem surrounding the wrecked distance plane. Suitably impressed with the historical importance of the venture, His Majesty waved aside the insurance requirement and generously announced that his government would assume all liability. Spirits soared from Sønder Strøm to Houston. And back in Rockford, a delighted Bert Hassell wondered whether King Frederick had a certain recollection when Commander I. H. Englemann of the H.D.M.S. *Ingolf* related the circumstances to His Majesty. Frederick IX had been the Crown Prince who had drunk a toast to him forty years earlier.

Because of the fickle weather, high winds, and treacherous landing surface, seven days were allotted for the recovery. That summer the Greenland climate had been milder than usual, and the wreckage was free from the grip of the ice pack. Sightings were now frequent, and two Danish coast guard crews landed nearby to inspect the plane's cabin. Commander Englemann entered the wreck and found personal items— instruments, documents, and a logbook—that left no doubt this was the Rockford-to-Stockholm ship. On their return, the pilots reported the good news that the natural cold storage had left the plane free of corrosion and very well preserved.

In mid-September 1968 the recovery began as a Greenlandaire Sikorsky S-61 from Sønder Strøm settled slowly on the ice a few yards from the overturned monoplane. Technicians dismantled the wings and tied them to the bare fuselage tubing. The plane's tail assembly was found nearby. It had been weakened when the Stinson overturned and was wrenched off by the years of fierce wind.

How well did the steel tube and fabric machine fare during its forty years in the ice wilderness? The bright yellow skin of the plane—its outer covering—was mostly gone. Rust was practically nonexistent on the steel parts, and the tubes of the antique radio transmitter were undamaged and operational. The windows were shattered, but the wicker seats were still intact.

The recovery team was surprised by the way the plane had weathered four decades in the Arctic deep freeze with its icy hurricane-force gales. "The aluminum frame was in top shape," Carlin said, "not corroded or even dulled. Instruments still functioned perfectly. Two of the flares in the plane ignited instantly, and an oxygen bottle squirted oxygen when its valve was opened."

A steel bridle was attached to the plane and with Greenlandaire's Captain Knut Solbakken at the controls, the big Sikorsky gently lifted the small airplane from the ice. Above, in the helicopter, were Hassell's son Vic and Parker Cramer's brother Bill. Less than an hour later the bundle of tubing and aluminum was gently lowered at Søndre Strøm Air Force Base, just forty years late for its scheduled refueling rendezvous. Hassell's last entry in the pilot log read: "24 hours, 12 minutes from Cochrane, Ontario, to the Greenland ice cap." The Danish helicopter pilot who made the recovery flight added this entry: "9-10-68. 59 minutes—55 N miles, S-61N—slinged by OYHAH to Søndre Strøm—Knut A. Solbakken."

In a formal base ceremony, amid toasts of friendship, the plane was turned over to Victor, who represented his father. Returning the plane to Rockford presented another problem, however. Because the *Greater Rockford*'s flight had not been of a military nature, the Air Force was reluctant to return the disassembled machine to the States. With the two Hassell brothers, Vic and John, Carlin arranged with Hemisphere Aircraft to fly their C-46—a private air transport—to bring the now-famous aircraft home. In the spring of 1969, almost two years after Carlin was caught up with the recovery idea, he and the two Hassell sons landed at Søndre Strøm Air Force Base to take delivery. In the background was the ridge that had been named Mount Hassell in 1928. On May 14, more than four decades after the *Greater Rockford* struggled heavily from Machesney Airport, the C-46 glided into the same field and pilot Monroe "Tex" Cauble touched the wheels of the transport briefly in tribute, at the point of the old plane's departure. Then they flew on to the new, larger Greater Rockford Airport. Full Circle. The final entry in the log read: "9-13-69. Søndre Strøm to Rockford via Sept Isle, Quebec, and Midway, Chicago. Return of *Greater Rockford* C-46-N68965—Tex Cauble."

Carlin has high hopes that the *Greater Rockford* will one day fly again and plans have already been made to restore it to its former glory before it finds rest in a museum. The retired air pioneer has revealed that it will be rebuilt by the Aviation Technology Division of Rock Valley College.

As old NX 5408 was unloaded on the ramp from the C-46 transport, Bert Hassell watched quietly with his memories. Then he rose from his chair and walked slowly around the plane. The once-blond mustache and distinctive beard of the grand old viking had turned gray. His shoulders were bowed with years and there was a cane in his still-sturdy hands. In the crowd were many who saw his takeoff from Machesney and there were a few who had helped to build the plane. There were youngsters, too—those who wanted a firsthand sight of aviation history and some with that same anxious, air-minded look he had seen so many times at grass strips and air training bases all over America. Perhaps he was thinking, too, of that day in the not-too-distant future when he and Mrs. Hassell would dedicate the *Greater Rockford* in memory of their youngest son, Lieutenant Peter David Hassell, a jet fighter pilot who was killed in 1961 while on an F-100 training flight at Luke Air Force Base in Arizona.

The veteran ran his hand carefully along the tubing, touched the ragged, brittle fabric that still clung stubbornly to the parts, and gazed into the cockpit at instruments he had last seen so long ago. In this quiet way, Bert Hassell welcomed his old friend.

His son Vic was standing at his side. "Pop, we brought her home," he said.

The old aviator blinked and was silent. There was an almost imperceptible nod as his hand went slowly to his eyes. For this reunion, there was nothing to say.

3

Auyántepuí—and the Bush Pilot of Angel Falls

He was quiet; very friendly with people he knew. His philosophy was to live today and let tomorrow take care of itself. Scrambled egg sandwiches and Scotch whiskey were his favorite foods. He was about five feet, ten and a half, heavy-boned, and weighed on the average about 180 pounds. There was a scar on his right cheek where a strut wire had gone into it during a crash in Chile. Dark hair and dark eyes. Always immaculately clean and slow to anger. Women were crazy about him."

Jimmie Angel. Aviator, soldier, air explorer.

These words of widowed Marie Angel, thirty-three years after she, her adventurous husband, and two others were stranded atop an isolated mesa in the uncharted wilds of the Guiana Highlands, recall the dash and daring of one of the most colorful of the early flying pioneers.

For centuries eastern Venezuela, shrouded in superstition and mystery, has been a tantalizing dream for ambitious men in their quest for gold and diamonds. Jimmie Angel did his best to wrest a fortune from the great mesa of Auyántepuí with an aerial expedition, but he fared little better than the others. Although he never gave up his search, the source of the gold nuggets he gathered with a fellow expatriate over four decades ago is still there for the taking—if you can only pinpoint his "stream of gold."

Because of Angel's insatiable quest for the riches of the mesas, he made a discovery more important than gold—the waterfall that bears his name, a plunging, breathtaking cataract that even today relatively few people have seen.

Jimmie Angel is numbered among the more daring of a generation of American bush pilots. He started flying at fifteen, lied his way into the Royal Canadian Air Force at sixteen, and was mustered out of service at eighteen, after shooting down three German airplanes and five balloons. Like many other ex-war pilots after the Armistice, he sought a steady flying job. For a while he barnstormed with his brother Eddie in "Jimmie Angel's Flying Circus." He was hired by Sun Yat-sen, President of the self-proclaimed National government in Canton, and in 1923 was bombing bandits in the Gobi desert. Soon afterward he helped to organize Chiang Kai-shek's air force. Back in the States he flew payrolls for oil companies. Then came stunt work in several Hollywood flying films, among them *Wings* and *Hell's Angels*.

This was the era of slowly developing bush flying in Canada and Alaska, but Angel set his sights on the more balmy climate of Central and South America. It was wide open for air links between the mining and drilling sites and civilization. The stocky, enterprising American established his flying headquarters in Panama, and hired out to airlift anything that would fit inside his planes. Payrolls, mining equipment, and an occasional mining engineer were his principal cargoes.

One day in 1928, while drinking Scotch in the cool interior of the Tivoli Hotel in Panama, Jimmie Angel became aware that a darkly tanned, red-bearded stranger was watching him. Angel judged the grizzled stranger to be an American of about sixty, and his weathered skin and sun-hardened features told the bush pilot that the man had spent many years outdoors. Presently he rose and walked over to Jimmie, hand outstretched. His voice was friendly.

"Jimmie Angel?"

Angel nodded and shook the calloused hand.

"I'm Bob McCrackin," the stranger said. "I've been prospecting to the south and I can use a pilot. I'm told you're the best."

Angel was always cautious with strangers until he knew their intentions, so he let McCrackin talk. Besides, the prospector had hinted at two things in which Angel was vitally interested: money and flying.

The man, Angel soon learned, was something of a legendary character, an Old Man of the Jungle who had tracked the rain forests of the Upper Orinoco, those uncharted lands that spread deep into Venezuela. Thousands of square miles of green foliage stretched from horizon to horizon. From the air it was an endless green carpet beyond which no white man before him had ventured. It was a jungle that harbored death in many forms—venomous snakes, insects, head-hunters, and the deadly piranha in its streams.

McCrackin told Angel that he had recently returned from a trip down the Caroni, a tributary that empties into the Orinoco. From his hip pocket he drew a well-worn map and spread it across the bar. His finger tapped a place in the east-central section of Venezuela. Here, McCrackin told him, was a mountain that was nine thousand feet high. The area under McCrackin's finger, however, was blank; no mountains were shown.

If Angel's expression told McCrackin that he had serious

doubts as to his sanity, the prospector took no notice but launched into a detailed explanation of his proposal.

"Lots of people don't believe it, but I do. I was there. I'd prospected all over Venezuela in the past ten years. In the rivers of the center there's gold—lots of it. I found it in the Caroní, but nothing really big. Then I got the idea if there's so much ore in the low regions, there might be a mother lode higher in the mountains—where the rivers begin."

Angel said nothing, but he listened intently as McCrackin continued.

"Last year, with two Camarata Indians, I hacked my way through the jungle and climbed to the summit. It took us more than two months. The Indians call the place Auyántepuí—home of the devil. I hit it big. I know you won't believe me, but I found a lode as great as any in the world."

Jimmie Angel looked searchingly at McCrackin. This man, Angel knew instinctively, was not lying. Nor was he playing a con game.

"At first," McCrackin went on, "the gold meant little to the Indians. But my actions must have given me away, and then they sensed the ore was valuable. I forced myself to stay awake for two days when we climbed down; I half-expected a poison dart in my back at any time.

"What kind of gold was it?" Angel interrupted. "A vein close to the surface?"

The prospector shook his head and took a soiled chamois sack from another pocket. He loosened the drawstring and spilled the contents. Angel stared at the dozen dull nuggets on the bar. "Not a vein—free gold in a stream. And there's lots more up there, but walkin's not the way to travel. We need an airplane."

Now Angel saw the picture. He asked McCrackin about the terrain and was told the mountaintop was largely flat, but cut up in places with deep crevasses and rock boulders. He said there were many level places where a small plane could land, load samples, and fly off. Angel nodded. It was a thousand-mile round trip. They would have to carry extra fuel in cans, but it could be done.

The ex-fighter pilot put his hard-headed business sense to the test. "O.K.," he told the old explorer, "I'm your man—for five thousand cash in advance."

McCrackin nodded. "It's a deal."

A few days later they were flying south in Angel's "Brisfit," a two-seater Bristol Fighter biplane. In short hops from one jungle clearing to another they made the week-long flight to Ciudad Bolívar, a small outpost on the Orinoco three hundred miles southeast of Caracas. There they stocked prospecting supplies: food, a shovel, and some tins for panning gold. McCrackin told Angel this outpost would be their final landing stop; the mountain lay a hundred and fifty miles south-southeast. They loaded ten five-gallon cans of gasoline and roared away.

As they droned over the most unbelievable country Angel had ever seen, he realized McCrackin was an able navigator. The ground below them was dense jungle, broken occasionally by stretches of low brush—savannah—and twisting, snake-like, unnamed rivers. Somewhere down there, obscured in the thousands of square miles of dense foliage, was the wreckage of Paul Redfern's green and gold *Port of Brunswick* that was lost in 1927. And now, in a region that furnished settings for two famous novels: Sir Arthur Conan Doyle's *Lost World* and W. H. Hudson's *Green Mansions,* a real-life drama to match the most imaginative of adventure tales was about to begin.

They had left the narrowing Caroni behind when Angel saw, rising straight up from the jungle floor, a great jagged mountain wall with its flattened top partially obscured by clouds. In the back cockpit, McCrackin leaned forward and slapped Angel on the shoulder. He pointed. *Auyántepuí.* It jutted into jagged rain clouds, a massive butte, an irregular ring of rock with sheer barren sides that towered more than a mile above the sweeping savannah meadows and undulating forest floor of eastern Venezuela. The untouched buttress of a mountain was a lost world beyond the steaming jungles. Here in the Gran Sabana, distances are deceiving. The six-thousand-foot mesas are separated by deep forbidding canyons that plunge to darkened depths. Everywhere, the terrain is difficult.

Angel scanned the great slabs of vertical granite that shaped the mysterious, uncharted place and decided it was everything his passenger said. He opened the throttle and put the Bristol into a climb. They spiraled upward, soaring higher on the jungle thermals, as the straining engine lifted them toward the stratus mists. Like a giant bird, it skimmed along the cloud line. Angel glanced at the altimeter. It read nine thousand feet and the Bristol was still below the mountain rim. Up, up through the vapor mists. As they drew nearer to the mountain's sides, vicious updrafts close along the granite walls caught them and tossed the light airplane roughly. The pilot struggled to keep the bobbing machine upright.

The small biplane, a little wobbly in the thin air, fairly brushed the rocky rim of the great butte and was over the top. These were the first men to look down on nature's edifice, Devil Mountain, the god to which the local Indians prayed. Here endless thunder rolled and shook the basalt cliffs until they reverberated again and again. So fearfully violent are the thunderclaps, that seasoned explorers will cringe at the deafening explosions surrounding them on the mountain. It was a place where mysterious animals scurried, where orchids and strange plants, found nowhere else on earth, thrived abundantly. Life here had been somehow set apart from the outside world since time began.

In the rarefied air at these heights the old Brisfit responded less quickly, but now that they were over the edge, the turbulence suddenly ended. McCrackin pointed south and Angel headed out, skimming the treeless, barren, rock-strewn tabletop. Here and there they saw a small lake or a meandering stream—perhaps the source of the Río Caroní—far below. There were stretches crisscrossed with fantastic gorges, grotesque and lonely sentinels of the unexplored. But McCrackin, oblivious to the magnificent scenery passing below him, looked straight ahead through the spinning propeller and occasionally directed Jimmie to change course with a jerk of his thumb. Soon after they passed over a deep canyon that separated the southern part of the mesa, at a place several miles from its nearest edge, McCrackin suddenly leaned outside the cockpit and into the propeller blast. He waved his arms wildly and pointed. "There!" he shouted over the engine's noise. "Land there!" And he indicated a small patch of bare ground through which a slender stream snaked. Angel flew low and studied the clearing carefully. He throttled back, brought the biplane into the clearing with its tail low, and mushed expertly onto its pebble-strewn surface. The Bristol hit roughly, but thanks to the oversize balloon tires on the slow World War I machine, it did not nose over as it came to a stop near a clump of bushes.

The propeller was slowing to a stop when McCrackin, with a shout, clambered to the ground and scrambled to the nearby stream. Angel, curious as to McCrackin's wild behavior, followed more slowly. There, under the old man's shoes, lay nuggets that ranged from the size of wheat grains to the size of walnuts. The surprised pilot dropped to his knees and helped McCrackin gather handfuls of the wet, precious ore, which they put into sacks.

In the late afternoon McCrackin suggested they leave the mountain before darkness came. Angel agreed. Ragged clouds, black and threatening, were building up and a light drizzle was already falling. He knew if they waited much longer, their landing patch would become a quagmire. Getting airborne with a load of ore in the thin mountain air would present enough problems. They refueled the plane from the cans, tied down the sacked ore, and backed the plane's tail into the bushes. With full throttle the machine lurched forward and gained speed slowly. The engine roared full out, and as soon as he dared, Jimmie Angel lifted the Bristol's tail into flying position. Then he urged the fully loaded machine into the air. The wings finally caught enough lift for buoyancy and barely cleared a copse of ironwood trees. In a few minutes they reached the fearsome, mile-high rim. They tipped over into the green-carpeted valley below, through the belt of turbulence and into an ear-congesting descent. Darkness descended but they flew on to Ciudad Bolívar in complete blackness and landed safely.

Overnight, thanks to the generosity of Bob McCrackin and the stimulating labor of one wildly exciting afternoon on an unmarked mountain plateau, Jimmie Angel went from an uncertain future to a degree of affluence. When the Bank of Panama converted their load of gold ore into cash for twenty-two thousand dollars, they had a nonstop, three-day celebration. Then McCrackin told the aviator: "I have some business back in the States, Jimmie. And when I've finished with it, I'll be back!" Angel never saw him again for, within a few hours of his arrival in Denver, the old man died of a heart attack. When the bush flier received the telegram from one of McCrackin's relatives, the heavy scar on his right cheek wrinkled. McCrackin dead? The blow was a staggering one; only the old prospector knew where the gold stream lay on Auyántepuí.

Determined, Jimmie resolved that he would relocate the site. He laid his plans carefully, and used his money to buy several airplanes and expand his business operations into that part of Venezuela. One plane was a Ford Trimotor, another a Hamilton, the third a Travelaire, and later he bought an all-metal Flamingo. All were workhorses with wings. From their profits he hoped one day to finance a sure-fire return trip to that clearing on Devil Mountain.

During one of his trips to Los Angeles, Jimmie met and became engaged to a nurse, Mavis Marie Sanders. In 1935 she flew south and they were married in Barranquilla, Colombia. His young bride proved to be adventurous, for she became his co-pilot on many South American flights. Then Jimmie extended his flights into Central America. They settled for a while in Managua, Nicaragua, where Jimmie established a commercial airline that flew passengers and mail between Managua and San José, Costa Rica. In March 1948 a revolution broke out while they were living in Costa Rica.

"It was terrible," Marie Angel recalls today. "Three thousand people were killed. Rolan, our youngest child, was born during the fighting in our apartment, which was a block and a half from the Presidential Palace. Most Americans had already fled the country, but we were within the area cordoned off around the building and we knew there would be difficulty leaving. Jimmie got word to us to get out at all costs. It was urgent, I could tell, for we were in no condition to travel, but he insisted, 'Get out, even if you have to walk . . . but get out!' Our chauffeur had been killed but we were able to get to the airport and were helped aboard an American government plane—our maid, Jimmie Jr., Rolan, and myself.

"When we got off the plane in Panama, there was Jimmie leaning across the wire fence, waiting. 'I knew you'd get out somehow,' he said. 'But what was the hurry?' I asked. He said, 'I'm supposed to bomb the palace tomorrow morning, and your apartment was too close. They promised me fifty thousand dollars and a brand-new Lockheed Electra.' But as things turned out, he didn't bomb the palace after all. Another pilot did, blew off one wing of the building and killed one person. Jimmie knew if he didn't do it, someone else would."

One of Jimmie's flying jobs was in Mexico, where he flew a payroll out of Tampico. He used a two-seater biplane for the deliveries and carried an armed guard in the front cockpit to protect the money sack. At the time a notorious and successful bandit named Monte was active in that part of Mexico. Over a desolate stretch, the guard rose in the front cockpit, turned and ordered Jimmie to land one a field below. Angel saw the picture immediately; the guard was highjacking the payroll. Angel, who knew what lay in store for him if he followed the turncoat's order, calmly drew his pistol and shot the man. The bullet also went through his fuel tank and he was forced to land, abandon the plane and dead guard, and make his way to safety as best he could.

As the years passed, the gold on Auyántepuí came to mean more than material wealth to Jimmie Angel. It became a challenge, a goal which he pursued with a driving, dogged persistence that would have exhausted a lesser man. His bush flying operation grew, and now he hacked airstrips out of the jungle as he ranged closer to Auyántepuí. He flew payrolls, equipment, and mining officials to remote camps and occasionally disappeared for days at a time on exploration flights into the Guiana jungle country of eastern Venezuela. Always, driving him on, was his belief that one day he would relocate his river of gold.

In 1934 he had established a base camp close to Auyántepuí, where he stored gasoline and supplies and cleared a rough landing strip. His skill as a bush pilot became as legendary as his preoccupation with the great mountain's treasure, and he was sought out by mining engineers for survey flights deep into the interior. One such engineer was a man named Curry. On a flight early in 1935, while scouting eastern Venezuela for possible locations of gold and diamonds, Angel, accompanied by his Mexican co-pilot and Curry, nosed his Travelaire cabin monoplane in and out of the great unexplored valleys around Auyántepuí. Suddenly, squarely before them, between the sheer, towering mesas, they saw a waterfall. It was so towering, so magnificent in its cascading plume of fog and billowing mists, that they could not believe their eyes. Angel flew level with the top and read the altimeter. Then he skimmed low across the valley floor, through the fine spray, and again checked the instrument. The water plunged downward more than a mile.

Unlike most cataracts, Jimmie saw that the water did not flow over the rim of Auyántepuí. Instead, it gathered its waters underground from the lakes and streams of the sprawling sixteen-by-twenty-two-mile plateau. Its water gushed from several crevices three hundred feet below the precipice and much of the time its head was hidden in the clouds. It would be fourteen years before a National Geographic expedition would make the first accurate measurements. In 1949 they found its main perpendicular drop to be 2648 feet. Added to the lower drop of 564 feet, the total fall of water is 3212 feet—the world's highest. Many explorers, impressed by its breathtaking grandeur, have called it the eighth wonder of the world. It is fifteen times higher than Niagara Falls.

The expedition ended disastrously when a coral snake killed Curry. When Angel returned to Ciudad Bolívar to tell others of the find, he admitted it all seemed like a dream. He told how the water dropped so far it disappeared into a foggy mist before it reached the valley floor. Many, who doubted his story of the gold stream on his uncharted, mysterious mountain to the south, refused to believe. But when the Venezuelan jungle frontier was forced back, the find was confirmed by a government official and two years after its discovery it was named Angel Falls. It was not until the late 1930s, however, that Auyántepuí appeared on maps. Jimmie suspected he had passed close to the cataract on his 1928 flight with McCrackin, but they failed to see it because of the almost continuous cloud cover.

Several close friends of Jimmie's knew that the bush flier's interest in the gold on Auyántepuí was not the result of a runaway imagination. One such person was the well-known American mining engineer Lee R. Dennison, who had worked with Angel from the small jungle hamlet of Paviche, on the Río Caroní. "Dennison was a very nice man," Marie Angel remembers. "A stalwart and rugged individual." Well-educated, Dennison's orderly and scientific mind could not be deceived by hearsay. His books, *Devil Mountain* and *Caroni Gold,* reveal his intimate knowledge of the terrain and of the great Gran Sabana and what geological surveys hinted that it contained. He hired Angel for numerous mining-survey flights, several of which took them over Auyantepui. Strapped tightly into the seat of Angel's high-wing Hamilton, they nudged over the top of the great fortress-like plateau. Dennison was awed by the desolate top that was strewn with rocks and stunted shrubbery. Later he said the millions of ounces of gold and diamonds that lie in the Caroní River at the foot of this great mesa likely had their source in Auyántepuí.

Another person who knew Jimmie well, Caracas businessman William Phelps, said the gold was very real to Angel. It was something, Phelps said, that his friend had personally seen and touched, and not imagined.

Two years after his discovery of the Falls, Angel made ready for his assault on the mountain. He had just the airplane for the job, an eight-passenger Flamingo. Slender, still-attractive Marie Angel says today: "That mountain had grown on Jimmie until it possessed him. It was a part of his life and he couldn't leave it alone. He always referred to Auyántepuí as 'she,' and I suppose if I were a jealous woman, I would have been jealous of it.

"The sole purpose of the flight was to try to find the creek from which he and McCrackin had taken the gold nuggets," Marie confirms. "It was October 1937 when we took off in Jimmie's Flamingo he had named *El Río Caroní*. We used a base known as Angel Camp near Hacha Falls on the sixteen-hundred-foot level of the Gran Sabana. Our party consisted of myself, Gustavo Heny—a well-known woodsman and explorer of Venezuela—and Miguel Ángel Delgado, a peon who had been with Gustavo for years. We had left a fifth man, Captain Félix Cardona, back at the base camp to keep radio contact."

The all-metal Flamingo was a large, high-wing monoplane with a powerful 450-horsepower Pratt and Whitney radial engine. It had a slow landing speed of sixty miles per hour and could carry a ton of cargo—an ideal choice for such an expedition.

The *El Río Caroní* spiraled steadily upward from the base camp and nosed over the mountain's edge. Jimmie set a course from landmarks he believed to be accurate. He droned on, making slight corrections here and there until finally, at a place fifteen miles from the edge of the nearest mesa, he sighted a small clearing that reminded him of the one where he and McCrackin had taken their bonanza nine years earlier. He throttled back, curved slowly into a gliding turn, and settled on the descent through the mountain air. Marie Angel tells what happened next:

It happened at the end of the landing roll. We had almost stopped when the wheels broke through the crust of gelatin bog and the plane nosed over—gently.

I can't remember how I felt when I realized we couldn't fly the plane out, but we all knew what it meant to be stranded there. Jimmie's first reaction was to try to save his plane. The propeller was undamaged and the plane could have been flown out if its nose could have been pulled from the bog. Gustavo's reaction was to get us out of the mess we'd gotten ourselves into.

We were not in radio contact with Cardona at any time while we were on top of Auyántepuí. We did some exploring nearby and found gold ore, but not the creek we were looking for.

The four marooned explorers faced what appeared to be a hopeless ordeal. The only way out of the trap was to abandon their stuck plane, select a few provisions to carry, and walk out. Gustavo Heny led the small troupe and under his guidance they set out for the northern rim of the mesa, across the miles of crevasses and jagged rocks. There the dangerous descent awaited them.

With ropes they edged their way carefully down sheer cliffs. The nights were bitterly cold and they were forced to sleep on narrow rock ledges. Torrential downpours soaked them and vicious insects harassed them. They fought away great black ants whose sting could paralyze a limb for hours. As they fell and stumbled through the wet, cloudy mists, always at their shoulders were the chilling fears of unknown dangers lurking around the next crag. "We climbed down a fifteen-hundred-foot wall mostly hand over hand on a rough manila rope," Marie Angel recalls. "We had plenty of rations to start with but after five days we discarded most of them and limited ourselves to bouillon cubes, chocolate bars, rice, and cheese. For protective gear we had oilskin coats, and three of us had sidearms.

"Cardona had radioed of our failure to return and a search was begun. At one time during our descent we saw a government search plane skimming the valley floor four thousand feet below us. We all screamed and shouted and waved, shot off our guns and the colored Very pistol flares in a desperate attempt to make him see us. But he didn't of course and flew on out of sight. We all sat down and cried because at that moment every one of us realized the simple truth that we might not make it out."

After incredible miles through dripping, steaming jungles deadly with venomous snakes and scorpions, and streams with piranha, they emerged miraculously safe to walk into their base camp fourteen days later and greet a surprised Félix Cardona. "But for months afterward," Marie Angel confides, "I woke up in shock many times at night." They were flown back to Ciudad Bolívar on an aero-postal plane piloted by José López Henriquez.

Still Jimmie Angel would not give up his dream of the lost gold mine in the sky. While he returned to his bush flying, Marie went home to California, where she had first met Jimmie after the war, and raised their two sons, Jimmie Jr. and Rolan. Angel returned often to the States, sometimes to raise interest in the gold that was still on Devil Mountain. Although new diamond fields had been opened in Venezuela—one of the world's largest not far from Auyántepuí—and uranium was discovered, he was only interested in the gold. Although he gave much thought to the loss of his abandoned Flamingo, he realized the futility of trying to recover it.

In 1956 he was making serious plans for another try at the gold. That summer, on a return trip from Venezuela, Angel was landing his Cessna 180 at David, Panama, for entry clearances. As he prepared to touch down, the plane was gripped by a sudden crosswind. It swerved and a wingtip touched the ground. A tool box slammed forward and struck him viciously on his head. Jimmie walked away from the plane thinking he had only a bad bump on his skull and a small cut on his finger, but a few hours later he suddenly fell unconscious. He was rushed to Gorgas Hospital in Balboa where for six months he lay in a coma. That December, following a cerebral hemorrhage, he died at fifty-six.

Almost four years later, in accord with Jimmie's wishes,

Marie and their sons flew over the Falls to scatter his ashes in the thunderous spume that bears his name. Shortly thereafter, the Venezuela government named his Flamingo a national monument.

"After Jimmie's death," Marie tells, "I opened a nursing home in Santa Barbara, which Jimmie Jr., now twenty-six, owns and operates. Rolan is twenty-two, and in the Air Force. Both are married. To start my new life I had to eat the diamonds that Jimmie gave me."

In July 1965, young Rolan made a pilgrimage to the lonely Flamingo atop Auyántepuí. With his mother waiting below at the base camp, "Jungle Rudy" Truffino led Rolan and thirteen others—including ten Waica Indians—up the rock. They reached *El Rio Caroni* on the seventh day. Despite thirty years' exposure to the raw elements, the silver plane had few marks of time on it. Rolan fastened a plaque on the side of the cowling which said in part: "... *in memory of his father by Rolan Angel, 1965* ..."

Early in 1970 a Venezuelan Air Force helicopter airlifted the famous Flamingo from the mountain and took it to Maracay, near Caracas, where a new museum of Venezuelan planes will be built. Tentative plans call for a replica to be made of the Flamingo, and the original returned to Auyántepuí as a monument to the bush pilot of Angel Falls.

Today, tourists can view Angel Falls on an inexpensive air excursion from the nearby jungle resort at Canaima Falls. The more ruggedly adventurous can trek on a four-day round trip to its base.

Men still roam the Gran Sabana in their search for gold and diamonds. The more daring have found them, and many have let the treasures slip from their very grasp. Jimmie Angel was one of these, and the secret of his lost stream of gold remains locked in the misty world atop Devil Mountain.

The urge for adventure was a profound driving force in

this bush pilot. It whetted his curiosity to a fine edge and compelled him to fly where no man had flown before—into darkened canyons where engine failure meant death. Because he dared, because he was an uncommon man, Jimmy Angel left the world richer than he realized. The Falls that bear his name give him, in death, an immortality that no store of riches on Auyántepuí could ever match.

4

Hell's Airport—and the Lure of Lassetter's Reef

In the ovenlike dead heart of the central Australian desert, men are still lured into danger in one of the most forbidding places on earth—Lassetter's Reef. A fabulously rich gold lode twelve feet wide, a hundred feet deep, and ten miles long, it beckons hopeful souls into the dreary, sun-baked interior with an irresistible lure for "the gold that must be there." A dozen men have died in the outback since it was first discovered in 1897, their bleaching bones strewn under the glaring sun in what is known today as Lassetter country. Five major expeditions and a half million dollars later it defies rediscovery as stubbornly as America's own Lost Dutchman mine. The men who went on three small-scale probes into the interior in 1969 returned empty-handed.

One day in May 1930 a small, bowlegged ex-sailor with scraggly black hair turning gray walked into the Sydney office of John Bailey, President of the Central Branch of the Australian Workers' Union, and said he had a story to tell. Bailey was accustomed to listening to hard-luck tales from unemployed union men and he prepared himself to hear another one. But this shabby little fellow was no ordinary out-o'-work with a tale of misfortune.

He said his name was Lewis Harold Bell Lassetter. In the presence of three others—Ernest Bailey, John Jenkins, and pilot-journalist Errol Coote—he told of a rich gold reef in central Australia. Its length would make it the world's largest gold producer.

Lassetter told how, as a twenty-year-old seafarer in 1897, he had heard a rumor about a bonanza of rubies in the Macdonnell Ranges not far from the settlement of Alice Springs. He left his ship at Cairns and trekked overland into the simmering wilderness, but after backbreaking months he found only worthless ruby quartz. He decided to quit and travel southwest from the Macdonnells in hopes of eventually reaching the distant coast. His maps were wrong and his sense of direction worse. In a few days Lassetter knew he was facing death—alone and lost. He came to a series of unmarked ranges in barren sandhill and spinifex grass country. A few waterholes allowed him to camp and feed his horses on the sparse grass.

One morning as he strolled a short distance from camp, he was attracted to a heap of odd-looking rocks—greenish, milky-colored quartz. Curious, he smashed one, and his bloodshot eyes widened as flakes of gold glistened in the harsh sunlight. He scanned the ground and slowly began to follow outcroppings of similar stones strewn about. On top of a small hill he shaded his eyes and squinted along the rough ground. It was then that he realized the lines of this yellow reef stretched for miles.

Highly excited, the wiry little man gathered several specimens into an oatmeal bag, broke camp, and headed for what he thought was civilization. A few days later his water gave out, then his horses died, and he became hopelessly confused in the blinding heat. He staggered aimlessly, growing weaker.

Near the Western Australia border a lone Afghan camel driver found the delirious and emaciated man on the point of death, but still clutching his bag of rocks. The Afghan carried him to the camp of a government surveyor named Harding who cared for Lassetter and puzzled over the rough specimens. Harding knew they came from a fabulously rich lode.

As Lasseter grew stronger, Harding asked him about the samples and the grateful sailor told him of his find. In a voice quavering with emotion Lassetter said, "Friend, there's so much gold out there, you have to kick it out of your way. But . . . I don't know where it is now!"

"What was the land like, thereabout?" Harding urged.

Lassetter described the ranges and the surveyor identified them as the Petermanns.

Harding wanted to return immediately to stake out a claim, but Lassetter would have none of it. His close brush with death had thoroughly shaken his confidence. He was weak; his nerves were shattered. "I can't face that desert again—not now." Harding begged and pleaded, but Lassetter stubbornly held his ground. "No, Harding, I won't go back. Perhaps later we'll go together. I'm going to have a long rest first."

While Lassetter worked in the Coolgardie gold fields for the next three years, the surveyor kept his ambitious proposal alive by correspondence, painting vivid pictures of the riches that awaited them at the lost reef. His health fully restored, Lassetter finally gave in.

In 1900, with a camel train packing supplies, the two men left Carnarvon on the Western Australian coast, bound for the Petermanns. For weeks they pushed into unexplored country. When they reached Harding's former camp, Lassetter began to recognize landmarks. Shortly after they made a base camp in the Petermanns, Lassetter's hardened hands grasped the gold-flecked rocks for a second time at his El

Dorado—the King Solomon's mine of Australia. Harding was jubilant. "It's ten miles long if it's an inch," the surveyor said; "and I'll wager it's a hundred feet thick!" In places, outcroppings protruded four feet above the surface. Harding made bearings with his watch and, weary but happy, the two men started back. Hundreds of miles from the reef they came to a small town. Lassetter headed for the saloon in the rough bush hotel. About to down his first beer in months, he was stopped short as Harding rushed in. "My watch!" he shouted. "Look at it! It's been losing time . . . it's seventy-five minutes late!"

Lassetter blinked, puzzled. "What's wrong with that?"

Harding explained there was no way to tell how far it had thrown off his calculations at the reef. Lassetter slowly lowered his mug. They were back at the beginning. The reef was just as surely lost as before. Weary and discouraged, they knew that to return to the Petermanns was out of the question. Their savings were gone and their supplies depleted. It seemed to have all been for nothing, but Lassetter believed he could find the reef again—bearings or not.

They trudged on to Perth, where their samples were assayed at three ounces to the ton. They tried to find capital for another expedition, but they were in the wrong place at the wrong time. The booming gold fields at adjacent Coolgardie and Kalgoorlie were making fortunes for anyone willing to work them. No investor would gamble on a lost reef hundreds of miles in the unexplored outback. In disgust, Lassetter gave up and returned to the sea. Harding stayed at Kalgoorlie, where he died a few years later.

The small audience in Bailey's office—and Errol Coote especially—listened carefully. Coote loved adventure. He loved to read about it and talk about it. He was, at that moment, unaware that the greatest adventure of his life was about to begin.

Lassetter continued his story. He told how, in 1911, he

interested a group in the gold field. "We started inland from Oodnadatta," Lassetter related. "Their interest waned as the days dragged on. When their booze gave out they all decided to go back to the Transcontinental Hotel in Oodnadatta."

The reef never left the little man's thoughts, for he had been fatally bitten by the gold bug. He fought in World War One, worked in the States, left the sea, married, and tried farming in New South Wales with little success. He was working in Sydney on the construction of the Harbour Bridge when, thirty-three years after he had found the reef, he decided to seek help from the influential Bailey.

There was silence in the room when Lassetter finished. Then Jenkins, an assayer and metallurgist who had mined gold with the young Herbert Hoover, questioned Lassetter on the terrain and gold. George Sutherland cross-questioned him and was satisfied Lassetter was telling the truth. After the small man left, promising to return in a few days, Jenkins studied a map of central Australia. He believed that the reef could well be an extension of the rich Kalgoorlie ore belt. But Bailey, ever cautious, decided to check further on Lassetter's story.

In a few days confirmation came from Western Australia, Harding's dusty government report that officially recorded their 1897 find was unearthed along with a 1900 record of assay on the specimens. Satisfied, Bailey invited investors to pool their resources and form a company. In two days three thousand pounds was available. The shareholders were to receive ninety per cent of the profits; Lassetter, ten per cent. It was named the Central Australian Gold Expedition Company, Limited.

A party of six was outfitted. Lassetter was to advise Fred Blakely, the leader, who was an experienced bushman and prospector. Others included George Sutherland; a gold-mining expert, Philip Taylor; engineer and aircraft mechanic,

Captain Blakiston-Houston, who was on leave from the 11th Royal Hussars, and Errol Coote.

The party was well provisioned. No foot treks into the interior; an English Thornycroft six-wheel lorry, especially built for desert exploration, had been donated, along with six hundred gallons of gasoline. They purchased a Gypsy Moth for reconnaissance flights. It would go ahead to locate water, routes, camping sites, and be their link with civilization. Aptly named the *Golden Quest,* it looked like a huge hornet, with its black wings, red fuselage, and gold lettering. This was the most modern-equipped expedition ever to probe the interior for gold.

After four of the party started overland to Alice Springs, the jumping-off place in the Northern Territory, Coote took off from Sydney on July 19 to pick up Taylor in Parkes. Together they flew fourteen hundred miles northwestward on a four-day flight. After the first day, mile after mile of sun-baked brown desert drifted under their wings, with not a patch of green to relieve the mountainous landscape. Ironstone hills with cut-off tops dotted the country, and the slanting rays of the sun struck the earth in a curious manner to make a floating illusion with the white salt and gypsum on the surface of Lake Frome.

Marree, then Oodnadatta near a low line of hills. Refuel, smoke, snack, then off again. Now they were over the pale-green spinifex that contrasted with the cinnabar-red drift of the sand hills. Each evening, high in the still air, they saw a striking panorama of deepening shadows that faded into the purple distance.

Across the James Range was a canvas and galvanized iron town on the banks of a dry creek in which stood tall gum trees. It was Alice Springs, a tiny township that governed a vast trackless region. The ground party was waiting.

Blakely hired a local driver, Fred Colson, who owned a

Chevrolet truck, to help transport their tons of provisions to Ilbilla, a speck five hundred miles to the west. It had a permanent well and would be their base. A few months earlier the McKay Aerial Survey Expedition cleared an aerodrome there six hundred yards square.

Coote found Lassetter in high spirits, but strange quirks in his behavior began to raise doubts in the party's mind about the chunky little man with the queer grin whom Sutherland had nicknamed Possum. Lassetter told them that when he had been to Alice Springs thirty-three years earlier there were only a few people there, but the postmaster later told the party this was not so, that there had been about thirty people in the town. Being a lonely outpost, then, the postmaster said no one could possibly make a mistake about the number of people. Then, one night at the Australian Inland Mission Hostel, Lassetter talked too much after a few drinks. Taylor brought word he was making a fool of himself and causing the expedition to look ridiculous. "If he's brought us out on a wild goose chase, we'll give him rations and water and make him walk back," Coote growled. The seeds of suspicion were sown.

On an afternoon in late July, with the plane safely stored, all departed from Alice Springs in two trucks. The journey lasted two nightmarish weeks. Progress was slow through the rocky, hilly country dense with mulga and brush. Paths had to be hacked with axes. Other times the paths lay on soft sand. The Thornycraft got temporarily bogged at Todd River and the first day they traveled only thirty-one miles. Flies and ants made eating difficult, and the nights were bitterly, painfully cold. No one slept except Lassetter, who for some reason preferred to snore away in the truck cabin surrounded with guns and ammunition. The farther west they traveled the more touchy Lassetter became.

When they reached Hamilton Dam, they had to spread

coconut matting to enable the heavily loaded vehicles to move. Branches were cut to make a corduroy road as the Thornycraft labored on at two miles an hour. Work was hard and tempers grew short. Virgin country was penetrated. The mats became heavy with sand as creek after creek was crossed. Logs were felled for bridges across the muddy streams.

One day, while the party was weary and exasperated, Lassetter pointed out a gnarled mulga bush as the one he had strung his hammock to when he first passed through here. As he moved on, Colson said to Coote: "Did you hear that? I do declare it must be the very tree. Bad luck though for Lassetter . . . that tree can't be thirty years old yet." They laughed, but not enthusiastically.

On an afternoon when only three men were in camp an argument broke out. Coote heard hot words and Houston snapped to Lassetter: "Oh, go away, you annoy me." In a minute Houston strode up to Coote. "That man is a blessed lunatic. Claims to have designed the Harbour Bridge . . ."

Later, as they tried to raise Wave Hill on their small wireless, a fight broke out between Taylor and Lassetter, who had neglected to get a speaker with the set. Only earphones were available. Coote told them neither one knew anything about the radio and this sparked more arguing. One member took Coote aside and said, "Look Errol, I've told Possum you and Taylor are a bit touched and he should humor both of you. Of course we all know *he's* the one who's mad and that's the best way out of the difficulty."

"Just as you say," Coote replied, "but I think he's a shrewder man than you give him credit for."

That night Lassetter's disposition improved and around the campfire he regaled the party with bursts of poetry.

"I always broadcasted Kipling," he said. "I made his works very popular."

"Oh, *you* were the chap responsible for that," Coote responded dryly. "I often wondered how Kipling became popular."

"Yes," Lassetter replied unsuspectingly, "I specialized in Kipling over the radio—and it went down well." Thereupon he gave an excerpt from "Mandalay." Then, breathless, he retired to his bed in the truck and was soon snoring away.

They passed Haasts Bluff and moved out of the dense mulga. For a short spurt they crossed easy country, with ample water, but soon the truck was bogged again and there was more swearing and sweating. The going grew murderous. At night the eerie quietness of the bush depressed them. Not a move—not a sound. Everything was deathly still. An owl flew low over the fire and sparked talk of evil omens and ghost stories. A long-drawn-out howl, mournful and low at first, then rising to a blood-curdling scream, shattered the stillness.

"Good God!" Taylor gasped and reached for his gun. "What's that!"

"Dingoes," Coote replied. "Calling for the kill. But don't worry, they won't attack."

Silence enveloped them again, as their thoughts turned to Lassetter, moving alone through this forsaken land thirty-three years earlier.

In trying to cross Aiai Creek, in the shadow of Mount Liebig, Colson's truck lost its differential. Colson and Coote readied the Thornycraft for the trip back to Alice Springs for parts, which Coote planned to fly to Aiai Creek. Houston decided to accompany them; his military leave was almost over. They reached the town in two days, got the parts, and said goodbye to Houston.

The next day Coote and Colson took off in the Moth, heavily loaded with parts. At Aiai Creek the party had cleared a postage stamp area and Coote set the plane down. Colson, Taylor, and Sutherland set to work on the damaged Chevrolet.

It was agreed Coote should take Lassetter for a recon flight, and the next morning Possum was waiting, decked out in helmet, goggles, and overcoat. Coote did not like the size of the clearing and decided first to take off alone to test how well the plane would lift. He roared directly toward the creek lined with tall gums and pulled up. The biplane faltered, stalled, and started to dive. Coote acted quickly, aimed through an opening in the gums, regained speed, circled, and landed. "No passengers today," he said. Had Lassetter accompanied him, both would have been killed on the takeoff. Coote tied the plane down, said a prayer that wandering bushmen would not camp under the wings with a fire, and the party pushed on to cover the remaining sixty miles to Ilbilla.

It was four days of grueling going. The spinifex grass and vegetation was thicker and everyone loked sharp for venomous spinifex snakes. Bright green, they lay coiled in the grass and struck at anything that passed. The men killed dozens. The Thornycraft bogged again, and in the shadeless desert the sun became hotter and hotter. They moved so slowly that the swarm of flies kept pace with them. The truck engine boiled, then caught fire. There were anxious moments until it was extinguished. The fear of being totally abandoned five hundred miles from the nearest civilization chilled them. On a night that turned bitter cold Blakely and Lassetter argued over a missing drinking mug, but they were separated before blows were struck. When Ilbilla was reached the following morning, spirits improved.

Colson's service ended, he headed back to Alice Springs, taking Coote as far as Aiai Creek to pick up the Moth and fly it to Ilbilla. They arrived in the afternoon and, finding the plane safe, began work with axes to clear a runway three hundred yards long.

They finished an hour before sundown and Coote decided

to make a dash for Ilbilla that evening. "There's just time," he said.

Quickly he checked the plane, pulled its tail into the bushes and gave it the gun. It accelerated sluggishly and twice Coote tried to make it lift. No luck.

At the end of the clearing was a fallen gum tree with a protruding branch. As it loomed toward the plane's nose Coote made a final, last-ditch effort to lift it over.

There was a clear patch on the other side of the fallen tree, so I held her off again, sawing her into the air. She was hurtling the gum tree like a giant race horse when, with a sound like a pistol shot, the right wing cracked against the dead limb sticking up from the gum. I had banked to dodge it, but too late. The banking only led to disaster. The machine slithered down on her left wingtip toward the standing gum tree on her port side. With a sickening rending and crashing I saw the left wing leave the machine. Quick in thought, I leaned over and knocked off the ignition switches, then pushed my goggles back over my head, flung my arms in front of my eyes, and ducked. All was perfectly still. I had finished my shortest flight.

The machine had struck the ground with the right wingtip first. Then the nose of the machine bored into the sand and she turned over on her back. I struck the instrument board with my head with such force that the board was smashed and the glass from the tachometer cut my left cheek under the eye. My head was doubled up against my chest and the blood streamed down into my eyes and helmet. I was upside down and could not move. My right arm was jammed by the starboard wing, my left leg felt numb and I could not move it. I felt an awful pain in my chest and it was with difficulty I could get my breath. All I could do was grunt. Petrol was everywhere. I was saturated with it. Terror struck my soul. The petrol was dripping to the hot engine and was sizzling. Any moment the machine would go up in flames. Frantically, I tried to move, but I was jammed in tight and upside down. Where was Colson? I tried to call out but could not get wind into my lungs. Then I heard Colson crashing through the mulga.

Colson pulled Coote clear. The pilot had face lacerations, a hole in his elbow, and a five-inch opening in his left thigh. "No chance for Ilbilla now," Colson said. "It's hospital for you." He helped the pain-racked airman onto the truck bed and as they started out Coote looked back at the wreckage. "It all seemed in vain now," he said later. "We'd come so far and now that the machine was about to do her real job, I had messed everything up."

Riding through the Central Australian wilderness was painful anytime, even in a well-loaded truck. But riding wounded on the broad of his back in the empty truck bed was excruciating torture for Coote. Colson dared not delay, however; it was a matter of life or death. In one torturous, two-hundred-forty-mile marathon dash, they reached Alice Springs in twenty-two hours—dog-tired, bruised and battered.

After medical attention, Coote wired the bad news to Sydney. As he rested and gained strength, a wire arrived from the syndicate to inform him that a second machine, *Golden Quest II*, was on its way to Alice Springs with another pilot, Pat Hall. Coote was to accompany Hall to Ilbilla.

Meanwhile, at Ilbilla, a worried Blakely, with Taylor and Sutherland, backtracked to Aiai Creek, found the bloodstained wreckage and feared the worst until they discovered the scribbled note left by Colson.

In a few days Hall and Coote flew the *Golden Quest II* into Ilbilla.

"Where's Lasseter?" Coote asked.

"Out taking a look at the country," Blakely replied.

Some Arunta and Luritya aborigines had come in from the Hermannsburg Mission with a young camel driver—a German named Johns who was a dingo shooter. Coote was suspicious of him and after a gentle hint Johns moved on, but, as events later showed, not very far, for he played a part in the tragic finish of the gold quest. A missionary native named Rolfe had accompanied Johns and it was later learned he did not care for the German either.

Pat Hall piloted Lassetter on a two-hour flight to scout the sand hills and to locate landmarks near the reef. When they landed, everyone was expectant. But Lassetter shook his head. "We're a hundred-fifty miles too far south," he said. Coote was suspicious and he led Lassetter aside. "Did you pick up your landmarks?" he asked.

"Yes, I did," Lassetter replied stiffly. "And what's more I saw the reef. It's there plain as a pike staff. We only flew about thirty feet off the ground when we were near it, but it's in the heart of mulga and timber country ... impossible to land there."

Coote became angry and reminded Lassetter of the company's rule that he was to reveal the location and landmarks when they were fifty miles out of Alice Springs. Words shot back and forth in a blistering exchange. Lassetter stoutly resisted because, he admitted, of his dislike for Blakely and Colson. Coote persisted until finally Lassetter told him of its location with respect to three hills.

Later, Coote cross-questioned Hall to verify Lassetter's story. Hall said, "We must have been gone an hour and ten minutes when he began to jump about in the front cockpit. He pointed to something, but I didn't know what he was trying to tell me. He almost popped out of the plane. There was no doubt that he was genuinely excited. Then he waved me to return to Ilbilla. There was no doubt he was very excited about something."

"Would you know that country again if you had to go out there?"

"I don't think I could ever forget it," Hall replied. "A man would remember every feature of that terrible place. I could go back there tomorrow and fly right over the spot. In fact, I could go there in twelve months' time and do the same thing."

Coote frowned. "Maybe the hills he saw were the Three Sisters—one of his landmarks. That was as good as seeing his reef. Was there a small lakelet anywhere near where you turned back?"

"Yes." Hall nodded. "Away on our right was a small circular lake. Looked as though one might tackle a landing there, too."

Next day a way was sighted through the sand hills and the party pushed off. The heat was intense; the truck finicky. Their enthusiasm waned rapidly. Lassetter was restless and argued with everyone.

Coote and Taylor flew back to Alice Springs and Coote traveled alone to Adelaide to have a larger engine installed and a twenty-five gallon fuel tank fitted in the front cockpit to increase the machine's range. On September 19 Coote left Adelaide for Alice Springs, four hundred miles distant. At Oodnadatta, where he was forced to wait three days because of gale-force winds, he received a wire from Bailey in Sydney saying the expedition was returning without Lassetter. He asked Coote to fly out and make contact with him.

Coote was puzzled. What had happened? Why abandon the man on whom the expedition had been formed? Why hadn't they brought him back with them? He wired Bailey he was prepared to carry on indefinitely and was flying on to Alice Springs.

Another wire awaited Coote at Alice Springs, suggesting he take Taylor if the mechanic was agreeable. Taylor consented and they made plans to establish a new base at Ayers Rock, 140 miles south of Ilbilla, where the earlier McKay expedition had found water. Taylor was to go in with the supplies by camel train, with Paddy Tucker, a half-caste driver.

Hell's Airport—and the Lure of Lassetev's Reef

The party had already passed through Alice Springs on the way to Sydney, and Taylor told Coote what had happened after they had left Ilbilla. When the party traveled west they ran into the sand hills and were stopped cold. Then someone discovered all the cans held petrol instead of water. Tempers were raw when they barely made it back to camp that night.

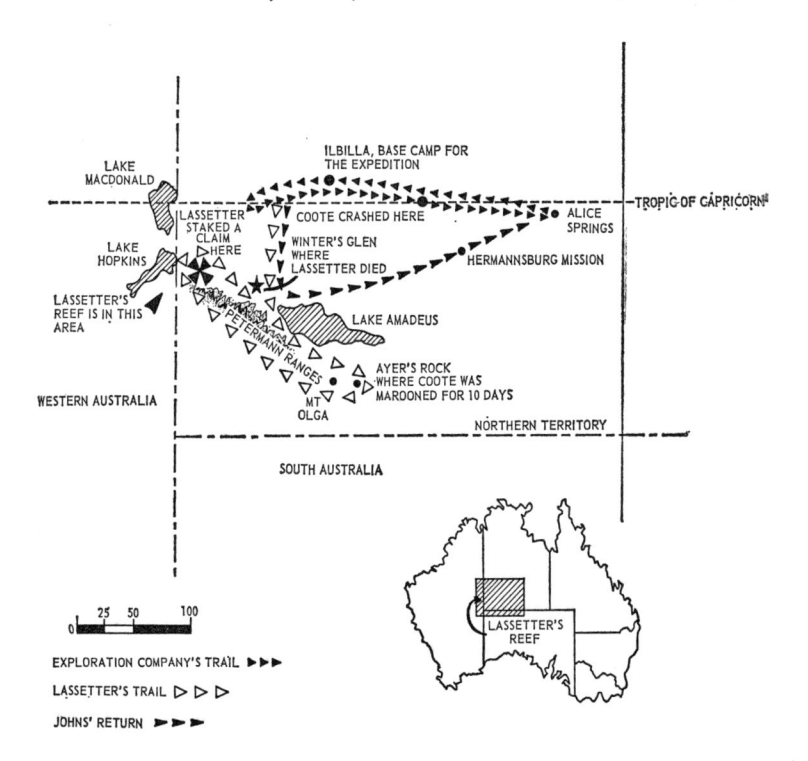

Map key:
- EXPLORATION COMPANY'S TRAIL ▶▶▶
- LASSETTER'S TRAIL ▷ ▷ ▷
- JOHNS' RETURN ▶▶▶

Next day another attempt was made to break through, but they were again halted at the edge of a plateau. It was the last straw. The truck was in bad condition, the plane was not available to act as their eyes, and the heat was unbearable. The majority voted to return to Sydney and reassess the situation. One member swore, "I'm not going to leave my bones to bleach on the desert for all the gold in Australia." But Lasseter, realizing the gold was again within his reach, was stubborn. "You chaps do what you like. I'm staying in this country until I get to the reef," he declared firmly.

Then, like a ghost out of the desert haze, Paul Johns returned to their camp with his string of camels. Lassetter made a proposition to the dingo hunter to use his camels on the gold trail. The others packed the truck and returned to Alice Springs.

A sudden tall spiral of sand—a willy-willy—wrenched the *Golden Quest II* from it tie-down, tumbled it thirty feet and smashed its engine mount. As Taylor repaired it he growled: "Planes are hoodoo in this country."

Finally, after rain and windstorm delays, Taylor, Paddy Tucker, and Dick, an abo, started south for Ayers Rock. Fourteen days later Coote set out to meet them, landing at Hermannsburg Mission on the first leg of the flight. There he engaged Rolfe to meet the camel train and join the search for Lassetter. From Hermannsburg he struck a lonely course southwest.

The country was flat, covered with salt bush and occasional spinifex. "I kept a sharp lookout for Taylor and the camel train," Coote recorded, "but not a moving object disturbed the peace of the sandy solitude. Now and then willy-willys careened in mad fashion over the landscape. Otherwise I was in a dead land."

The salt hills disappeared and the dreadful sand hills came over the skyline. He crossed the tip of Lake Amadeus that had the appearance of a terrible place. After four hours in flight Mount Olga was passed on his right. Then, like a red specter emerging from the haze, came Ayers Rock, square and stark. The huge monolith rises 1143 feet from a ten-thousand-square-mile flat plain. It is five and a half miles around its base. Twenty miles away is the only other elevation of any prominence, the Olgas, a weird jumble of rounded rock knobs. Coote's plan was basically sound, for Ayers Rock and the Olgas are today the jumping-off place for gold hunters.

Coote circled the rock looking for the camel train. He circled wider. Nothing. He flew to nearby Mount Conner and back without sighting people or a camp. Two hours of fuel remained, not enough to return to Hermannsburg Mission. The smoothest patch he could find was five miles from the rock so he throttled back, glided in, and touched down carefully. The Moth had almost stopped rolling when *whack!*—something struck the propeller. When he stopped the engine he discovered he had lost four inches from the edge of the propeller when it struck a stick. He was marooned, hundreds of miles from civilization, entirely alone in the desert. An extremely precarious situation.

Coote realized the ground party was already five days overdue. Were they lost? Still struggling? Had they gone past the rock? Had they turned back?

The pilot took stock of his supplies. One bottle of medicated wine, a two-gallon demijohn of water, milk tablets, beef cubes, eighteen eggs, two pounds of sugar, one pound of tea, two small fruit cakes, some carrots and cabbages.

Trailing a stick in the sand, Coote walked the five miles to the Rock. He found water in several places; also an abo's footprints and rock paintings. Overhead, eagle hawks soared silently over the peaks.

He started back to the plane as the Rock slowly turned a brilliant pulsating red—a giant, glowing coal—in the desert sunset. Knowing the Rock was sacred ground for natives added to his uneasiness. Before climbing into the plane to sleep he fired three shots as a signal to the ground party. No reply. He settled down, nervous and edgy in the trackless solitude.

It must have been about half past eight when I heard a growl like distant thunder. It was coming steadily closer and I wondered whatever it could be. I was not left long in doubt. Like a stinging fury the wind had arrived for its nightly sonata at the Rock. Playing an accompaniment to the chorus of the ghosts of departed aborigines which are supposed to dwell in the cavernous heights of the desert monolith. It howled all night, ripping the sand up in great clouds and swinging it in blinding clouds against the plane. At the crack of dawn I crawled from my cramped position in the cockpit and lit a tiny fire. I did not want to attract the natives. My breakfast was a cup of tea. Eats were reserved for the night meal . . .

Next morning, carrying a can of red paint, Coote hiked around the Rock to pinpoint water holes. The ground crawled with lizards, snakes, huge flies and ants. At a dozen places on the rock wall he wrote a message for Taylor's party.

S.O.S. Plane 5 miles
SW rock.
Coote 29-10-30

After twenty miles of walking he was back at his plane. Day after day passed and in the terrible heat of day he lay under the wings of the plane. He had a pint of carefully measured tea each morning, and at night a slice of cake, an egg, and another pint of tea. He perspired profusely and felt himself grow steadily weaker. By day he fought off the giant red ants and at night the tiny black ants. Lizards scampered over the plane. As the water diminished he made plans to leave the plane and make camp at the Rock's northeast corner, where he would prepare smoke fires.

Carrying the remainder of his water in a small bottle, he set out at the crack of dawn on the ninth day to take his belongings—in relays—to the Rock. The sun beat mercilessly on his trebled journey over the blast-furnace desert floor.

Hell's Airport—and the Lure of Lassetter's Reef 89

When he finally reached the water hole at two-thirty that afternoon, he discovered that it was dry.

I nearly collapsed as the thought struck me with overwhelming force that this had probably happened to all the other holes.

My mouth dropped open and I jabbered like an ape. My breath came in short gasps; I was going off my head . . .

I staggered back from the hole. I was almost frantic now and my tongue had risen to the roof of my mouth. It was swelling rapidly.

"Cool down, don't make such a fool of yourself," said a small still voice in my brain. I did. Looking up at the Rock I saw a particularly wide, dark scour extending right down its face. At the foot of the scour was dense undergrowth. Perhaps there was water there. Eagerly I tore through the bushes. A snake reared and hissed. Madly I struck at it with a stick and flung it several yards away. It was a black snake about four feet long. Hundreds of birds rose chattering shrilly. There at my feet was clear blue water. I bent down and plunged my face in and drank and drank. Then I ran back to my flag [marker] and brought it over to a cave that was nearby. The snake had disappeared and I was not worrying about it very much. I had found water and that was the main thing. I took my pannikin and procured more water. Critically I examined it as I raised it to my lips. It was full of little red leeches. Climax and anticlimax. Now I was going to bleed to death.

I waited the regulation quarter of an hour that it is supposed to take according to schoolboy dictum for a swallowed leech to kill you, then I boiled some water and made myself a cup of tea. It was 2:30 P.M.; I had left the plane at 4 A.M. My progress had certainly been slow.

I came out of my soliloquizing with a jerk as I got another whiff of sweat and stale medicated wine. Comforting thought. If I was as savory inside as I was externally, those leeches were undoubtedly dead meat.

Coote crawled into a nearby cave and smoked his last cigarette. Where was Lassetter? Had he passed here? He watched a horde of big black ants strip a large dead lizard to a skeleton in two hours and knew that would happen to him if he died there.

Determined to hold out as long as possible, he moved to the cooler northeast corner. The moon that night rose high and full and bright as daylight. As he walked to the water hole he drew up short. There were a dozen fires there. Wild blacks! he thought. He ducked back, automatic in hand, and lay still. Then he heard a strange call. *Kura kai, Kura kai*—an abo call for certain.

Unable to sleep, he lay sweltering in the ninety-degree night heat until his thirst became unbearable. At dawn he decided to make a break for the water a couple of hundred yards away. He staggered forward. Nothing stirred. As he rounded a rock he saw some camel tracks, then a man bending over a fire. It was Taylor, with Rolfe and Paddy Tucker. They had not been lost after all—only delayed.

Taylor straightened, mouth agape as Coote staggered up. It was a welcome reunion for both. After some damper (bread baked in flat cakes), beef, and tea, Coote knew things were at last looking up.

Taylor told Coote of their difficult journey. Their camels had floundered, stalled, and threw their loads. The party became lost and arrived at Mount Conner with canteens almost dry. No water there. Tucker went ahead to find water at Ayers Rock. It was he who had built the fires and sounded the eerie calls.

With rivets and a bit of benzine tin, Taylor repaired the plane's propeller and Coote flew the Moth to a clearing near the camp. The supplies were unloaded from the camels, stockpiled, then Tucker left for the return trip to Alice Springs, leaving Rolfe and two camels with which to scout for the missing Lassetter.

Leaving Taylor and Rolfe to finish clearing the airstrip,

Coote fueled the Moth and took off for Alice Springs and Adelaide for a new propeller. The air was thick with yellow sulfurous dust and he was glad to see the Rock grow smaller behind the plane's tail. Apart from being a hell for him, it had been—unknown to Coote—a port of call for Lassetter, who had passed just over the western horizon to his final camp. Coote later commented: "Ayers Rock was a place as near the 'nether regions' as I ever wish to be."

On reaching Alice Springs three hours and forty-five minutes later, the propeller vibrated so badly Coote decided to wire Adelaide for a new one by rail, rather than risk the flight. Shortly after his arrival a wire from the directors told Coote to pick up Taylor, return to Sydney, and leave Lassetter to shift for himself. The pilot was unhappy with the instructions and three days later, as he pondered the situation, Paul Johns arrived in town with three ragged, footsore camels. He came to Coote's tent and told him what had happened in the desert.

Lassetter and Johns headed south into land that was wild and unbroken, where the Petermanns shimmered in the far distance through the intolerable desert heat. They swayed on atop their camels, into the vast, silent land of canyons, rock monoliths, and salt lakes. They crossed the Low Bluff Hills, drank at Petarde Spring, moved around Mount Peculiar, pitched camp at weird Lake Amadeus, and stopped at Ayers Rock. Finally they trekked into the wild, broken Petermann Ranges. Water became a problem but fortunately Johns knew where to find native soaks—springs—spaced three to four days apart. Their camels developed sore feet and travel was slowed.

As they drew close to the area of the reef, it became increasingly apparent that Johns was suffering from the gold fever. He tried to suppress his eagerness, but continued to hound Lassetter with questions about his reef. Lassetter's suspicions of Johns grew, and the strain of their long journey began to surface. They argued and Lassetter went on alone. Two days later he returned with a sack of rocks and told Johns he had found the reef again.

"I questioned him about the country," Johns said, "and he told me such an absurd story I called him a liar. He bellowed that anyone who called him a liar would have to fight him. We were eating at the time and he threw his plate of food in my face.

"I told him the only thing I'd fight with was my gun and I drew it."

They grappled. Lassetter overcame Johns and threw his pistol in the mulga. Then he packed his gear and said he would camp alone, but the next day he was back, willing to make amends. He asked Johns to bring more supplies and gave him a letter to take to the government resident in Alice Springs. Johns started back after leaving Lassetter with two camels.

Coote saw Lassetter's letter at the resident's office. It said he had found the reef, pegged six leases on it and made photographs. He needed fresh camels and supplies and asked that Johns bring them out. He would wait a week or two at Ilbilla, then go south to Lake Christopher to meet a man named Johannsen. Coote wired this news to the directors but they were adamant. Return to Sydney. Resignedly, Coote shrugged, and when the new propeller was installed he took off for home on November 20.

Meanwhile, at Ayers Rock a willy-willy had blown hot ashes on the stockpiled supplies and burned them. There was no choice but for Taylor and Rolfe to strike out for Bob Buck's place—four days of slow traveling in the intense summer heat. They arrived more dead than alive.

There were more upsetting days ahead for the directors of the Central Australian Gold Expedition Company. In late December they sent out another plane with Leslie Pittendrigh as pilot and a mining engineer named Hamre. Taylor was directed to go to Ilbilla and re-establish the base there for them. They failed to arrive and on December 26 it was evident the men were down somewhere in the wasteland inferno of the Macdonnell Ranges. Royal Australian Air Force "Wapiti" machines searched steadily from January 1 to 10, when the men were found in open country, weak but alive, where they had landed in mulga scrub ten miles east of Haasts Bluff, out of petrol. In an average daytime temperature of 115 degrees they had walked thirty miles to find water. Rain saved them.

Nothing was done for Possum—the lonely man in the desert upon whom the very existence of the venture depended. What happened to him?

Paul Johns emphatically declared Lassetter would not reach the rock hole sixty miles south of Ilbilla, the Rawlinson Range, or Lake Christopher because he lacked knowledge of the country. Johns was wrong, as pieced-together events later proved. Traces of Lassetter's camp were found in the Warburtons and in the Rawlinsons. Explorer Michael Terry found traces of Lassetter's camp on the shores of Lake Christopher.

Johns was to have followed Lassetter to the lake with fresh supplies but did not go. Lassetter took his camels there, but Johannsen failed to meet him. He and a companion were speared by blacks and their bodies afterward found by a police party. Lassetter was returning to Ilbilla for more food when his camels bolted near the Petermanns in a maze of sand hills. It must have been a terrifying predicament; he was too far from base, marooned. There, eighty miles west of Mount Olga and Ayers Rock, he must have sensed the veil of death closing in.

Fortunately Lassetter had removed his packs before the animals bolted and was able to reach the Petermann Ranges, where there was ample water. He found a cave near Winter's Glen and made camp. Soon Eumos tribesmen—black brethren of the Petermanns—came in to share his camp. Lassetter was always finicky about blacks, but in his diary and letters, found later, he said they were friendly, especially one old man he called Warts.

But no help came. Overcome with dysentery, almost blind with sandy blight, and suffering the agony of hunger, he clung grimly to life until the end of January. By then, with ants and flies eating at his face, he had become an emaciated and helpless skeleton of a man, although he remained rational until the coma of death overtook him. His diary and a letter to his wife, found in a hole in the cave where he held grimly to life for eight weeks, showed little Possum's tremendous tenacity and clarity of mind. He spoke of his reef and how it would provide comfort for his family. He wanted his son to be a civil engineer. He was content when the end was near, hopeful the reef's discovery would bring the tremendous development he envisioned. In his letter he wrote, in part:

I'm dying . . . Good-bye Rene, darling wife mine, and don't grieve. Remember you must live for the children now, dear. My last prayer is "God be merciful to me a sinner, and be good to those I leave behind."

Harry

Eventually, Johns and Taylor set out from Ilbilla to find Lassetter, but the marooned man was then in the comatose state. Shortly afterward he was dragged by a native and his lubra [woman] to Shaw Creek, where his body was eventually found and buried by Bob Buck. After fencing the grave around, Buck carved the one word LASSETTER on a nearby tree.

Men of the 1933 McKay Aerial Expedition found the lubra who helped carry Lassetter to Shaw Creek. They also found the cave with his last pathetic message: "Sixty days without food. Cannot last much longer."

Lubras in the area had torn the film from his camera and wore it as belly bands.

The tragic failure of the expedition should logically have checked gold exploration in Centralia. It didn't; it stimulated it. In August 1931, enterprising Leslie Bridge hired Bob Buck to guide him into the Petermanns. They came to within sixty miles of the reef before they turned back due to lack of water and incompatibility. The expedition cost two thousand pounds.

Late in 1932 an expedition entered the Warburtons and returned empty-handed. In the winter of 1933 Charles Cable and a friend found a small gold reef in the region described by Lassetter. His companion strayed from camp and died of thirst. Cable returned, vowing the country was hoodoo.

A. V. Foy led an expedition in 1936, and the Cutlack Air Expedition made two probes that year. Gold Reefs Investigators Company, Limited, went into the Petermanns twice in 1937 and again in 1939. In March 1951 W. N. Harding led an expedition toward the reef. He planned another journey as late as March 1967.

Some people are convinced Lassetter never saw a reef worth a nickel. Some who knew him said he was an aggressive, self-opinionated crank, full of hopeful visions. And some suggested his reason for telling the story, risking his own life and endangering the lives of others in his pointless quest for the phantom gold, lay in his heart, not his imagination. Lassetter had a wife and children whom he dearly loved. With the Harbour Bridge nearing completion, he again faced unemployment. The privations his family would suffer were thought by some to have driven him to put up any despairing bluff that would provide them with shelter and food. As long as he was out on trek for the Gold Company, he earned twenty-five dollars a week which was paid to his wife. He knew his family was safe. But although it is certain to exist, the reef Lassetter claimed he found has never been positively located. As time passed, however, more and more about Lassetter was found to be true. Coote reflected years afterward: "Too many people, including myself, were confident Lassetter could not do anything right out there. It was we who were wrong, not Lassetter, who died alone in the desert after finding three times what should be Australia's largest gold reef."

Part Two

World War I and II

5

O'Brien Outwits the Huns

P̄AT O'Brien fought in France with the Royal Flying Corps before his countrymen went "over there." He downed three German airplanes, was shot down, wounded, imprisoned, escaped, and was back in the United States seven months before the Armistice. In his struggle for freedom, despair joined forces with the enemy and despondency pushed him to the brink of surrender. But in those moments O'Brien heard a faint voice say: *Get up; go on*—and he did.

At eighteen, he began flying in Chicago. It was 1912. Four years later he joined the American Flying Service, but after eight months his impatience over America's delay in entering the war caused him to resign his commission. In Canada he joined the R.F.C. and in May 1917 the strapping six-foot-two Yank from Momence, Illinois, sailed aboard the *Majestic* with eight other Americans and nine Britishers. By August 1 all were flying fighter patrols. By December 15 only one had escaped the casualty lists.

The 66th Squadron was quartered at Liettres in France, and O'Brien flew a Sopwith Scout, a light, sensitive fighter with one machine gun. He returned from his first low-level strafing mission with several bullet holes through his plane.

"Before we started out on one of these jobs," he wrote home, "we made sure our motors were in perfect condition. They told us the war bread in Germany was bad." On one morning patrol his flight sighted four German artillery planes. O'Brien's group was six miles behind the German lines, high in the sky to keep the sun behind them so the enemy couldn't see them. They selected three of the machines as targets and dived. O'Brien went right past the man he had singled out. The observer in the rear seat pumped lead at him, but not one shot took effect as O'Brien zipped under him. The American turned, gave him another burst from his synchronized Vickers, and the two-seater went down in a spinning dive, one wing going one way and one another.

Another victory followed a few days later, but it was the events of August 17, 1917, that were indelibly impressed in O'Brien's mind. He brought down a two-seater in the morning, then enemy "archie" knocked out his engine and forced him to land barely inside his lines. Shelling demolished his plane and from a nearby infantry post the young officer wrangled a ride to base. His return brought boisterous rejoicing, especially when he learned his closest friend, Paul Raney, had told Major G. L. P. Henderson, their C.O.: "Don't send for another pilot. That Irishman will be back if he has to walk!"

In the early evening O'Brien's flight prepared to go again, but his name was not marked for duty. He asked why, and the C.O. replied he'd done enough for one day. O'Brien insisted, and the Major reluctantly consented.

The five-plane flight, droning along at six thousand feet, had ten minutes remaining in a thus-far uneventful patrol when they dived into a fight below. Four Germans converged on O'Brien's Scout. Their tracers zipped past, closer and closer. He flipped his light machine into an Immelmann turn that put one plane squarely across his gunsight, barely ten yards away.

I can still see his white face and startled eyes. He knew beyond question his last moment had come. My first tracer passed within a yard of his head, the second looked as if it hit his shoulder, the third struck him in the neck, and then I let him have the whole works—and he went down in a spinning nose dive.

Meanwhile the other Germans converged their fire on O'Brien. He could hear their bullets strike his machine, one after another. As he glanced at the instruments he had time to notice his altimeter indicated eighty-five hundred feet—then the whole works disappeared. A burst of bullets into the panel blew it to smithereens, another bullet went through his upper lip, came out the roof of his mouth, and lodged in his throat. The next thing he remembered was coming to in a German hospital at five o'clock next morning. He was a prisoner of war.

German officers who watched his plane spin eight thousand feet and smash into the ground were dumbfounded to find the pilot alive but unconscious—and without one broken bone. O'Brien had to be cut from the wreckage. His leather helmet was split from front to back by a bullet and the star on his right shoulder had been shot cleanly away. He was unable to move without intense pain.

The hospital was a four-room brick house, low, dirty, and near the front. As his pain-racked head cleared he could make out the orderlies. A German doctor who spoke perfect English removed the bullet from his throat and, reading O'Brien's identification disc, tongue-lashed him. "You Americans who got into this thing before America entered the war are no better than common murderers and deserve to be treated that way!" O'Brien could not reply; his throat wound made it impossible.

On the fourth day he was allowed to relay a brief message to his squadron informing them he was a prisoner of war and "feeling fine." He later admitted, "I was never so depressed but I realized the message would reach my mother. It was enough for her to know I was a prisoner; she didn't have to know I was wounded."

Outside, high in the sky, an air battle raged. With the help of an orderly, the still weak officer was helped outdoors. Six British machines were fighting sixteen Germans. The end came quickly as two Allied and two German planes crashed to earth. O'Brien asked a German officer to learn the identity of the English pilots. He returned with a photo taken from the body of one. It showed O'Brien with Paul Raney. Unknown to O'Brien, Raney had gathered his belongings and sent them back to England, little realizing a few days later he would fight his last air battle with O'Brien a helpless onlooker.

German intelligence got nothing from the young flier and sent him to the officer's prison at Courtrai, Belgium. Its heavily barred windows told O'Brien he could easier escape from Hell.

Courtrai was bombed day and night—twenty-one air raids in the fourteen days he was there. One night, during an unusually heavy raid, several German officers entered his room— all clearly shaken. O'Brien jokingly remarked it would be fine if a British plane dropped a bomb squarely on the old prison. The percentage would be highly satisfactory—one Allied officer and ten German ones. They didn't appreciate his humor.

Rations were poor: near-coffee (chicory and cereal), boiled beets, soup, and occasional pickled meat. A third of a loaf of bread a day, heavy, black, and sour. At every opportunity O'Brien bought food, mainly small, hard pears. These he ate, and hoarded his bread for the day of escape.

The prisoners were occasionally paraded through crowded streets to impress the Belgian populace. German soldiers smirked, but large numbers of townspeople watched in sympathetic silence. One day O'Brien smiled and spoke to a pretty Belgian girl. When she replied a German made a dash for her, but she stepped into a house before he reached her.

The popular topic was escape. One officer suggested stealing a Gotha bomber in which seven or eight could escape. O'Brien was elected to fly it. Neutral Holland was the goal, separated by miles of German-infested Belgium and a triple barrier of electrically charged barbed wire. He waited, and his leap for freedom came earlier than expected.

Early on September 9, O'Brien learned he and six others were being transferred to Strassburg, Germany. A train took them to Ghent under heavy guard where more prisoners joined them. They were herded into a fourth-class compartment of an ancient coach with hard, wooden seats and a solitary candle for light. "From the moment the train started," O'Brien recalled, "the thought kept coming to mind that unless I made my escape now, the war was over for me . . ."

Village after village slipped past. Each click of the wheels brought confinement nearer, freedom farther. O'Brien's only chance was through the window with the train traveling at a good speed. Otherwise the guard could shoot him easily. He opened the window and because the compartment was warm and smoky the guard made no objection. The train's clatter was thunderous, its speed about thirty-five miles an hour. O'Brien weakened. He closed the window.

The urge returned, stronger than ever. So close was the guard sitting opposite, his boots and the stock of his Mauser occasionally bumped O'Brien's shoe. He was middle-aged, homeward-bound on leave. O'Brien smiled at him. Quietly the lieutenant told his plan to the English officer beside him.

"For God's sake, Pat, chuck it!" he said. "Don't be a lunatic! You'll knock your brains out against the rails, or hit a bridge or a whistling post . . . or a train on the other track. You haven't one chance in a thousand!"

O'Brien murmured that he was going. Where they were headed, he wouldn't even have these odds.

It was 4 A.M. Dawn soon, so it was now or never. Feigning throat irritation from the smoke, O'Brien began to cough. He opened the window again. This time the guard frowned. The wheels rattling over the ties seemed to say over and over: *You're a fool if you do; you're a fool if you don't! You're a fool if you do; you're a fool if you don't!* Over one shoulder of his trench coat was slung a knapsack he'd fashioned from a gas mask bag. It held two pieces of bread, a piece of sausage, and his flying mittens.

He made his move. Casually, as though to place his knapsack on the overhead rack, he stood on the bench. With his left hand on the rack and his right hand clenching a strap that hung from the coach ceiling, he suddenly pulled himself upward, stiffened his body, shoved his feet and legs out the window, and let go.

There was a prayer on my lips as I went out. I expected a bullet between my shoulders, but it was all over in an instant. I landed on my left side and face, buried my face in the rock ballast, cutting it open and closing my left eye, skinned my hands and shins and strained my ankle. I was completely knocked out.

I came to within a few minutes and, finding no bones broken, didn't stop to worry about cuts and bruises. I jumped up to put as much distance between me and the track as possible before daylight.

He bled profusely from his wounds but managed to check the flow with handkerchiefs held as pressure bandages. To prevent telltale traces on the ground, he held the tail of his coat to catch the blood as he stumbled along. He limped a mile, stopped, took his bearings from the stars and headed west for two and a half hours. Although weak from loss of blood, he unhesitatingly swam a canal just before daybreak. It ruined his watch and map. In a small woods he found a hiding place where he lay down and took careful stock. He was sore, caked with mud and blood, his clothing soaked through. His ankle pained, and the jump had opened the wound in his mouth. He could not have swallowed the bread if it hadn't been water-softened.

Sleep was impossible and when darkness came he dragged himself to his feet and stumbled on. More canals. Another ten miles. At dawn he found a clump of bushes and dozed in his wet clothes. Before he started out at nightfall he finished the last of his rations—the sausage. That night, after walking several miles, he became ravenously hungry and thirsty.

For the next six days O'Brien lived on cabbages, sugar beets, and an occasional carrot, always raw, just as he pulled them from the fields. His drinking water, often rank, came from canals and pools. One night he lay in a cabbage patch for an hour to lap the dew from leaves with his tongue.

His many detours to avoid detection almost doubled the distance to freedom—to at least 250 miles. With clear skies the North Star guided him, but he reflected later, "I think it rained almost every night I made my way through Germany and Luxembourg."

He had to find a hiding place by six every morning, and invariably sleep came only from exhaustion—and always toward dusk when it was time to move on. By the sixth night O'Brien was so groggy he was tempted to sleep through the night, but he stumbled on until, at eleven o'clock, he sank wearily into a clump of brush to rest from the drizzling rain. He awakened in broad daylight in a German's backyard! It cured further temptations to sleep at night.

On the ninth night the young flier crossed into Luxembourg; it offered no safer haven than German-occupied Belgium. Although he had covered seventy-five miles, the scarcity of food, constantly wet clothing, and lack of sleep weakened him gravely; he entertained doubts as to his survival. He crossed a river and lost a shoe in eight feet of water. For an hour he strained to dive for it. Eventually he found it and, completely fatigued, struggled on after resting only fifteen minutes. In an hour he came to a river much like the one he had crossed. He walked along the shore to find a boat or bridge. Then he realized it was the same river he had swum earlier—at a bend! Had he followed the shoreline, he could have avoided a three-hour delay. Now he had to cross it. Angrily, he sloshed into the water.

Under an overcast sky one evening, he left a woods and struck off in the direction he thought was north. He trudged through a labyrinth of canals, rivers, and swamps. Toward morning he estimated that he had covered seven or eight miles. Then he frowned. The landmarks . . . something was wrong. He entered a nearby woods and waited on the edge of the forest until dawn. "Imagine my disgust and discouragement when I came upon the exact place I had spent the day before," he said later, "and realized all night long I'd been circling the very woods I was trying to escape. Such ill-fortune and discouragements were harder to endure than the hunger. At times I was furiously angry with myself for the mistakes and foolish things I did. But I always tried to see something funny about the situation. It relieved the strain and helped pass the time." Paradoxically, O'Brien later discovered the greater part of his journey was made during this time.

Blisters appeared on his legs; his knees swelled painfully. He was convinced he had lost the sight of his left eye; he had seen nothing with it since his leap from the train. Crossing back into Belgium he narrowly avoided German guards for the next four days while he traveled due west. At a place between Namur and Huy he encountered the Meuse River where he came nearest to giving up the struggle. The Meuse there was a half mile wide—as wide as the Hudson at West Point. Normally, O'Brien would not have hesitated. He had swum San Diego Bay and the San Joaquin, each a mile and a half wide, but in his weakened condition the Meuse looked like the Pacific Ocean. Unable to find a boat, or even a scrap of timber to buoy him, he waded in at 3 A.M. After an hour's struggling in the current he was exhausted and began to doubt that he would reach the opposite bank—a mere thirty feet away. He choked and gasped; his arms and legs were stiffening, almost immobile. He sank, tried to touch bottom, and failed.

O'Brien prayed for strength to move those few yards and, with all the will he could summon, struck out. It seemed a lifetime before he finally felt the welcome bottom mud and dragged himself out. The bank was high, and he shook so violently when he took hold of the grass it slipped from his hands. He was afraid he would faint and slip backward into the water, but he kept pulling and crawling frantically up the slippery bank, and finally made it. Then, for the first time in his life, he fainted from utter exhaustion.

For two hours O'Brien lay in a stupor. Then he crawled to shrubbery where he hid for another day without food or water. That night he made little headway and by morning had a high fever. Delirious, he talked with himself, arguing back and forth with an imaginary Pat O'Brien whether to continue or simply lie down and quit. Following each spell of foolish chatter he regained his senses for a while, relocated the North Star, and trudged on until his fever returned. "I feared another day of this would finish me," he said. "I had to have food; I was on my last legs."

In desperation, O'Brien decided to approach the nearest

house and get food—or die trying. He wrapped a rock in his khaki handkerchief, fully prepared to kill the occupant if necessary to get something—anything—to eat. At one o'clock in the morning he walked boldly to a door and knocked. An old lady—she must have been seventy-five—came to the window and looked out. She couldn't imagine what was dressed in the bulky overcoat. She gave a cry and her husband and a boy came to the door. They couldn't speak English and O'Brien couldn't speak Flemish, but he pointed to his flying coat and then to the sky and said *fleger* [flier], which he thought would identify him.

O'Brien could not tell whether they understood him or were intimidated by his hard-looking appearance. He reasoned that the old man and the boy would have to be brave to start an argument with such a villainous-looking character as stood before them that night. He hadn't shaved in a month, his clothes were wet, torn, dirty, and his leggings were gone. His hair was matted, and his cheeks were flushed with fever. In his hand was the rock. He made no effort to conceal it or its purpose.

A fearful pause, then they motioned him inside and gave him his first hot meal in more than a month. It was only leftover potatoes, but the old woman warmed them in milk— in the dirtiest kettle O'Brien had ever seen. He asked for bread, but she shook her head. "It was for lack of it rather than because she begrudged it to me," O'Brien said, "for if ever a man showed he was famished, I did that night. I swallowed those warm potatoes ravenously and drank four glasses of water one after another . . .

"As I approached the door I got a glance at myself in a mirror. I was the awfulest sight I'd ever laid eyes on! It startled me as much as a dreaded German helmet! My left eye was fairly well healed by this time, and I was beginning to regain the sight of it, but my face was so haggard and my beard so long and unkempt I looked like Santa Claus on a bat."

Constant exposure and exhaustion forced O'Brien to discard unnecessary weight. His clothes were tattered and threadbare and on his fifth night in Belgium he stole a pair of overalls from a clothesline. An overcoat was confiscated the following night, and the flier could now replace his uniform. He buried it. "I never realized how much I thought of that uniform," he remembered. "I felt I was abandoning a friend when I parted with it. I was tempted to keep the wings off the tunic, but thought it a dangerous concession to sentiment in case of capture."

He moved cautiously along a road to emerge in a village main street. Within twenty feet of him, sitting on a pile of bricks, was the dim outline of a man wearing a German spiked helmet. He backtracked with two lost hours.

At a cobblestone road he paused, listened carefully. On such a road a horse or wagon could be heard a mile away. All was silent, and he started to cross. Then he froze dead in his tracks, for as far as he could see in both directions it was lined with German infantry. More backtracking.

At eight o'clock one evening, with hunger pangs gnawing at him, the Lieutenant approached a small house, handkerchief-bound rock in hand. He knocked timidly. The door was opened by a Belgian peasant, a man about fifty. The fugitive pointed to his ears and mouth, pretending he was deaf and dumb. He opened and closed his mouth to convey hunger. The man beckoned the disguised officer to sit at his rough table and put a plate of cold potatoes and stale bread before him. He warmed some milk. As O'Brien wolfed the food ravenously, from the corner of his eye he saw the peasant watching him. In a minute he touched O'Brien on his shoulder, leaned over to where his lips almost touched his ear and said in broken English: "You are an Englishman—I know it —and you can hear and talk if you wish. Am I not right?"

O'Brien stopped chewing. He stared searchingly at the Belgian. There was a smile on the man's face and a friendly attitude about him. Instinctively O'Brien knew he could be trusted. "You've guessed right—but I'm an American, not an Englishman." The Belgian looked at him pityingly, nodded, and refilled his cup with warm milk. "You will never get into Holland without a passport," he declared flatly. "The closer you get to the frontier the more German soldiers you will encounter and without a passport you are a marked man."

"What can I do?"

"If you will call on this man," the peasant replied, mentioning the name and address of a Belgian in Brussels, through which O'Brien had to pass, "you can arrange for a passport. He can get you out of Belgium."

O'Brien's spirits soared. He thanked the man profusely and tried to pay him for his kindness but he would accept nothing. He covered several miles that night and at dawn hid in a wooded area. At dusk he begged bread from an aged peasant couple. Now, instead of adding two or three miles skirting each village, O'Brien walked boldly through them. In one village he walked directly past two German soldiers leaning against a bicycle. They didn't turn a hair and the incident gave him a world of confidence. It demonstrated there was nothing in his appearance to attract their attention. Apparently the escapee looked like a Belgian peasant.

At the next village more German soldiers stood at the curb. He was fifteen feet past them when:

"Halt!"

I couldn't describe my feelings. The thought that the jig was up, that all I'd gone through and everything I'd escaped was lost, mingled with a feeling of disgust because of my foolish risks in going through the village, combined to take all the starch out of me. I wilted as the soldier advanced to where I stood rooted in my tracks.

I had a bottle of water in one pocket and a piece of bread in the other, and as the Hun approached to search me I held the bottle up in one hand and the piece of bread in the other so he could see it was all I had. I knew he would frisk me, then arrest me and march me off to the guardhouse. I knew I was captured and there was no use resisting. I was unarmed and two other German soldiers were within a few feet of us.

Then, it suddenly dawned on me that for all this soldier knew, I was a mere Belgian peasant. His sole object in searching me was to determine whether I was smuggling potatoes!

He felt my outside clothes and pockets and, finding none, seemed satisfied. He said something in German and then some real Belgian peasants came along and attracted his attention. I put the bottle in my pocket and walked on. I took a furtive glance backward and saw him rejoin his comrades at the curb and stop another fellow. I disappeared in the darkness.

At the entrance to the city, O'Brien shuffled along and mingled with a group of Belgian women. "I imitated the slouching gait of the Belgians, and we walked right past three German guards under a bright arc-light. They paid no attention. If ever a fellow felt like going down on his knees and praying, I did at that moment!"

It was almost midnight when O'Brien found a landmark his Belgian benefactor described. A few minutes later he knocked quietly at a door. The man, Huyliger, was not disturbed when aroused from his sleep. Briefly, O'Brien explained his plight. His contact spoke fluent English, drew O'Brien inside, gave him food and listened patiently to his story.

"I'm going to help you," he said. "It may take time, but eventually we'll get you into Holland."

"I don't know how I can possibly repay you."

"Don't think of that," the Belgian replied. "Knowing I've helped put one more Hun victim beyond their reach will more than repay me for the risks." He rose. "Turn in now, O'Brien, and in the morning I'll tell you the plan."

When he undressed, O'Brien noticed his knees were still swollen to twice their normal size, his left ankle was black and blue from the wrench he'd given it when he jumped from the train; and his ribs protruded. He'd lost forty pounds since his capture. It was his first relaxed rest in two months; he slept for twelve hours.

His host provided a sumptuous breakfast of real coffee, bread, eggs, and potatoes. Huyliger sat on the edge of the bed, watched him eat, and outlined O'Brien's escape.

"We are going to conceal you in a convent temporarily; I'll find a priest's garb for you. You say you can speak a little Spanish, so when the time comes to leave the city you will go as a Spanish sailor—otherwise it would mean disaster."

O'Brien listened carefully and nodded.

"You'll be given sufficient money to bribe the guards at the Dutch frontier," Huyliger continued, "and everything will work out."

"I'll follow your instructions," O'Brien said. "I want to rejoin my squadron as soon as possible."

Huyliger filled in a blank passport. Occupation: sailor. Birthplace: Spain. Age: 30. He repaired a damaged official rubber stamp the Germans had discarded and photographed O'Brien for the forged passport. That night the Belgian moved O'Brien to an empty four-story brick house in a fashionable part of the city. The pantry was bare—except for eighteen hundred bottles of choice wines. A door led to a dark sub-basement—an excellent hiding place. Every mattress had been removed from the beds so O'Brien slept on the floor.

Huyliger suggested O'Brien go out by himself and buy food at the stores, asserting it would build his confidence.

But the American thought it safer to remain hungry rather than risk his ignorance of Flemish or German to a bystander. The Belgian told him of a motion picture house in town. "It's free every night except Saturdays and Sundays. Once inside you're not likely to be bothered. Of course, patrons are expected to eat or drink while watching the pictures." O'Brien learned to slip quietly from the house at night and scour the darkened streets for scraps of food. Occasionally he worked up enough courage to beg from a passing peasant. He realized that he was worse off in the city.

The first night O'Brien passed the picture house he was tempted to enter. He was famished, and he might buy something to eat, although he had no idea how to ask for it. He had screwed up his courage and was about to step inside when he ran full tilt into a German officer just leaving. "It settled my hankerings for moving pictures that night," he recalled.

The next morning his fright seemed foolish. He reasoned he needed confidence. He would confront soldiers often near the frontier and his safety would depend on the calmness he could display. He struggled to overcome his terror at the sight of every spiked helmet, reasoning that with his dirty and unshaven appearance he could easily pass as a poor Belgian peasant. He also noticed the people, although careful to obey the orders of the occupation troops, showed little fear of them. He argued the theater was safe to attend, the last place the Germans would expect to find an escaped American R.F.C. pilot.

The next night, determined to enter the theater regardless, O'Brien cleaned himself as well as possible, brushed his hair, and trimmed his beard with a pair of rusty scissors. To his amazement he looked no worse than the next man who was as poorly dressed. He walked slowly down the alley, imitating the indifferent gait of the townspeople. Once inside the building he saw he could select his seat because not half a dozen persons were there. He slouched over a table in the back with a seat next to the wall. From here he could see everyone and no one would notice him—except those at his table who would have to turn around to do so.

The room filled rapidly and every other person seemed to be a German soldier. A Belgian and his wife sat at his table. Every new uniform caused O'Brien to worry until they were settled. Just before the lights lowered two German officers paused inside the door, looking for seats. They made a straight line for the vacant chairs at O'Brien's table and sat down in front of him. The fugitive could have reached over and touched one on his bald head. They ordered some light wine, but O'Brien's Belgian neighbor ordered bock for himself and his wife, which was what he decided to order anyway, as it was the only thing he could say. He would much rather have ordered something to eat, but the bill of fare meant nothing to him, and he was afraid to pronounce the names of any of the dishes listed. When the waiter came to him, he said bock as casually as he could, relieved to get through this part of the ordeal so easily. A glass of beer cost eighty centimes, but the smallest change he had was a two-mark paper bill. Apparently the Germans were similarly fixed, for the waiter handed their bill back with a remark. O'Brien took it to mean he couldn't make change.

O'Brien was in a quandary. To offer the waiter his bill after he had just told the officers he didn't have change would seem strange, yet the flier couldn't explain it was also the smallest change he had and the waiter would have to return to him later. The only thing to do was to offer him the two marks as though he hadn't heard what the waiter had said to the Germans. The man said the same thing to him, a little more sharply, and handed back the bill. Later he returned with a handful of change and they closed the transaction silently.

For the first half hour the daring impostor was on pins and needles. With over a hundred soldiers in the place and two Germans at his table he considered leaving several times, but when the lights dimmed he felt better. Between pictures the lights came on, and now reasonably composed, O'Brien studied the people. At one table was a German medical officer with three Red Cross nurses. The soldiers drank bock quietly, conversed, and were quite orderly. There was no hilarity or rough-housing. As he sat there within arm's reach of the German officers, he realized what they would have given to know they could have captured an escaped British flier. He smiled to himself, but when he thought of the unnecessary risk he was taking he wondered whether he had acted foolishly. Nevertheless, the evening passed uneventfully. When the show ended he mixed with the crowd and left casually, feeling proud of himself—and considerably more confident.

O'Brien lost no time in putting his new-found assurance to use. After British bombers raided the city he ventured out to inspect the damage. He mingled with crowds, largely soldiers, moved from one bombed-out area to another, and carefully avoided speaking to anyone. He gained military information useful to Allied intelligence. It amused him, while gazing into shop windows, to stand next to German soldiers doing the same, consider how near he was to them and realize they had no way of knowing. But the thought was always tempered with the knowledge that discovery with the forged passport—and his military knowledge of the city—meant he would be shot with little ceremony.

The young escapee was unprepared for the exchange one morning when Huyliger brought breakfast. When O'Brien finished eating Huyliger asked coolly: "I want to know how far you're prepared to go to compensate me for the risks I'm taking and the service I'm giving you."

O'Brien could scarcely believe his ears. "I'll pay you as

well as I can, Huyliger," he replied, trying to cover his disappointment over the Belgian's sudden turn. "But is this the time to discuss compensation? You needn't worry about me showing my gratitude—substantially."

"That's all right, O'Brien," he persisted with a knowing manner. "Perhaps you will and perhaps you won't. I'm not satisfied to wait. I want to be taken care of now!"

"What do you want me to do? How much compensation do you expect? How can I get it to you? I'm willing to do anything reasonable."

Huyliger mentioned a fantastic figure in English pounds. O'Brien was staggered. Was Huyliger joking? He collected his thoughts and said, "You don't really mean that, do you?"

"I certainly do. And what's more, I intend to collect every centime—and you're going to help me get it!" From his coat he took an agreement and demanded O'Brien sign it. O'Brien waved it aside and replied, "Now I see your motive. I don't intend to be blackmailed. I won't stand for it!"

"Very well. As you say. But before you make up your mind so obstinately, think it over. I'll be back this evening." Before the Belgian left he told O'Brien there was a change of plans about the convent. "The Cardinal has issued orders to his priests," he explained. "They're to help no more fugitives. It will be best now if you stay alone rather than mingle with people."

O'Brien's first impulse was to leave quickly. He had the passport and considered Huyliger's help unnecessary in getting across the border. He could use his own ingenuity. But he had turned his personal papers, photographs, and identification disc over to the Belgian when they met. He wanted them back.

All that day O'Brien had no food. In the early evening, famished, he noticed a cat with something in its mouth run down the steps of the opposite house. Throwing caution aside he burst out the front door, ran down the steps, across the street, and pounced on the surprised cat before it could get away. It had a piece of stewed rabbit. O'Brien grabbed the meat, hurried back inside the house and ate it. "I felt sorry for the cat," he said later, "but had no qualms about eating its dinner."

Huyliger returned at eight o'clock. "Well, O'Brien, will you sign or not?"

O'Brien's Irish temper had simmered all day over this man who ostensibly had befriended him and now tried to extort money because of his plight.

"No, Huyliger," O'Brien said. "I've decided to get along without your assistance. Furthermore, you'll return all the photographs, papers, and belongings I gave you."

"Sorry, O'Brien, that's something I can't do."

"If you don't," O'Brien said angrily, "I'll take steps to get them—and damned quick!"

"What could you do?" the Belgian asked. "They're out of the country. I couldn't recover them if I wanted to."

O'Brien knew he was lying. Slowly, deliberately, he advanced and laid his huge hand on Huyliger's shoulder. He glared straight into the man's eyes. "Huyliger, get them by midnight. If you don't, at eight o'clock I'll go straight to the Germans, give them the false passport, and tell them where I got it!"

There were no lights in the house, but they stood where the moonlight streamed through a stained-glass window, and O'Brien saw Huyliger's face go pale. The Belgian spun on his heel and started down the stair.

"Till the city clock strikes twelve," O'Brien called after him, "or the next time you'll see me is with the German authorities. I mean what I say!"

For two hours O'Brien sat on the staircase, musing. His threat to surrender was bluff of course, but would Huyliger dare to steal the jump and get first word to the authorities so as to discredit the story he had threatened to tell them? O'Brien was sure he had detected a yellow streak in the blackmailer.

He had. Before midnight Huyliger returned with most of the flier's things. He apologized and told O'Brien the idea of the agreement was not his. There was another plan to get him to Holland and he asked O'Brien to meet the two other men.

"All right, but meanwhile I need food."

"Sorry, I'm afraid you'll have to get along as best you can. It's too dangerous risking discovery by entering here with food. Until tomorrow then."

One of the men who came the next day was Huyliger's brother. He said they had another passport for him—a genuine one—much safer to use than the counterfeit. O'Brien saw through their game at once.

"Of course you'll have to return the original passport before we can give you the real one," Huyliger's brother concluded.

"No objection . . . let me see the new one."

"That isn't necessary, Mr. O'Brien," the man hedged. "Give us the old one and we'll give you the real one. Fair enough?"

"You'll get this passport"—he patted his breast pocket—"from my dead body!"

O'Brien knew the three could have made short work of him with no one the wiser, but at that moment he felt so mean toward the whole world, he was determined to sell his life dearly.

"The passport's here," I repeated, "and I'm going to keep it. If you 'gentlemen' think you can take it from me, you're welcome to try!"

I was spoiling for a fight. The walls were lined with great pieces of earthenware which had every earmark of great value.

They certainly had great weight. I figured it would come in handy; a single blow with one big vase would put a man out neatly, and as there was lots of pottery and only three men, I knew I could hold my own in the fight I'd flatly invited. I selected the first vase, got up, back to the wall, and told them if they wanted the passport, this was their chance.

They realized the officer meant business and all three immediately began to expostulate on his attitude.

"My dear fellow," said the third man, "for our own protection you owe it to us to proceed as best you can without it, because as long as you carry it, you jeopardize our lives too. Isn't it fairer that you should risk your own safety rather than place the lives of three innocent men in danger?"

"That may be, my friends," O'Brien replied as he edged his way cautiously toward the door, "and I'm glad you realize your danger. Keep it in mind should you feel inclined to notify the Germans. If they get me, they get the passport, and your lives won't be worth a damn. I'll implicate all of you, and they'll take the word of an officer before yours. Good night!"

The bluff worked.

The days spent in the house seemed like years. Improved sleep and security did not offset the hunger that continued to gnaw at him. To pass the time he crouched behind the keyhole and watched soldiers that passed the house frequently. On his last afternoon, while gazing through the keyhole, he heard a squad of approaching soldiers following a military truck. They halted in front. O'Brien fled to the extreme rear of the pitch-dark wine cellar and wedged himself between two cases. German boots tramped up the front steps, there was a crash at the front door, guttural commands, and the clatter of heavy feet overhead scurrying from room to room. Banging and hammering. Smashing and crashing. O'Brien was convinced Huyliger and Company had betrayed him, that it was only a matter of minutes . . . He clutched a wine bottle in each hand and waited. Nervous rats and mice scurried across the floor and over his shoes.

Twenty minutes passed before a detail clomped noisily down the cellar steps. O'Brien stiffened. No sooner were they in the cellar than a guttural order caused them to file back up the steps, out the front door—and away. An hour later O'Brien ventured upstairs. Water faucets were ripped from sinks, pipes torn from walls, and every gas fixture and cooking utensil of brass and copper had been carried away. Germany was desperately in need of critical metals.

It was time to break for the frontier. His health improved, wounds healed, and ankle stronger, O'Brien felt better than at any time since his jump from the train. He left the city and traveled faster, day and night. Feigning deaf-muteness, he begged food from peasants and planned how to outwit the Huns at the most hazardous point of his entire flight—the barrier.

A pole vault? But where to get a pole? Six feet on each side of the electric fence were six-foot barbed-wire fences. A twelve-foot broad jump? This idea was abandoned.

Stilts? As a boy he was skilled in stilt-walking, but again, where could he get the material? He decided speculation was cheap; it would be better to inspect the barrier before making a firm plan.

That night brought a close encounter. Looking for a decent place to sleep, he crawled under a barbed wire and snagged his coat. When he tried to pull it free, he shook the fence for several yards. Out of the darkness came the shattering command: "Halt!" Again he knew he was done for. He hugged the ground in the blackness, undecided whether to run and trust the German to miss him in the night if he fired, or stay where he was. It was foggy as well as dark, and although the sentry was only a few feet away he decided to be still. He thought his pounding heart was as loud as the rattling of the wire, and it was a tense moment. The German muttered a few words to himself and then made a sound as though to call a dog, apparently thinking it had made the noise as it passed under the wire.

For five minutes O'Brien lay motionless before he crawled carefully away. Later that day he knocked at a house for food where the occupants were a father and mother and ten children. He pressed a mark on the man and indicated he was hungry. They invited him to share their meal—a huge bowl of soup served in ordinary wash basins. The father and eldest son were uneasy; they obviously suspected he was not a deaf-mute. While he lingered after the meal a young neighbor called on the eldest daughter, a girl of about eighteen. The suitor eyed the stranger suspiciously and conversed with the family. He seemed antagonistic toward O'Brien and appeared to argue with the family against him. Then the escapee knew why; he wasn't wearing wooden shoes as were ninety percent of the Belgians. When the young swain left, O'Brien departed soon afterward.

After darkness, the long-suffering fugitive arrived at the frontier of Holland to find that the barrier was indeed formidable. Stilts or a pole vault were out of the question, and a brief glimpse was all he got before the measured stride of a sentry caused him to retreat to the fields. "It was disheartening. Only a few feet away was liberty, and the only thing that prevented me from reaching it were three confounded fences!"

One afternoon, as he sat in a clump of bushes and stared morosely at the frontier, he wished some miracle would put his Sopwith Scout before him for three minutes.

Day and night he edged westward. He begged for food but fared badly. Troops were quartered in many houses and people were terrified. Every few miles he approached the barrier to see whether conditions improved. They had not.

A huge ladder! He searched for hours in the forest for pieces of fallen timber. Nothing. There was only enough lumber for a simple ladder that could be leaned against a post where the electric wires were strung. He might climb to the top and jump over the charged fence.

All night long he assembled the crude ladder from small, damp, fallen pine trees. He attached the rungs with grass and strips of his handkerchief, then tested it against a tree. It wobbled threateningly.

All day he huddled in the woods and counted the hours until the supreme test. When night came at last he made for the barrier and waited. After the sentry passed, he hurried across the clearing, shoved the ladder under the barbed wire and tried to follow it. His clothing caught, but he wrenched it clear and crawled to the electric barrier.

He intended to lean the ladder against one of the posts, climb to the top and jump.

O'Brien put his ear to the ground and listened for an approaching sentry. Not a sound. Eagerly, carefully, he placed the ladder against the post and started up. Now only a few feet separated him from liberty. He climbed three rungs before he realized a serious difficulty.

The ladder was slipping!

Just as he took the next rung the ladder slipped and touched the live wire. Current passed through the wet sticks and into his body. There was a crackling blue flash, his grip on the ladder relaxed, and he dropped heavily to the ground, unconscious.

He did not receive the full force of the current; it would have killed him. He came to in time to hear the German guard approaching. He dragged the ladder from the sentry's path and lay flat on the ground, not seven feet from the passing sentry. The German passed so close he could have pushed the ladder out and tripped him.

The mishap convinced O'Brien this way of escape was not feasible. The electric shock had so unnerved him he was afraid to risk it again.

Another way of crossing occured to him. If he couldn't get over the barrier, what was wrong with going under it? The bottom wire was only two inches from the ground and he dared not touch it. With only his hands to dig with, he began eagerly. Fortunately the ground was not very hard. When he dug about six inches he uncovered an underground wire. O'Brien knew enough about electricity to realize it couldn't be charged, being in contact with the ground, but there was still insufficient room for him to crawl through. It was either pull the wire up, or continue digging deeper and crawl under it.

He continued digging. When the distance between the live wire and the bottom of the hole was thirty inches he pulled on the ground wire with all his strength. It wouldn't budge. He was about to give up in despair when a staple gave way in the nearest post, allowing him to pull the wire through the ground slightly. After another vigorous tug, a staple on the next post gave way. The work became easier. There was more leeway now. He tugged again and again until all eight staples had given away. Each time a staple snapped off it sounded like a gunshot to his ears, and he put his head to the ground each time to listen for the guard before he resumed work.

Now he could drag the wire far enough through the ground and away from the fence to dig more freely. Several times he stopped cold, imagining he heard the sentry approaching.

I suffered enough that night to last me a lifetime, with a German guard on one side, death from electrocution on the other, and starvation staring me in the face. The deeper I dug the harder was the work because now my fingernails were broken and I was highly nervous—afraid every moment I'd slip and touch the charged wire. But I kept at it, my mind constantly on the hole and the freedom almost within reach.

Finally I figured I had enough space to crawl under with a few inches between my back and the live wire. I lay face down. On my stomach I writhed under the wire, snakelike, feet first, hugging Mother Earth as closely as possible. To touch the wire with my back meant instant death.

When I finally got through and straightened up, there were still several feet of Belgium between me and liberty—the six feet separating the electric barrier from the final barbed-wire fence. But before I took another step I went down on my knees and thanked God for my long series of escapes. Then I crawled under the barbed wire and breathed the free air of Holland.

O'Brien had no idea where he was and cared less. He was free, and that was enough. He heard the sentry pass the ladder and hole without noticing them. It was November 19—seventy-two days since his final leap from the train thirty-five miles from Strassburg.

O'Brien moved through the darkness, overjoyed with his new-found freedom. Then, thirty minutes later he ran squarely into a three-section barrier fence exactly like the one he crossed. While he tried to puzzle it out, he heard an approaching sentry. The man walked briskly, unlike the slower German guards, and O'Brien assumed it was a Dutch sentry. Bewildered, he moved in the opposite direction. Half a mile away he saw a sentry station light at a crossing point. Thinking to tell his story to the Dutch guards, he approached the sentry box and faintly made out three men in gray uniforms—the regulation Dutch color. On the verge of shouting to them, caution, born of ten weeks' bitter experience, prevailed. As he moved behind nearby bushes, out of the blackness came the German command: "Halt! Halt!"

He froze. Hollanders or Huns? He dropped to his belly as another man ran up. There was considerable talking, but finally one laughed and walked back to the sentry station. O'Brien inched nearer. Then, silhouetted between the light and the sentry post, he noticed the stooping figure of a man—with a spiked helmet. This crossing point was manned by Germans!

O'Brien knew the guards would have shot him without ceremony had he foolishly revealed himself. He would have been buried at once—on the spot—with no one the wiser.

He was completely disoriented now. There appeared to be a frontier behind him and a frontier before him. His faithful guide, the North Star, had disappeared; the entire sky was pitch black. His jumbled brain could bring forth only one thought: Have I wandered in another circle?

In the dim distance he could make out the faint glow of village lights. It had to be a Dutch village; all Belgium was blacked out.

He made straight for the lights, through marsh and swamps, and occasional waist-deep water. In three hours he reached firm ground, found a path and followed it into the village. He approached a little workshop where a bright light burned outside. It was after midnight and three men and two boys who were making wooden shoes were just quitting work. It wasn't necessary to explain he was a refugee; he was caked with mud to his shoulders, and his face told them his experiences of that night. He simply said: "I want the British Consul."

In the village the Dutch family fed him a hearty meal. He slept in their house that night and after breakfast his new friends escorted him to the railroad station. He didn't have the price of his fare to Rotterdam, but they pooled their money for a third-class ticket. As they waited, a crowd gathered and the whole town turned out to see him off. O'Brien recalled: "As the train pulled out of the station the crowd gave a loud cheer, and tears almost came to my eyes."

At Rotterdam he told his story at the British consulate and a bath, shave, fresh clothes, and warm food restored his spirit. The technicalities of internment were somehow bypassed, and the following night Lieutenant O'Brien was aboard a boat for England under destroyer escort.

In busy downtown London the returnee found his nerves in a bad state. It was impossible for him to cross a street without the fear of being run down. He would stand helplessly at the curb, like an old woman from the country on her first visit to the city, afraid to venture across until an understanding bobby, recognizing his condition, escorted him across. In a few days he regained full control of himself.

As soon as possible, the Lieutenant sent a wire to Mrs. M. J. O'Brien in Momence, Illinois.

> Just escaped from Germany. Letter follows.
> Pat

For five days Intelligence officers at the War Department questioned O'Brien on his escape. Ten days after his arrival in England, he told his experiences to His Royal Highness, King George V, in an unprecedented fifty-two-minute interview. That evening he was given a banquet at the Hotel Savoy by a fellow who had wagered with three of O'Brien's comrades that the American would be home by Christmas. The escapee learned of the bet and before the dinner had sent this telegram to Lieutenant Lewis Grant:

> War bread bad, so I came home.
> Pat

In March 1918 Lieutenant Patrick Alva O'Brien relinquished his commission because of ill health and sailed for

Canada and home. On the boat he saw an R.F.C. man, Lieutenant Lascelles. He walked over, held out his hand. "Hello!"

Lascelles stared. "I can't believe my eyes," he said.

"The last time he saw me," O'Brien recalled, "I was going down to earth in a spinning nose-dive with a bullet in my face. He later read I was a prisoner of war, but never believed it; he said it was impossible to survive that fall. Lascelles was one of the few men living of the eighteen original pilots in my squadron."

Back in Canada, O'Brien was met at the King Edward Hotel in Toronto by his brother. Fifty-two years later, Jack O'Brien recalled their reunion.

"The first night he told me the story of what happened to him. He was extremely nervous and paced the floor most of the night while relating his story. The next morning he told his story to a literary agent in New York City, then left Toronto and went to New York to write *Outwitting the Hun.* From then on, Pat lectured throughout the country and occasionally came home to Momence for brief visits. I saw him several times, then I came to California and never saw Pat again."

At a meeting in Kankakee in December 1918, O'Brien announced his intention to become the first man to fly the Atlantic solo. The war flier revealed plans for a twin-engine hydroplane with great fuel-carrying ability. This was nine years before Lindbergh's epic air crossing.

The handsome hero became popular with the Chatauqua circuit. His welcome at the Palace Theater in New York and the Majestic Theater in Chicago was overwhelming. He traveled widely, and while in Cuba in January 1920 he married Virginia Livingston Allen, an American motion picture actress. There were no children and the marriage was destined to be short-lived. Soon afterward, in California, he appeared in the movie *Shadow of the West.*

Today, only one man can be located who remembers Pat O'Brien, the war flier. He is Emerson A. L. F. Smith of Victoria, British Columbia, who says: "I knew him while in Canada. He was an honest, clean-living gentleman who would mix up in any fun or devilment that was going on. Everyone in the camp knew Pat O'Brien and liked him."

Three years after his nightmarish escape, on December 17, 1920, Pat OBrien died from a bullet wound while a guest at the Alexander Hotel in Los Angeles. The act was reportedly self-inflicted; some believed he could never quite escape the memories of his nightmarish war experiences. But a mystery shrouded his death; family and friends refused to believe it was suicide. There was serious speculation about a "suicide note" that his family declared was not in his handwriting. He was buried in Momence with the largest funeral the town had ever seen and the eulogy was given by a member of the Royal Canadian Air Force, representing the Crown.

In his quiet moments this restless man often expressed his belief that he was spared to convey a message of hope to others destined for similar trials. Following his return from Japan on a diplomatic mission for the government, he predicted: "Our next war will be with Japan." Now, in retrospect, it is known that he had strong suspicions of World War II in the Pacific, that he foresaw the hundreds of prisoners who, like him, would risk everything for a try at freedom. For those in generations yet unborn who would fight in Korea and Vietnam, his message was: "Never give up—no matter what happens."

6

A Hero's Life—A Flier's Luck

ENGLISH aviation journalist John Hook once described Ernst Udet as a "great adventurer and a true knight of the air." Twenty years earlier, Udet's captain, annoyed that his reckless young plane-crashing observation pilot had been rewarded with a transfer to single-seater fighters, remarked: "More luck than brains."

Both men were right.

Few airmen loved the rush of a slipstream as passionately as Ernst Udet, and fewer still packed as much high adventure into their lives. Although his postwar reputation as a charming roué followed him round the world, his fame for feminine conquests ran a poor second to his adventurous life in the air. It began in a burst of glory and when World War One ended, he was the highest-scoring surviving German ace —second only to the redoubtable von Richthofen.

At first thought, this man who sent sixty-two Allied planes smashing to earth might be regarded as a hardened killer, a Prussian martinet with little concern for enemy and compatriot alike. But paradoxically, stocky, short, square-shouldered Erni Udet was a man who loved life and his fellow men. Flier, explorer, photographer, cartoonist, and author, he had a rare capacity for enjoying people. Throughout his life he had a zest for adventure. His sensitive and humane nature entered easily into the feelings of others and in his daring, romantic bent he is remembered as the jovial, balding aerial daredevil of four continents. Because he liked people more than power, he was not a disciple of Nazi invincibility and this, finally, was his undoing.

Born in 1896, young Ernst developed into a slightly built youth who designed model airplanes and, later, a man-carrying glider that refused to fly. When the war came he repeatedly volunteered for service but was turned down. Undismayed, and as the owner of a fast motorcycle, he volunteered as a dispatch rider. A few weeks later, speeding on a forward road, his motorcycle struck a shell hole. He took a bad tumble and broke his shoulder. When he was released from the hospital he pleaded with his father, who was financially well off, to let him take private flying lessons. As soon as he had soloed he was accepted by the Imperial Air Service and sent to Darmstadt for advanced training. Here began a hero's life with a brand of luck in war and peace that was to become legendary—and he would need every scrap of it he could get.

The rash Private First Class lost his overconfidence quickly with Fliegerabteilung 206, a photo and reconnaissance squadron. In September 1915, *Gefreiter* Udet, with his commander, Leutnant Bruno Justinius in the observer's cockpit, met serious trouble. Part of their Albatros BII's flimsy structure failed over enemy ground. Miraculously, they managed to edge their crippled bird home, for which they were awarded the Iron Cross. A few days later Udet took off in an Aviatik overloaded with bombs and armament, foolishly made a steep turn after takeoff and reduced the two-seater to a heap of scrap. He was charged with carelessness and sentenced to seven days of military confinement.

A new assignment followed with the maneuverable single-seater E-3 Fokker. Now an acting sergeant-major, Udet was in his glory. One Sunday afternoon in March 1916 he was alerted. French bombers were crossing the front. He raced to the field at Habshiem, clambered into his machine and droned away to intercept them. The light Fokker climbed well in the cool air and at eight thousand feet he turned toward Altkirch. Agonizing minutes passed before he sighted the enemy over Mulhausen—a veritable armada of Farman and Caudron bombers herded overhead by their leader, a great Voisin biplane. Udet, nine hundred feet above them, stalked the fleet cautiously.

The moment had come. My heart beat furiously, and the hands which held the joy-stick were damp. It was one against twenty-three!

My Fokker flew above the enemy squadron like a hawk singling out its victim. The hawk followed, but did not pounce. But even as I hesitated, I realized that if I failed to open the battle immediately I should never have the courage to do so afterwards. In that case I would land, go to my room, and then in the morning Pfalzer would have the task of writing my father that there had been a fatal accident while I was cleaning my revolver.

The Fokker tipped down, plunged. In the cockpit Udet watched through the blur of his propeller as he closed on the back of the Farman that was squarely in the center of the formation. At ninety feet he tripped his gun. *Tack . . . tack . . . tack.* The bomber faltered. A blue flame flashed from its engine, followed by a thin stream of white vapor. Smoke billowed and the bomber tumbled earthward, burning. It was Udet's first victory. He was pleased that in the moment of decision he had confronted his fear and conquered it. Pfalzer would not have to write condolences to his father. One thing young Ernst could not deny was his honor. In 1916 he was ready to take his life to appease the disgrace of a personal failure. Twenty-five years later he had cause to reflect on that moment over Mulhausen.

Victory followed victory, for Udet had found his element and rode the crest of joyous flight. He was given command of Jagdstaffel 15.

Over Lierval in June 1917, Udet, now a leutnant, crossed machine guns with the famous ace of the "Storks." As he maneuvered tightly with the Spad, they passed so close he felt the propeller slipstream of the French machine and saw every detail of his opponent's thin features under his goggles. On the side of the enemy plane were two boldly lettered words: *Vieux Charles,* with the silhouette of a flying stork. It was France's famous son and leading ace—frail, deadly Georges Guynemer, the man who had shot down Udet's close friend, Puz, a few days earlier.

The Frenchman was skilled. Udet half-looped; Guynemer easily half-rolled away. Udet looped, rolled, and sideslipped; Guynemer followed with lightning speed and a hail of bullets rattled and spattered against the German's upper wing. Udet was perspiring. "Gradually I realized he was more than a match for me. Not only had he a better machine, but this Frenchman was the superior duelist. But I had to fight on; to turn away would be fatal."

Udet threw his machine into a steep turn and for a fleeting moment had the helmeted head in the Spad's cockpit squarely across his gunsight. He pressed the Spandau triggers. Nothing. His guns had jammed. Furiously he hammered the breech with his fist. He shook them. They wouldn't clear.

Panic was coming on. He thought he might dive to escape, but wisely he changed his mind. The stronger Spad could outdive any fighter on the Western front.

We still flew in circles round each other. It was a wonderful flying experience—if one could forget that one's life was at stake.

I have never had to deal with a more skillful opponent, and for a while I completely forgot he was Guynemer, my enemy. It seemed to me, rather, that I was having some practice over the aerodrome with an old friend. This feeling, however, did not last for very long . . .

Suddenly Guynemer looped and flew on his back over my head. At that moment I relinquished hold of the stick, and hammered with both hands at the machine guns. It was a primitive remedy, but it sometimes worked.

Guynemer had observed my actions and now knew that I was his helpless victim. He passed close over my head again, flying almost on his back. And then, to my great surprise, he raised his arm and waved to me. Immediately afterwards he dived away toward the west . . .

I flew back home, stupefied.

There are some people who believe that Guynemer himself had a machine-gun stoppage at the same time. Others claim that he feared that I, in desperation, might ram him . . . I do not believe any of them. Rather do I believe that Guynemer gave proof that even in modern warfare there is still something left of the knightly chivalry of bygone days.

Udet was so emotionally shaken by Guynemer's merciful act that he asked for a short leave. Now he could feel complete justification in the words he once spoke to Gontermann, his squadron leader: "If I could only hate them . . . perhaps it would be easier. But they are a magnificent bunch."

Composed, he returned to command Jagdstaffel 37 at Wynghene, a little village in Flanders. His opponents were courageous English fliers who took up every challenge, against all odds, and fought in old, clumsy machines that were no match for the sleek bullet-nosed Albatros.

Flying slackened as the winter of 1917 closed in with snow and rain. The clouds hung so low that flying came almost to a standstill. There was one gray-leaden day Udet remembered well.

I was living in a house owned by a lace manufacturer. The son of the house was serving in the Royal Flying Corps, and his parents made a point of reminding me of it: "He is doing his duty; and you are doing your duty." That was their view and they cared not who knew it.

On his sister's birthday, this Belgian airman flew over the house and dropped a bouquet of roses. They fell right on the roof. I climbed up and got them, and took them to the young girl, who was just eighteen. As I handed her the flowers, I noticed tears were in her eyes. *"Merci, monsieur,"* she said, *"je vous remercie mille fois."* And I was glad too.

On patrol above Albert one crisp morning in early March 1918, Udet narrowly dodged a sudden, withering attack from an aggressive pilot in a Sopwith Camel. The ace was flying a Fokker triplane, a maneuverable match for the fiesty Camel. The Britisher, however, instead of falling into the usual tail-chasing act, preferred the head-on attack. Again and again they dashed straight toward one another, firing furiously, swerving aside at the last moment.

"It appeared as though we would ram one another each time," Udet recalled. "A quick movement, and he passed just above my head. I could feel the draught of his propeller and smell the oil fumes from his engine."

During one rush, the Camel's wheels almost skimmed the triplane's top wing. Udet saw the black fuselage number "8224" as it flashed past.

As they began the fourth rush, Udet felt his hands go damp on the controls. Opposing him was a brave and desperate man. He knew before this battle ended, both might well be dead.

On the fifth rush, Udet sensed the decisive moment was at hand. His engine sounded muffled in cotton; his own frantic heartbeat drowned out its roar. He aligned the oncoming Camel squarely in his sights and gritted his teeth; he was determined not to turn aside this time, come what may. If each man kept his nerve, both would die.

The Camel rushed on; two hundred feet . . . a hundred. At fifty feet the olive-drab biplane loomed. Then, as it swerved slightly, Udet tripped the gun triggers. The Spandaus shook on their mounts as twin tracers flicked ahead. The Camel shuddered, stalled, turned lazily on its back and plummeted toward a huge shell hole, where it exploded in a dirty fountain of earth and smoke. Udet swooped down and saw men in field-gray running to the wreckage. They waved.

No matter how many men Udet shot down, his struggle to be outwardly unaffected about them never lessened. For some reason, he felt a compulsive urge to learn who his rash opponent had been. That evening he went to the crash site. Nearby was a field dressing station where he knew the pilot's body had been taken. Leutnant Udet asked for the Medical Officer. In a few minutes the man appeared in the door of the dugout and in the hard light of the carbide lantern his white coat had an uncanny appearance.

"Your opponent, Herr Leutnant? Dead. Shot through the heart. Death was immediate."

Udet nodded. The doctor turned to a box that held the dead flier's few possessions. "Here are his personal things," he said, and handed Udet a wallet.

On a visiting card I read: *Lieutenant C. R. Massdorp, R.F.C. 47.* Also in the wallet was a picture of an elderly woman—and a letter. It said: *Don't be too reckless . . . Think of Father and me.*

A hospital orderly brought me the number of his aeroplane, which he had cut out of the wreckage. It was covered with little spots of blood.

I drove back to my unit. Somehow one had to try to get rid of the thought that a mother wept for every man one shot down.

During the German spring offensive, the Kaiser's deadliest and most decorated ace, Manfred von Richthofen, personally

invited Udet to join his famous group. Udet had twenty victories and was elated with the prospect of becoming a member of Jagdgeswader Number 1. On his arrival at the new post, Udet learned the Rittmeister operated differently.

I had not long been a member of the Richthofen Squadron before I began to discover the secret of its success.

Other squadrons lived in castles or small villages fifteen or twenty miles behind the lines, but Richthofen's unit was housed in corrugated metal buildings that could be taken down and re-erected in a few hours. It was seldom more than fifteen miles behind the front line trenches. Whereas other units took off two or three times a day, Richthofen and his men made five or more flights in the same period. In bad weather the others ceased flying, but Richthofen's machines were nearly always in the air.

But what surprised me most were the pilots' seats on the aerodrome. They were an idea of Boelcke, Germany's master airman, and the scheme had been adopted by Richthofen, his most brilliant pupil.

A few kilometers behind the front, often within reach of the enemy shells, we used to sit, in flying kit, in deck chairs . . . in the middle of the aerodrome. Our machines stood close by with their engines running. As soon as a hostile plane appeared on the horizon we took off. Sometimes only one went up, sometimes three, and at other times a whole flight took off.

When the battle was over we landed, again reclined in our deck chairs, searched the sky with binoculars, and waited until the next opponent put in an appearance. Richthofen permitted patrol flights, but he did not encourage them. "Sentry-go in the air damps the pilot's fighting spirit," he said. And so we seldom took off unless there were definite prospects of a fight.

Udet developed a serious ear infection that caused Richthofen to order him on leave for treatment. In Munich he spent happy days with his family and his beautiful fiancée, Lolo Zink. But there was something else he had to do—visit the father of his dead friend.

In the afternoon I visited the Bergens. I could no longer postpone my call. The maid took me straight into the living room, where I found old Bergen reading a paper. He was quite alone: Hans and Claus were at the front, and his wife died some years ago. He lowered the paper, and looked at me over the top of his spectacle. His face had an alarmingly old appearance—it seemed lifeless—and his gray imperial, usually so smartly trimmed, looked bedraggled.

How hard it is to say the right thing on painful occasions . . . I blurted out something about having called "about Otto."

He nodded.

"That's all right, Ernst, you wanted to pay Otto another visit. Come along then." He stood up, shook hands with me, and led the way upstairs.

We stood in Otto's room, the little room which had been his den when he was a schoolboy.

"There you are," said old Bergen, "have a look at anything you want to see." Then he left the room and I heard the retreating steps as he descended the staircase. I was alone with Otto.

The room had been left exactly as I remembered it in the "old days." On the window sill and bookshelf were models of airplanes Otto built. They were wonderful models, representing all types known at the time, and every little detail had been patiently carried out. When he attempted to fly them, however, they dropped like stones. That was ten years ago.

I went up to the child's desk with its green-baize, ink-stained top, and lifted the lid. Inside were a number of blue exercise books and the diaries of the Aero-Club München 1909 [Munich Flying Club]. Our members were between ten and thirteen years of age and we met each Wednesday in a big barn to discuss model building, and each Saturday for the big flight contests at the Stadtbach on the River Isar. Otto's machines were always the best-looking, but mine, which were as plain as rain-soaked sparrows, invariably flew the farthest. The results were all recorded in the precise and, for a schoolboy, excellent handwriting of the club secretary. "Aviator Herr Ernst Udet is awarded first prize for a successful channel crossing with his U-II model." This was the testimonial I received for flying a model plane, without breakdown of any kind, across the River Isar. It read:

> Munich, 9 January 1911
> The Munich Air Club's official certificate of airworthiness has been granted to Herr Ernst Udet, pilot, for his "M.V.G." constructed "Dornier monoplane." The prescribed course of 3 meters was flown in the presence of the Chairman and Secretary.
> Munich, January 1911
> Chairman: W. Götz
> Secretary: Otto Bergen
> Pilot: Claus Bergen

The desk was a model of neatness and order, as though he had tidied it up before leaving for the last time. The letters I had written to him were tied in a neat bundle with string, and arranged in yearly series. Right on top was the last one. The envelope was still sealed. The letter stated that I had at last managed to arrange for him to join my flight. It concluded: "Hurra, Otto!"

I found records of the many things we did in our childhood days, including a description of the *Flugtag von Niederaschau* [Air Day at Niederaschau]. I took to the air with the first glider constructed by the club. We crashed, and the bird broke its beak. Then I discovered groups of pictures which ranged from our first lessons in dancing, to the days of the war. One showed me as a motorcycle dispatch-rider; another was a picture taken just after I brought down my first opponent. Each picture bore a date and a note, in white letters, explaining the contents. He had followed every step of my life.

There is something unique about a friendship between youths. We would rather have bitten our tongues out than said a single word which might have suggested we were in any way fond of each other. Yet, now, I realized how true it was.

I closed the lid of the desk, and descended the stairs. Old Bergen was still seated behind his newspaper. He stood up, and gave me his hand, a hand without strength and without warmth.

"Erni, if there is anything of Otto's you'd care to have," he said, "by all means take it. You were the favorite among his friends."

He turned away and began to polish his spectacles. I had no spectacles to polish, and a few tears ran over my cheeks. I had to stand on the porch for a few minutes before I felt capable of walking out into the street.

I was twenty-one at the time, and Otto Bergen had been my greatest friend.

On June 29, 1918, Udet had one of the war's luckiest escapes from death in the air. Fortunately, the German Air Service had recently adopted the newly designed parachute and supplied them to its pilots.

North of Villiers-Cotterets forest he found a French Breguet two-seater directing artillery fire from twenty-six hundred feet. Its crew was two Americans. On his first pass he fired into the fuselage and appeared to seriously wound the observer-gunner, who disappeared into the cockpit. Udet assumed the machine's rear was now unprotected and swooped in for the *coup de grâce*. When his dive narrowed to twenty yards, the gunner suddenly popped bolt upright in the cockpit like a jack-in-the-box and sent a hail of lead into the triplane at point-blank range.

Udet's machine reared up on its tail, went out of control and began a long, spiral dive to the trenches. He tried frantically to regain control. It was useless; the crippled triplane plunged on unchecked. Udet scrambled over the side. The wind blast slammed him into the tail planes where his parachute harness became tangled. Desperately he struggled to free himself as the earth rushed up. At a scant two hundred fifty feet he pulled free, the chute opened with a *crack!*, swung once, and he landed roughly in the midst of whining shells and a gas attack in no man's land. He had wrenched his ankle. Bursts of machine-gun fire from the Allied trenches spattered mud around him but after a painful two-hundred-yard crawl, he reached the safety of his front line. Fourteen years later, in a crowded Chicago convention hall, he sat dumbfounded and heard a much different version of his escape.

Udet's flamboyant Fokker became well known along the front because of the huge monogrammed "LO!" painted on its side. It was for his love, Lolo—a personal insignia and good luck talisman.

When Richthofen was killed in April, Overleutnant Reinhard took command of J.G.1. In June, Reinhard died testing a radical new fighter. Ernst Udet and Erich Lowenhardt were each qualified for the command and each, sparked by a mutual personal dislike, were bitter rivals for the highest victory score. To avoid friction in the Jagdgeschwader, the High Command wisely selected an outsider, Hermann Goering.

Goering was a disciplinarian. Jealous of Udet's popularity and victory score, he displayed an open animosity toward the mild-mannered pilot. In later years it grew to dangerous proportions.

Early one balmy summer morning Udet was awakened by the rattle of antiaircraft fire. "Berend!" he shouted to his mechanic. "Get my machine ready!" He pulled boots and flying gear over his pajamas, double-timed to the tent hangars, leaped into the cockpit of his idling D-7 and roared off.

It was bitterly cold at ten thousand feet but bursting "archie" shells warmed the sky. Ahead, a flight of Fokkers had already engaged a patrol of Nieuports flown by Americans. Udet saw one Nieuport fasten hotly to Lowenhardt's tail. He fired a quick burst into the Nieuport's rotary engine and the machine promptly nosed into a dive, smoked, and crashed behind the German lines. Nearby was a clear place free of shell holes where Udet landed his Fokker. He walked over as the pilot crawled clear of the wreckage and lay on the ground, racked with pain. Soldiers ran up as the German victor knelt beside his mud-spattered victim and offered him a cigarette. "I'm Ernst Udet," he said, feeling somewhat foolish to stand on formality under the circumstances.

"Thanks," the American replied. "I'm Walter Wanamaker —U. S. Air Service."

"So I see," Udet said pleasantly. "You've come all the way across the ocean to fight us." Then, seeing the downed airman was doing his best to hide the pain, he asked, "Are you injured badly?"

Wanamaker pointed at his thigh. It was fractured.

Udet ordered a soldier to summon an ambulance. Medics arrived and Ernst Udet saw that Wanamaker was moved carefully onto the field stretcher. A man in field-gray hurried past and called something excitedly in German.

"What did he say?" Wanamaker asked. Udet translated. "Three Americans have just been shot down."

"Well . . ." the Lieutenant remarked dryly, "sounds like we're having a pretty good morning." As he was loaded into the ambulance he waved to Udet. "But don't worry—we'll do better!"

In August, Udet shot down an S.E. 5 near his airfield and was afterward greeted by admiring infantrymen. Allied pressure was intolerable all along the front, and gasoline for the planes was sharply rationed. The Fatherland's days, he knew, were numbered. Yet, there was no choice but to fight on. He saw these ragged troops move down the roads daily; their uniforms could barely be distinguished from the mud. They trudged wearily behind the lorries that carried their rifles and tents. The water bottles and mess kits made their belts sag on their ill-fitting uniforms.

One infantry officer complained to Udet that they were strafed incessantly, but the most galling insult was the two Sopwith Camels that appeared regularly before sundown to drop surrender leaflets. He gave one to the ace. The paper had a black, red, and yellow border, and was obviously written by deserters who implored their comrades to defect.

Udet planned his ambush. That evening his comrades pooled their gasoline to give him enough and, as the sun dipped below the western horizon, he roared into the deepening dusk.

There they were, south of Foncaucourt. The fading daylight cast a dull red glow on the surrounding clouds as Udet pounced on the two unsuspecting Camels. One turned tail for the west; the other flew on. A short distance behind the German positions the British pilot dumped his leaflets. As they fluttered down several flew into the ace's face.

The chase began. Udet's heavier Fokker was not as maneuverable as the Camel, so when his opponent looped at three hundred feet, he followed with a slightly larger circle. At the bottom of the maneuver Udet felt his D-7's undercarriage strike the Camel's upper wing. He banked and when he looked below he saw the pilot, on the ground, scramble awkwardly from his wrecked fighter. German infantrymen rushed forward, rifles leveled, and the injured pilot surrendered.

Three days passed before Udet could visit his opponent in hospital. They had a pleasant chat. "I wasn't prepared for a fight at such close quarters," he told his victor with a laugh. Udet liked the tall, lanky fellow immediately. He was a student from Ontario.

Leutnant Udet left, but he was to hear from his fifty-first victory again. Fifteen years afterward, while taking part in a flying competition in Los Angeles, he was reminded of this incident. Roscoe Turner landed from his nonstop dash across

Courtesy Colonel Hassell

The *Greater Rockford* in 1928 shortly before it took off for Stockholm.

SAS-Greenlandaire Photo

The Greenlandaire Sikorsky helicopter lifts the bundled *Greater Rockford* from the ice cap in 1968.

Marie Angel and her husband, James Crawford Angel, in Venezuela a month before their landing on Auyántepuí.

Courtesy Marie Angel

Lieutenant Pat O'Brien as an instructor in Canada with a Curtiss JN-4.

Ernst Udet during World War I.

Below: Lieutenant Ira Sussky stands on the wing of the PT-17 Stearman biplane trainer as Lieutenant Melvin B. Kimball shakes hands with Captain Charles P. Colwell, the pilot who first sighted Kimball's downed P-40 in the Burma jungle.

U.S. Air Force Photo

World War II Collection of Seized Enemy Records in the National Archives

Hanna Reitsch converses with an unidentified man at a glider demonstration meet shortly before World War II. In the background is a high-performance sailplane of the type in which she won many gliding laurels.

Staff Sergeant Klier, a flight engineer-gunner, says, "It isn't often a person has a picture of himself being shot at! But here I am in the top turret of our Martin B-26 over France. There are five bursts of 88mm flak around our tail."

A 20mm cannon shell hit the tail gunner of the B-26, September 19, 1943.

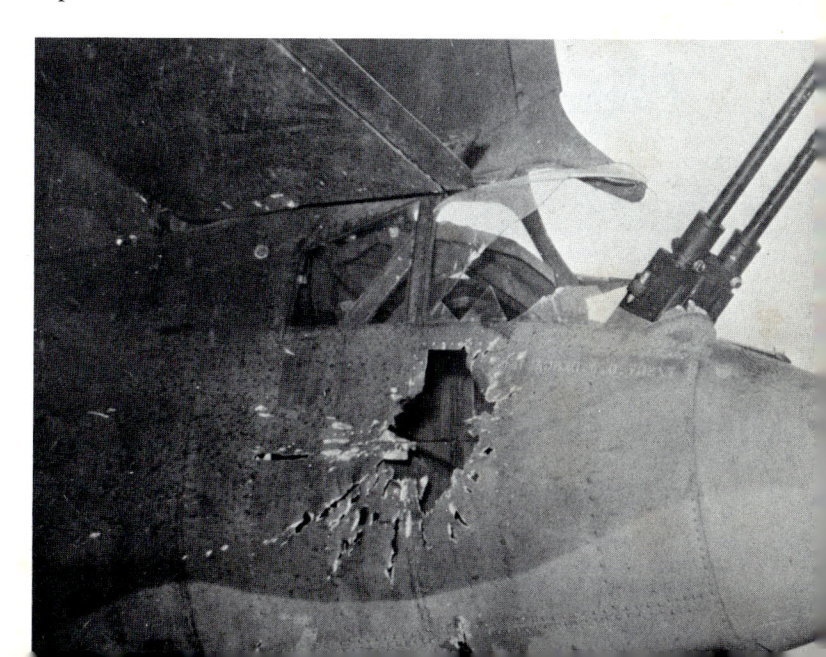

The DeHavilland 9, "P.D.," at one of its stops in Australia shortly before
Royal Canadian Mounted Police Photo

Photo courtesy of the Australian War Memorial

it crashed on its flight to Melbourne.

Royal Canadian Mounted Police Photo

Left: Aerial photo shows scene on the Eagle River where Albert Johnson made his last stand. Dark spot in the lower center of picture is the trapper's body. February, 1932.

Right: Death photo of Albert Johnson, the Mad Trapper of the Yukon.

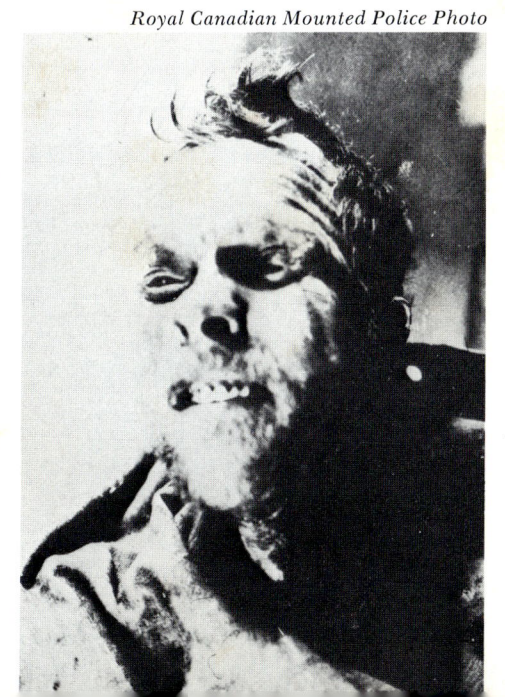

Twice a day Fred Key had to perform the routine engine servicing on the Wright J-6-5. For safety he wore an ordinary lineman's harness with two straps that could be clipped to the catwalk railing. The sliding fuselage panel is shown just aft of the top window.

the continent and brought a present for the jovial German. "A fellow back East asked me to give you this." The strapping race pilot grinned as he handed Udet a folded piece of paper. "He said he forgot to throw it to you that day in 1918." Udet unfolded it; it was a leaflet, with a black, red, and yellow border.

At the Armistice, Udet was the highest-ranking living German ace. To survive he barnstormed, designed airplanes, and entered racing competition. Flying was his life. He knew —and wanted—nothing else. In 1920 he married Lolo, but the adventurous spirit developed during the war years made him a playboy, and the marriage failed in 1922.

It was Udet who perfected one of the most famous aerobatic planes of all time, the "Flamingo." In it he polished his already superb stunting skills to thrill millions of spectators. In Italy he won a two-hundred-mile air race in another plane of his design. During a brief South American racing tour he gained the reputation of the "world's greatest flier."

Then, at an airshow in the Rhön Mountains in 1924, the debonair flier met a svelte woman in a leopard coat, the Countess Margot von Einsiedel. She told him her husband had no use for women at all. Udet smiled. "Women are my seventh sense."

"What's the sixth?"

"Flying."

The Countess became Udet's frequent companion on his flying jaunts, but in early April their passions got out of control and she stabbed him in the chest. As the doctor dressed the wound in his hotel room Udet showed him a long manicure file. "The whole affair is like the Italian opera *Rigoletto*," he said, holding up the weapon. "Exhibit A. You meet in the hotel; you dance; you are together. Curtain. The next morning you breakfast together in the same room. She accidentally finds a photograph of another woman—and acts as though you were her first love affair."

The doctor wiped the file carefully and put it in the bedside table drawer. "Half an inch higher, Herr Udet, and . . ."

Udet nodded.

From 1925 to 1929 Udet, with his partner and manager Walter Angermund, toured Germany presenting airshows until, late that year, the films discovered him. *The White Hell of Pitz Palu*, a mountaineering script, was written by Dr. Arnold Fancke and starred Leni Riefenstahl and Gustav Diessel, but Ernst Udet stole the show in his Flamingo. While cameramen gasped, he maneuvered his plane through the steep mountain ravines. When the film was previewed in the studio, critics shook their heads and said, "Trick photography."

A year later the Fancke unit hired him for *Stürme über dem Mont Blanc (Storm over Mont Blanc)*, to be shot at St. Moritz on fourteen-thousand-foot location.

Then, in 1930, European newspapers carried the headline: UDET MISSING IN AFRICA! The search for something different in flying had lured Udet on an East African expedition. Two airplanes, thousands of feet of film, and the latest motion picture equipment were shipped to a remote campsite six thousand feet up the north side of Lake Manyara in Tanganyika. Udet liked the work; he also enjoyed the company of one of the girls on the expedition—Frau Felsing.

His job was to fly over the great African "ditch," an enormous game-filled hollow that traverses much of the continent. The two planes roared over herds of giraffes, great swarms of gnu, and prides of lions. All fled from the fleeting shadows of the noisy Klemm and DeHavilland Moth. The expedition pushed into the Congo to film elephants and the lumbering, thick-legged rhinos. For three months its members photographed wild animals and native tribesmen.

"Papa" Siedentopf was the leader and advisor of the expedition. Once, he owned an estate in East Germany as large as a principality. It was filled with rich ore and well stocked with game and fish. Now he had nothing.

Schneeberger, the hero of Castelletto, was the cameraman, a small, wiry individual. He spoke little, but what he said was brief and to the point. With eight soldiers—and fifty-two corpses lying around him—he had held a position for six weeks.

A third member was Suchocky, like Udet, a pilot.

In the evenings the four gathered round their tent, a few paces from which they could see Lake Manyara shimmering in the moonlight. They listened to the breeze whistle softly in the treetops, like a gentle tide breaking on the seashore. Hyenas laughed; jackels howled; and Siedentopf told stories in the dying glow of the campfire. When he drew deeply on his curved pipe his thin, leathery features were faintly visible.

Their work went well. Visibility was unusually good in the clear air, and they could see for miles, easily spotting the great herds. There was one problem: in photographing from the airplane, the scenes below swept past so quickly Schneeberger could not capture them all. "Too fast!" the exasperated cameraman signaled. "Too fast!"

To solve the problem Udet was forced to fly low and slow, a dangerous practice in any airplane. He throttled back, flew into the wind and, at a few miles an hour over the plane's stalling speed, staggered along just above the heads of the wild animals. Now Schneeberger smiled; this was *much* better. Udet sweated; this was *very* dangerous.

Over the Serengeti, Udet flew alone in the DeHavilland. Following in the Klemm were Suchocky and Schneeberger. Udet came upon a group of lions lying down, two males and three females, and decided to photograph them. With the control stick held by his knees, he dropped to within eighteen feet of the ground and began snapping pictures. The males only turned their heads to watch the popping airplane. The females, however, were enraged. They rose to their feet in a crouch, tails thrashing the ground nervously, their eyes fixed on the tightly circling biplane. Udet was not concerned; his experiences indicated animals were likely to attack a plane only after it landed, not in flight. Nevertheless, one lioness sprang suddenly into the air and nearly touched the lower right wing. Udet was so surprised the camera fell from his hands. He thought of the Klemm behind him and realized their danger. He looked back at the second machine and sure enough, Suchocky was flying very slowly, barely ten feet above the grass. Udet opened his throttle quickly, turned, and tried to warn them. Too late. Like a streak, another crouching lioness hurled herself at the Klemm. Her paws struck the lower wing and caved it in. The plane wobbled, dipped, and scraped the ground.

Suchocky fought for control. Slowly, groggily, the Klemm staggered into the air again. It headed for camp, very low, streaming a long, tattered ribbon of fabric.

At base, pale and shaken, Schneeberger and Suchocky climbed from their machine. The force of the blow was terrific and the Klemm was considerably damaged. "It was a miracle you could stay airborne!" Udet said. Claw marks, hair, and bloodstains spattered the wing.

A few days later they were out again, scouting the valleys of the Esimingor. Again Udet was alone in the Moth; Siedentopf was in the repaired Klemm with Suchocky. Below, desert cactus and the dull, dusty green of the euphorbia plants slipped slowly past their wings. When they reached the area they were to photograph, Suchocky made the first landing attempt. Udet watched. His friend swooped down toward a clearing, flared smoothly out, and touched down. Then Udet saw the Klemm's flicking propeller dissolve into a sudden blur again as Suchocky gave the machine full power. A round, flat rock nearby suddenly came to life and rushed the plane— a snorting, furious rhinoceros. Suchocky had disturbed its afternoon nap.

The emergency ended quickly. Suchocky failed to regain flying speed and the Klemm reeled into a giant anthill to crash in a great cloud of powdery brown dust. When the air cleared, the plane's tail pointed skyward.

Udet landed hurriedly beside the up-ended machine as the snorting rhino circled, each time drawing nearer. He fired several pistol shots at the armored beast, none of which did the slightest damage except sting its thick hide. The rhino pawed the earth and, with a final snort, disappeared into the underbrush.

"Suchocky! Siedentopf!" Udet switched off the Gypsy engine and vaulted from the still-rolling Moth. As he ran to the wreckage he heard a mournful groan from inside the fuselage. "Here we are . . ." It was Suchocky, pushed inside the fuselage by the impact. With his bush knife Udet slit the fabric and helped Suchocky out. The stunned and dazed pilot crawled away with difficulty, stretched prostrate on the ground and moaned softly. He was thoroughly shaken and bruised, but otherwise unhurt.

Siedentopf! Udet dashed around the wreckage and saw, protruding from underneath, a motionless hand. Frantically he shoved against the side of the plane. "Siedentopf!" he bellowed. "Siedentopf! Can you hear me?" No answer. Udet dropped to his knees and from under the machine heard the old man mutter: *"This place stinks like the plague!"*

In five minutes Udet freed Siedentopf. Then, making two trips, he flew the men to camp. "Suchocky had to go to bed," Udet recounted, "but Papa Siedentopf appeared as usual for our evening meal in the tent. He was bent and lame, and swore fearfully, but nevertheless ate enough corned beef for two ordinary men.

"Three months later I visited Suchocky at the hospital in Hamburg," Udet said. "His face was as small as that of a ten-year-old child and he weighed less than eighty-five pounds. 'Diseased liver,' the doctors said.

"Suchocky showed me a letter Siedentopf had written from Dar-es-Salaam. With it was a photograph which showed the old campaigner, too, had grown exceedingly thin. The doctors said his liver was diseased.

"The two men died almost on the same day. I can't explain the coincidence," Udet said, "but I believe the place where they crashed was poisoned with carrion. The doctors with whom I discussed their cases shrugged their shoulders. What it was, they couldn't tell me."

As soon as Suchocky and Siedentopf were hospitalized, Udet and Schneeberger resumed flying. They moved their camp to Babati in the region of the Ufiume. The Figtree Hotel, a curious complex of four small, round, straw-thatched huts beside a long, flat building, was their headquarters.

"Ah, civilization," said Schneeberger as they stepped into the room and scanned the well-stocked bar. They sat on the tall stools and sipped brandies. Through the open door and across the shady forecourt lay the far distant expanse of the colorful steppe country. It melted gradually into the hazy horizon.

The hotel, established years earlier by Lord Lovelace, was a stopping place for motorists and airmen. Udet found it the strangest place he had ever been. Curious individuals stopped there; secretive, sinister characters with mysterious business among the tribes of the deep interior. There were a few farmers. "Anyone who lives in this godforsaken place year after year," Udet confided to Schneeberger, "and keeps going in such loneliness, has to be a man—or go to pieces."

They slowly realized the sky was darkening. "Part of that ominous-looking cloud bank we saw in the northeast," Udet commented. Schneeberger frowned. "It's a solid wall now." A blue shadow slowly drifted over the sun-baked yellow earth. "We'd better get the Moth under cover," Udet said.

As they hurried to their plane the sky suddenly turned dark. They had almost covered the engine and cockpits with canvas when the roll cloud churned overhead. They struggled to hold the airplane but a whirlwind caught them up and, like dry leaves, cartwheeled them—and the Moth—before it. The heavens opened with a deluge and soaked them to the skin. A minute later the cloudburst had spent itself and a steady downpour set in. Udet staggered to his feet. A hundred and fifty yards away were the battered remains of their camera plane. He looked around but his companion was nowhere in sight.

"Schneeberger!" Udet howled, stumbling toward the wreckage. The cameraman weaved drunkenly from behind the twisted and tattered remains, his hair covering his face, looking like a drowned rat. "I'm all right, Erni. I just didn't want to let go. What a ride!"

The muddy pair sloshed back to the bar to find the bartender had removed their drinks. "Oh, you're back," he said. "I thought you'd left." They ordered fresh brandies and drank morosely. Outside, the storm had passed as quickly as it came and the evening sun shown brightly in the west. Steaming mist rost from the puddles and steppe grass.

In Arusha they hired mechanics and, during the several days required to repair the Moth, Schneeberger phtographed the slim Babati girls, their proud, broad-chested warriors, and hordes of children. "They're so nice," Schneeberger grinned, "if you don't notice the dirt."

The Moth repaired, they continued their work over the African terrain. The rainy season came and heavy mists hung on the horizon. At Arusha the main body of the expedition broke camp and returned to the coast by car. Udet and Schneeberger preferred to fly.

The plains fell behind; ahead were the ten-thousand-foot peaks of the Mau Range. Soon they saw the sprawling, silvery stretch of Lake Victoria and away to the north stretched the green foliage of vast, virgin forests. Skimming over the treetops, from which rose a putrid, sickly sweet odor, they suddenly felt a jolt. Udet glanced forward to see their reserve fuel tank wrench loose from its mounting and swing free in the slipstream.

We were two hundred fifty feet above the trees, with no sign of an opening or native settlement where we could land. To our right was Lake Victoria, and in nearby shallows the crocodiles drifted like floating logs. I saw them quite distinctly.

A nasty crack-up seemed inevitable, then Schneeberger rose up, stretched as far forward as he could reach, wrapped his arm around the tank and held it. If he could keep it there until we reached Jinja . . . We were just above the trees and the stench from the forest was almost unbearable. Higher up it was cooler, and perhaps Schneeberger would be better able to hold out. I eased into a gentle climb. He held on to the tank like grim death.

Jinja . . . the Ibis Hotel . . . a remnant of civilization in the African jungle. We shut off and landed. I had to help Schneeberger out of the machine, for he was so stiff he could hardly move. That night he developed a high fever.

A Ford agent helped with repairs, but he was dubious of their chances. When they were ready for takeoff he said, "Better follow the motor road through the Sudan." He shrugged. "You know . . . just in case . . ."

For several miles the flight went well, then, over the Lado grasslands, where a huge elephant herd had stamped over the brown earth and kicked up great clouds of dust, the gas line broke. As the propeller slowed to a muffled, windmilling paddle, Udet scanned the ground for a clear space. He was glad he had taken the agent's advice; below, beside the road, was an open patch.

As they rolled to a stop, the heavy, oppressive jungle heat settled over them. They were stranded until a car passed. With no shelter in sight, Udet helped the feverish cameraman from the plane. With a tarpaulin, he made a lean-to against the wings and they crawled under it to escape the burning sun.

Schneeberger's fever mounted. Now semidelirious, he begged Udet for water. The aviator found a hollow place in the ground filled with stagnant, vile-smelling swamp water and filtered it through his pajamas. It was neither cool nor palatable, but Schneeberger drank it greedily in long, thirsty gulps.

Toward evening some natives moved cautiously past. When Udet called and signaled, they disappeared in the tall grass. Then one, the son of a local chief, to demonstrate his bravery, approached warily.

Through sign language Udet learned they were in the land of the Lau tribe. The natives were much afraid of airplanes, but when the chief's son learned the "bird machine" was crippled, their attitude changed. The Laus made it plain the fliers were in their power.

In the tropics there is no twilight and darkness fell like a black curtain. The war bird had been in rough spots before, but this was something else. In two days not a car passed. Schneeberger's fever grew worse; he was now completely delirious. And the Laus grew more impertinent by the hour. Udet remained near the tent to prevent them from stealing their possessions. The heat became intolerable, water was short, and the strain on his nerves began to tell. "Gradually,

I began to despair," he said later. "My friend was ill, we had no provisions, and were surrounded by inhospitable natives. Moreover, the rains were due at any moment, and weeks might pass before a car came along the road."

On the morning of the third day, Udet began to daydream. The shimmering grass flats were a furnace. He imagined there was a snowfall and through it he could hear the drone of an engine. Then a fleeting shadow crossed the sun and with a roar a Puss Moth swept into view and passed low over them. Udet waved the tarpaulin frantically as the plane banked and landed. A wiry young Englishman strode toward them with a smile and an outstretched hand.

"Campbell Black," he said.

Udet and Schneeberger grinned weakly. The Laus had vanished. Black had cigarettes, food, and fresh water. Years afterward Udet said, "I'll never forget the debt we owed that gallant, quiet Englishman. He told us the Shell petrol station where we'd last refueled had—after we'd left—telegraphed to inquire whether we'd arrived. When they learned we were overdue, a search party set out."

That afternoon an R.A.F. plane landed with tools to repair the gas line, a supply of fuel, and the personal invitation of Wing Commander Sholto-Douglas to visit him in Khartoum. Late that evening they arrived and Sholto-Douglas greeted the disheveled pair with a broad smile. Udet started to thank him but the tall, distinguished officer interrupted with a wave of his hand. "We were on the same sector of the front in 1917," he said, "and that's good enough—even though we were on opposite sides."

Udet arranged to enter the aerobatic competition at the Cleveland National Air Races in 1931. He had just arrived when a practicing racer zoomed low over his head. As it curved gracefully around the pylon he saw it was trailing a thin wisp of white smoke that puffed quickly into a dark, thick stream. The plane was on fire, but the pilot was quick. He rolled the plane on its back, pushed its nose skyward, and catapulted from the cockpit. His tumbling body was only a few yards above the ground when the parachute snapped open, and the pilot landed a hundred and fifty feet from Udet. The German, with a swarm of mechanics, rushed to the man who stood brushing the dust from his clothes.

"Anything damaged?" he asked a man in coveralls.

"No. Thank God it missed the buildings."

"O.K." The pilot took a pack of cigarettes from his pocket and slowly lighted one. Udet watched him and later said: "The hand that held the match was steady as a rock. Cool customers, these Americans."

In aerobatic competition with superb pilots of international fame, Udet knew his small, old, and underpowered Flamingo could not compete in their class. He gave much thought to his tactics and when the announcer called, "Ernst Udet from Germany," he had an idea.

I planned to fly very slowly, close above the heads of the spectators—the very opposite type of flying that had hitherto been seen.

I flew on my back close to the earth. I looped with the engine shut off, climbing again when my machine was only a few yards from the stands. Then I finished with a "plate" landing on the very spot from which I'd taken off.

As Udet rolled to a stop, the crowd went wild. People sprang from their seats, shouted and waved their hats. A reporter seized him by the arm and dragged him to the microphone, where he came face to face with a tall, spare man who looked, said Udet, like a white Indian. He was America's top ace, Captain Eddie Rickenbacker. They had met before, in 1918 over Soissons. Rickenbacker held out his hand. Cameras clicked and his voice boomed across the stands: "Now we can shake hands and show young Americans that honorable opponents can be honorable friends when the fighting is over." The crowd thundered its approval and Udet was thoroughly stunned by his American acceptance. He later remarked, "Then Rickenbacker bent down, grinned, and whispered in my ear: 'Got a drink here for afterwards.' He tapped his hip pocket. It was during Prohibition."

On this occasion Udet again met his thirty-ninth victory, Walter Wanamaker, now a judge in Akron.

Wanamaker duly arrived, accompanied by his wife, and he had evidently already made up his mind what he was going to say.

"Hello, Ernst," he said into the microphone. "Why, you've gotten quite fat!" The crowd roared; they rather enjoy personal remarks in America.

I then produced a piece of canvas, which I had been hiding behind my back. It was the number of Wanamaker's machine, which I had cut from the wreckage of his Nieuport soon after he had crashed. At the sight of this grim relic of the past his carefully prepared speech was forgotten. "Say . . . that's mighty nice of you . . ." he stammered, ". . . fine of you to think of that."

After the air races, Udet was the Wanamakers' guest. On his first night he looked at the Wanamaker family pictures on his bedroom wall. *Had Wanamaker died on that cool mornin of July 2, 1918,* Udet thought, *I should never have visited this comfortable home, and the woman with the fair hair would have hated me as the man who had killed her husband.* "I switched off the light and went to sleep."

Soon afterward, the ace appeared before five thousand German compatriots in Chicago. Many months were to pass before Udet told his close friends of its most poignant incident, and even then he used a fictitious name to shield his recipient's feelings.

The chairman raised his voice. He was a man of dignified appearance, with a long, white beard.

". . . and now I have a pleasant surprise for our airman friend. Among us is a man, a fine fellow, who in 1918 rescued Herr Udet from the enemy's bullets. Herr Grabe, come forward please!"

There was a roar of applause from the assembly. A man ascended the platform. His manner was hesitant and he was embarrassed. Rather under average height, he was thin and pale—he looked underfed, and I could have sworn I had never set eyes on him until that moment.

"Now, Herr Grabe," said the chairman encouragingly, "we want you to welcome Herr Udet."

Grabe began to speak in an almost inaudible, shaky voice. "I am delighted," he said, "to have this opportunity of meeting you again, Herr Major."

I examined him more closely. His sleeves were frayed, and his shoes were patched and down-at-heel. There was an expression of anxiety in his blue, protruding eyes, the fear of a broken-down man whom life had served very harshly. He was a man staking everything on a last hope. "Give him a chance," I thought, and advanced toward the platform.

"Many thanks, Herr Grabe," I said and shook hands with him. Thunderous applause broke out in the hall. Grabe turned red but began, in a stronger voice, to relate his story. He described how he found me lying unconscious on the barbed wire, how he picked me up, and carried me back through a hailstorm of bullets. When he ended, there was such a tumult of cheering that it was a long while before the chairman could make himself heard again.

Below, in the body of the hall, I could see Grabe in the center of a crowd of reporters. Occasionally he looked in my direction and smiled in a rather pathetic sort of way. Then he continued answering questions.

A few days later one of my friends wrote saying that Grabe had been given a job in a German slaughterhouse. Before that he had been unemployed. It was his first job for many a long day.

"Give him a chance," I thought. It was America's favorite election slogan, and a pretty good slogan, too.

American International Film Company wanted Dr. Arnold Fancke to make *S.O.S. Iceberg*. From May to October of 1932 Udet was again teamed with Schneeberger—this time on location in North Greenland. In the short summer sunshine at Igdlorssuit, pilots, mechanics, and cameraman awaited instructions. Sixty kilometers up the fjord at Nûgâtsiak was the main camp where Dr. Fancke and the film company were shooting the script. When colored rockets arced in the northern sky it signaled filming was about to begin; a pilot and cameraman were needed. The men donned their furs and in minutes the little pontoon-equipped Klemm was off.

Despite the isolation and shortage of activity, Udet found much to interest him at the settlement. Occasionally a giant iceberg "calved"—or split—on the gray-green waters and there was a mighty roar, like the firing of artillery. It resounded through the fjord, echoed and re-echoed across the perpendicular basalt cliffs. Then giant waves, fifteen feet high, roared onto the beach in a thunderous rush.

Their quarters were in the upper story of the village's only church, a weathered, wooden structure. For nine months of the year an American, Rockwell Kent, lived at the village. He had helped improve the postal communications with the filming camp. Mailbags were suspended between two tall poles at Nûgâtsiak and a hook on the plane picked them up as they dropped their own letters. A great nature-lover, Kent had a heart that understood simple people. The Eskimos loved him.

In the evenings they all sat on a little bench outside the door, played an accordion and talked. The girls, dressed in their gayest clothes, would gather and listen. Sometimes the men sat in silence and smoked. It was then old Daniel came. He sat beside them and cast longing eyes at their tobacco, but he was too proud to beg.

One evening, after the fliers gave him a drink of schnapps, old Daniel grew cheerful and talkative. He told the story of his fight with a great polar bear, and Rockwell Kent translated for him.

"He was alone with his dogs, far away on the fringe of the inland ice. The dogs crouched around the bear in a half circle and growled. One of them rushed up and hurled itself at the white bear but was thrown aside on the snow with a broken back. Another charged, and the bear's paw killed it. A third dog was also killed. Then Daniel himself attacked the bear with a harpoon. In those days there were no guns for hunting."

The old man took up a paddle that was leaning against the wall and began to spar with an imaginary beast. His actions were weird, but not ridiculous; he was a brave hunter re-enacting an heroic deed of his youth. Kent translated:

"The bear grasped the harpoon in his powerful teeth and paws, and it broke like an icicle in a child's fingers. Then he took his long knife from his boot and rushed at the bear. He kept from the wild animal's deadly embrace long enough to plunge the blade into its heart. Blood spurted all around him. The bear sank to the ice and the dogs rushed in...."

As the old man finished speaking, he was seized by a coughing fit. He coughed so violently he had to lean against the church. Then he spat blood on the sand. He shook his head at the fliers, grinned, and walked slowly to his hut. He had tuberculosis and would not live long.

One evening, toward the end of summer, when the filming was almost completed, David approached Udet. He said his father was dying and he had one last wish: to be taken aloft over the fjord and Igdlorssuit in the white man's bird.

Udet nodded. "All right, David. Tell the men to get their waders and prepare the machine. Then bring your father to the beach."

Two hunters bore the old man and lifted him gently into

the plane. Udet put a flying helmet over his head and adjusted the goggles. Old Daniel laughed like a child. They skimmed over the water, took to the air and climbed smoothly into the evening sky. Below them, the sea lay in the light of the sinking sun. The year was growing old, and winter, to the north, was harnessing its black steeds for the long night.

We climbed higher, and still higher. The mud huts of Igdlorssuit had grown as small as worm casts, and the church spire looked like a finger pointing towards the sky. The mountains were below us, and looking into the North one saw a vast expanse of inland ice stretching as far as the horizon, glittering in the light of the setting sun. White, remote, and filled with melancholy peace.

It was wonderful to see how the old man in front of me followed each movement of the machine, and how he "went with" her as each change of direction was made. The hunter who is accustomed to handling a kayak in all sorts of weather is at home in all the elements.

Udet found it strange to fly over the ice with a dying man. Once the old hunter raised his arm and pointed down with a yellow-gloved hand. They were over the fjord, and below a few kayaks were speeding through the green water to leave a white, foaming wake.

The engine droned on. Land and sea slipped smoothly below us. Then, suddenly, came a human voice, gradually swelling, rising above the noise of the engine.

Old Daniel was singing.

He was still singing when we landed and he continued to sing as they lifted him from the machine. His face was leathery, burned from wind and sun, but his eyes were radiant. The old man spoke.

"What did he say?" I asked.

David replied: "He said it was good to have led a life of which one had such fine memories."

They took him to his hut and, still singing, he disappeared into its dark interior.

Next morning David was waiting outside my door. "My father died during the night," he said.

I gave him my hand.

"You are my friend," he said. "You can stay with me as long as you wish."

But I had to be going on. Soon the long night would fall, a long night in which life stands still in the North.

Back in the States in 1933, Udet did more stunt flying in Cleveland and Los Angeles. His favorite trick was to roar across the field inverted, roll upright and adroitly scoop up a lady's handkerchief with his wingtip, a feat that required perfect timing and coordination. He became highly intrigued with the Curtiss P-26 Hawk as a dive bomber and purchased two for testing in Germany. They proved to be the forerunners of the dreaded Stukas six years later.

In 1934 Udet met smart, fair-haired Ingelein Bleier, who became his close companion until the end. He seemed to have no regard for his life and few friends would fly with him, believing his phenomenal luck would surely run out. In July he pulled the wings off one of the Hawks in a test dive over Tempelhof Airport. He parachuted to safety.

Germany was on the rise. Hitler came to power and everywhere the factories hummed. Goering, as Udet's commander in 1918, was not overly fond of Ernst's flying success. But as he struggled to put the fledgling Luftwaffe together, he found himself in need of this man's technical skills. He offered the ace a high position in the new air service. Udet hedged. He was never interested in politics and was not a Nazi, but finally, convinced by Goering that it was his patriotic duty, he accepted. In 1936 he became Inspector of Fighters and Dive Bombers and soon afterward was promoted to Director of the Technical Department in the Air Ministry. Responsible for the design and production of all aircraft, it was the Udet talent that made German air power second to none. His brilliance was in the cockpit, however, not behind a desk. He remained a man of action, hated paper work and loathed making decisions based on theory. He continued to fly, for this was the part of his job he enjoyed most—testing new planes purchased by the burgeoning Luftwaffe.

Udet's closest brushes with death came in 1937. During a demonstration in Zürich he flew a low-wing Messerschmitt ME-109 smack into a thirty-thousand-volt trolley wire. The impact jerked the cable car violently uphill but slowed his plane like an aircraft carrier's arresting cable. Udet stepped from the wreckage without a scratch. Then, in July of that year, a Heinkel HE-118 prototype dive bomber he was testing, failed and crashed. He was rushed unconscious to the hospital at Rostoff but in two days gave his doctors the slip.

The pursuit of the "good life" had altered the playboy pilot into a balding, stocky man. In 1938 Udet, now forty-two, was promoted to Lieutenant-General. Despite his successes, he remained an outsider at the Air Ministry. Goering's State Secretary Colonel-General Erhard Milche was the direct antithesis of Udet; a hard, cunning, and brilliant organizer, and a man too discreet to show open hostility to the trusting, optimistic Udet.

On the evening of August 31, 1939, Ernst and Inge dined at Horcher's with Ernst Heinkel and his wife. Next morning the couples breakfasted in Udet's apartment in the Pommerschenstrasse. A terse, official announcement came over his radio: "German troops crossed the Polish border at 05:45 hours . . ."

A cloud crossed the veteran airman's face. He came to his feet and turned off the radio. His voice was flat. "Let's have a drink."

Berlin was blacked out as he escorted Inge to her apartment that evening, through streets blustery and wet. He was a man of many moods and Inge—although she had long known him—could admit she truly did not understand him.

"What's wrong, Erni?"

He shook his head. "I can't help it, you know," he said. "We can't win this war. It's already lost."

Soon afterward, the pressures and tensions of high office began to tell. In July 1940 he became Colonel-General. A month later the Battle of Britain began—and failed. In one month Goering's proud Luftwaffe lost 786 fighters and 811 bombers. Udet's unsuspecting nature and straightforward personality kept him from recognizing the political maneuvering behind his back. Goering and Milche needed a scapegoat for their mistakes and for the Luftwaffe's shortcomings. Udet—never one of their breed—was it.

Udet recommended a large-scale repair organization to put damaged planes back into action. Inspector-General Milche said no. In October, Udet suffered a mild stroke. Goering intended that he remain in the hospital for six weeks, but with his distaste for hospitals, Udet remained seventeen days.

He began to drink heavily and now became aware of the political intrigue around him. In June 1941 Hitler launched his senseless invasion of Russia, and Udet, knowing the war would now be a long one, realized a drastic command decision must be made quickly. A superior aircraft would have to go into immediate development. With Willi Messerschmitt he proposed an immediate change to jet airplane production. Again Milche said no. Air historians ponder how the course of the air war might have been changed if Milche had listened to them and put the deadly ME-262 jet fighter into operational squadrons a year earlier. But Udet knew Germany would not win a war with *ifs,* and the Panzer divisions and Luftwaffe squadrons were already committed to a struggle he knew would fail. Frustrated, disgusted with Hitler, the war, and his country's leaders, he flew from factory to factory to keep up production. The strain was weakening him and he quarreled often with Inge.

In the early morning hours of November 17, 1941, while holding the receiver of his telephone as he finished talking with Inge, he committed suicide with a Mexican Colt revolver. Radio Berlin announced General Udet had a fatal accident while testing a "new weapon." A state funeral was ordered and Goering delivered a glowing funeral oration.

The flying general, Hermann Dahlmann, who had been Ernst's friend since the First World War, walked to muffled drums as the procession moved to Invaliden Cemetery.

I saw a woman who had once been very intimate with Udet. It was a long time ago. She was a certain Frau von Langen . . . About 1930 her picture was on the front page of nearly all the German illustrated weeklies . . . In those days she was often photographed with Udet. Now, as the procession passed the Kaiserhof she stood there on the plinth of a statue and wept.

And then I suddenly noticed other people to right and left of us in the street. I have seldom seen so much genuine mourning in my life.

Udet wrote in one of his books: "I have been in many foreign parts. Wherever I went I sought men and comradeship of hearts which had not given up faith. I sought and found them. In the African jungle and in the Greenland ice."

A hero's life; a flier's luck. He liked to be complimented on his racing prowess and speed records. "Yes," he would say, "it was fast, but Death flies faster."

7

Burma Rescue

AIR rescue by helicopter in the jungles and bordering coastal waters of Vietnam is almost commonplace today. During the Korean War downed pilots were frequently plucked from the reach of communist troops as they steadily tightened their circle around stranded airmen. But it was during World War Two in the China-Burma-India theater, that an Arkansas flier pulled off a rescue stunt as daring as anything Hollywood ever filmed—and he used an old, unarmed Stearman biplane to do it.

In March 1943 the Japanese were hanging tenaciously to Burma and trying to organize a drive north to Fort Hertz, located in the triangle of Burma between India, Tibet, and China. To lose the fort would be a blow to British prestige in the sight of the local guerrilla fighters. And it was important for other reasons: it was a forward emergency base for P-40 patrols, an important radio and weather reporting link, and a main center for collecting native intelligence on enemy activity. But most critical, should the Japanese reach Fort Hertz, they would outflank the Ledo Road that General Joe Stilwell had begun earlier—a supply route carved through the jungles and over the mountains to connect with the Burma

Road that was to supply China. Daily, elements of the 14th Air Force in China and the 10th Air Force in India pounded enemy airfields and staging areas to keep the Japanese off balance.

The stage for the singular rescue was set early in the day when four fighter pilots took off in their Curtiss AVG (Flying Tiger) P-40s at Kunming, China. They were to refuel at a stop in Assam, India, en route to Karachi at the far western end of India. There they would exchange their old pursuits for newer models and return to Kunming. Shortly after takeoff, Lieutenant Melvin Kimball, a husky, fair-haired twenty-six-year-old fighter pilot, had engine trouble and turned back for repairs. The other three pilots flew on. When his engine trouble had been remedied, Kimball took off alone, realizing he would have the sky all to himself. An hour out of base, he was bobbing in the turbulent currents over the Hump—the rugged Himalayan range that separates China and India—and encountered some cloudy weather that diverted his attention from matters of navigation. When he broke out of the clouds, the Himalayas were behind him. He peered ahead expectantly for sight of the large Brahmaputra River that was a prominent checkpoint for all pilots flying through that part of the China-Burma-India theater of operations. His fuel was running dangerously low and his well-worn engine gave occasional signs of running rough again, but the thought that he would soon be in the Assam province of eastern India where there were half a dozen American airfields reassured him.

As minutes passed, however, the countryside became even less like the topography shown on his chart. Realizing that he had wandered astray while in the clouds, he reasoned his drift must have been south of his almost due westerly course from Kunming to Dinjan. Kimball felt certain he must already have passed over the tip of northern Burma and was now into

Assam, but too far south of the Brahmaputra to see it from his present altitude.

After checking his fuel gauge again, Kimball knew he would soon be forced either to bail out or to land. Hitting the silk would be the safest move, but with American fighter planes still badly needed "at the end of the line" in this part of the Asian struggle, a crash-landed P-40 could at least be salvaged and its parts cannibalized to repair other Tomahawks.

Nothing familiar came into view, and when the 1150-horsepower Allison engine finally became starved for fuel, Kimball selected a dry rice paddy with a nearby road leading to a village, and decided on a wheels-down landing. Gear down and locked, landing flaps extended, Kimball hung the fighter on the edge of a stall and glided it over the edge of the trees and onto the small field. Although the ground was spongy and uneven, the bouncing P-40 rolled to a stop, right side up. He was lucky, for now he saw the surface was a pocked mass of holes and ruts, made by the heavy tracks of elephants and by the wallows of water buffaloes that were used to cultivate the field. In the bottom of the holes was sticky mud.

Kimball breathed a sigh of relief, pushed back the cockpit canopy, released his safety harness, and looked around. Where were the natives? Usually a downed plane brought them out in droves. In the distance he saw the native village, a cluster of huts. Now he would find out where he was, get word by runner to the nearest telephone or telegraph, and wait for the pickup truck.

The young officer strode across the rice paddy, and after several hundred yards arrived at the row of bamboo bashas on stilts. Oddly, not a person was to be seen or heard. Kimball looked around in the eerie stillness, singled out what appeared to be the main bungalow, and marched boldly up the wooden steps. He knocked on the door. No answer. The entire atmosphere reminded him of an abandoned ghost town of the Old West. Even the women and children were missing. Were they all working in the fields? Still alert for some sign of life, he walked toward his plane. It was not long in coming. He had almost reached his fighter when several rifle shots cracked from the surrounding jungle. A fountain of earth was kicked up near the propeller; one bullet smacked solidly into the airplane's fuselage. Kimball unholstered his .45 and scanned the circle of underbrush. Why were people shooting at him? Assam was in India, and the natives knew an American plane.

A volley. Kimball dropped into the nearest depression and tried to puzzle out the confusing state of affairs.

Operations for the 10th Air Force's 51st Fighter Group was in an old tea planter's bungalow a little way from Dinjan Field, where part of the Assam Dragon's 25th Squadron was located. Dinjan was known by the local residents as the Polo Grounds—a holdover from the earlier, happier days of the British tea planters. The whole of northeast India, in which the province of Assam is located, is a tea-growing area. It was developed by the British and despite the war and uncertain conditions, many of the planters were still there. It was too early for the wet monsoons of summer, when two hundred to six hundred inches of rain normally fell in Assam.

Elements of the 25th Squadron were scattered out to several fields at that time; one was at a grass field at Sadiya, the jumping-off place for missions into Tibet. Another field was at Sookerating, which, like Dinjan, was one of the several western terminals for the cargo airlift over the Hump. From there, C-46 transports kept a stream of supplies moving to Chennault's 14th Air Force. Because of frequent bombing and strafing by hit-and-run Japanese raiders, it was decided to disperse the Dragon Squadron's P-40s. Half the Dragon pilots were always on standby alert. Some days before, a large flight of Zeroes and Bettys had flown on a low-level run through the mountain passes to hit the Air Transport Command fields in northeast Assam. A transport pilot who had bumped into them and had been shot up before he could duck into cloud cover, alerted the 25th Squadron by radio, and the Dragons were able to roar off in force to cut up the invading force before they reached the airfields.

Because the Burma Road was still in its early stages of construction, one of the main missions of the 51st Fighter Group, ever since former C.O. Colonel John Egan moved it from Karachi to Dinjan six months earlier, was to defend the ATC bases ahead of the Burma Road as well as the transports running the gauntlet of Japanese interceptors over the Hump. Egan had brought the Group to India a year earlier, fresh from its training at March and Hamilton Fields in California. One of his pilots was twenty-eight-year-old Captain Charles H. Colwell of Park River, North Dakota, a West Point graduate.

On the large screened porch of the planter's house that afternoon were twenty-eight-year-old Major Howard Wright, Group Operations Officer, and Major Paul Droz, Commanding Officer of the 25th Squadron. The drama began when the clear, readily recognized voice of Captain Colwell broke over the radio. He was about a hundred miles to the southeast, still over Japanese-held Burma, and was returning home in his P-40B from a strafing mission on a target in the south. The men listened intently as Colwell reported that a P-40 was on the ground in a rice paddy near Maingkwan. The plane appeared intact and the pilot was outside and had just waved to him as the Captain zoomed low overhead on a close pass.

Major Wright looked at a map to confirm the location. It was a Japanese field headquarters that probably housed a sizable detachment of Japanese infantry. As Colwell circled lower to try to pick out details, Wright asked him to report on his fuel and ammunition reserves. Colwell replied he was low on both. Wright instructed Colwell to remain in the area as long as it was safely possible, and if the downed pilot were threatened, to fire into the jungle and keep the enemy at bay. He added that reinforcements were on the way, and, turning to a sergeant, told him to alert Colonel Sanders, the Group C.O. Then Wright ordered four P-40s into the air to relieve Colwell. Within minutes the Tomahawks roared off and were racing to where Colwell was guarding the marooned flier.

Minutes later Colonel Homer Sanders entered the operations room from his quarters down the hall. Sanders, a longtime Army Air Corps officer, later to command the Tactical Air Command at Langley, sized up the situation quickly. "Probably one of Chennault's men," he decided.

Colwell's voice broke in again. He reported that dust was being kicked up all around the pilot and plane. Sanders asked Colwell if the Squadron PT—primary trainer—could get in and out of the field. Colwell assessed the probability and, considering the field allowed the heavier, faster P-40 to land without nosing over, replied in the affirmative.

The Stearman biplane was the type then used at stateside training bases to give aviation cadets their first flying lessons. It had a 220-horsepower engine that turned a metal, fixed-pitch propeller and cruised at ninety-five miles per hour. Major Droz had used it to drop onto a river sandbar in a hemmed-in canyon of the Naga Hills to pick up several airmen who had parachuted from a transport flying the Hump. War or no war, the Naga hill country between Assam and Burma was still the home of roaming headhunters.

At the Dinjan flight line the Dragon Squadron's operations officer, Lieutenant Ira N. Sussky, had recently landed in the Group's PT-17. The twenty-three-year-old graduate of Arkansas Tech was a cool, calculating pilot with a year and a half of air interdiction missions into northern and central Burma, bombing and strafing Japanese targets. He was tall and trim, one hundred and fifty pounds, with thick black hair and heavy eyebrows over hazel eyes. A few days earlier a flight of P-40s from Sussky's field shot up twenty Japanese trucks on a supply road. When they had finished their job, Sussky dispatched another P-40 whose pilot reported eight more Japanese trucks had been brought in to clear the debris and remove the casualties.

The soft-spoken native of Little Rock was at Dinjan on a volunteer flight to make a short passenger run in their PT. He was preparing to leave when he was called to the field telephone.

"This particular day was my day off," Lieutenant Colonel Sussky recalls today. "I wasn't standing alert and had no mission scheduled. The portion of the squadron where I was flying from at the time was based at nearby Sookerating, and earlier in the day Group called over and wanted someone to fly the PT to Dinjan, pick up a mechanic there and take him to a field to the west where one of their P-40s was out of commission with a rough-running engine. I didn't have anything else to do, so I volunteered to fly the mechanic to the grounded plane. A short time after I arrived at Dinjan, and before I could take my passenger to the P-40, I got a call on the hot line from Group Operations. They told me a pilot was down in the northern part of Burma and gave me the location of the plane and the details they had on it. They wanted to know whether I'd consider going down there and try to pick him up.

"Well, what do you say to someone when they ask you to go pick up a downed pilot? Naturally your first thoughts are: 'Hell yes, I'll go!' Later on, when you're completely involved in it and the fur begins to fly thick and fast, you ask yourself:

'How the hell did I ever get into this!' But I was glad to do it.

"There were a few of the silver-gray, fabric-covered PTs in the area. Although they weren't assigned to us for rescuing downed pilots, they had been used a few times for this. We flew them mainly in administrative support between the outlying fields, to ferry mechanics in repairing planes and for personnel transport. They were only two-seaters so they didn't have much airlifting capability, but they could land and take off in small clearings.

"Over the phone I was told there'd be some P-40s flying air cover for me. Colwell, whom I didn't know too well, was then circling the downed plane but he couldn't remain there indefinitely. As the whole thing was unannounced and unplanned, all I had was my flying suit and my .45. We didn't wear a parachute in the PT and there was no radio of any kind. I just got into the rear cockpit, strapped on my helmet and goggles and took off, alone, heading southeast. There was no P-40 escort and I saw none en route.

"The PT's tanks had been filled before takeoff, and this would give me about three hours air time. As things developed, I found out I needed it all. I climbed to clear the mountain ridges by about a thousand feet as I crossed the Naga Hills. Then, as the hilly country gradually flattened out as I got deeper into northern Burma, I dropped down and held two hundred to three hundred feet for protection.

"I had flown about an hour in the direction of the reported position when I saw four P-40s circling and I knew they were over the stranded pilot. As I flew nearer, I saw the plane on the ground about a mile northwest of Maingkwan. It was an active enemy field headquarters, but I didn't recall any recent air strikes against it; most of our air operations at that time were farther down in Burma."

Sussky made one low, quick circle of the field to select the best landing area. It was a couple of hundred yards long in both directions, and from the air it appeared to him to be fairly flat and smooth. There were a few old, scattered bomb craters in the general area, but none in the field itself. He clearly saw the pilot near the plane, waving. To all appearances the field was safe; it looked like an abandoned, dried-up rice paddy. Sussky decided to chance it. Turning on the carburetor heat, he closed the throttle and put the trainer into a glide. The seven-cylinder radial hushed to a whooshing rumble and the wind sang through the brace wires as the young lieutenant broke his glide over the edge of the trees and flared out for touchdown. Immediately on contact Sussky knew the surface was not all it appeared to be from the air, and suspected he would have difficulty in taking off. The Stearman bounced and bucked over the buffalo wallows and deep elephant tracks. Each hole the wheels struck threatened to snag the plane and overturn it. As the plane slowed, Sussky seesawed the rudder right and left to avoid the largest depressions. The biplane rocked awkwardly to a stop—one wheel in a pothole—a few yards from the P-40, which, Sussky saw with some surprise, had made a successful wheels-down landing. It appeared to be in good shape, except for having been riddled by Japanese rifle fire. And its engine, he noticed, was smoking slightly although there was no fire. That was when the Arkansan realized there was Japanese ground action—lots of it.

Sussky jumped out of the PT and saw that he had landed squarely in the middle of a Japanese assault on the downed pilot. Only the circling and diving Warhawks overhead were forcing the troops to keep their distance a hundred to a hundred and fifty yards away.

"Kimball came over to me immediately," Sussky said. "He was about my height, with a crew cut, and was dressed in khakis with a leather jacket. He was a stranger to me, as I'd never been to Kunming and hadn't had a chance to meet him.

I can't recall our first words at that time; I didn't give him a chance to say anything and there certainly wasn't time for introductions. Bullets were smacking into both planes now, but he seemed very calm about the whole thing. Listening to the bullets rattle around while we were there, I couldn't understand why he didn't suspect something was wrong when he saw his plane being shot up. I can only surmise now that he didn't realize where he'd landed until some time later.

"I let the PT's engine idle; if I'd shut it off, it would have to be cranked by hand and I didn't want to risk not getting it running again. I told Kimball to help me get the airplane moving."

The drone of the P-40s overhead and their occasional peel off for a blistering strafing run on suspected pockets of enemy snipers was reassuring to the two men. The Stearman, however, refused to move when Sussky gave the engine full power. It was stuck in an elephant pad. The pilots jumped out and, with each grasping a wingtip, rocked, tugged, and seesawed the wheels from the depression. Then they were back in the cockpits for another try at taxiing. The airplane lurched forward again, but before it could gain enough momentum to carry it up and over the next depression, it would stop suddenly. The tail would lift dangerously and the plane would threaten to nose over. Sussky and Kimball sweated and flinched as the bullets continued to whine, slap into their plane and slice through the fabric. There were now eight or ten holes in the small trainer, but no vital part of the engine or controls had been damaged. The less than outstanding accuracy of the Japanese fire was due, Sussky knew, to the P-40s that were keeping the snipers dug in and pinned down.

Sweating from their constant and strenuous exertions to move the plane, both men again jumped to the ground and rocked and pushed the PT free. Back in the cockpits. Power.

Another roll of a few feet before a wheel lurched into another hole. Sussky's concern mounted.

In the now-packed operations office at Dinjan the men heard one of the pilots report Sussky's repeated attempts and frustrating failures. The protective umbrella of fighters that had relieved Colwell continued to relay a blow-by-blow account of the struggle on the ground. Someone muttered: "Now there are *two* pilots stuck."

But one officer huddled around the "squawk box" in the crowded room was betting on the men making good their escape. He was Group A-2 (Intelligence) Officer Lieutenant Colonel Harold L. Buckley. Although the two American planes stuck beside a Japanese headquarters were a tempting plum ripe for capture, he suspected the enemy was thinking twice before rushing out pell-mell into the open to capture the poorly armed pilots. The tall, gangling, gray-haired Buckley, who had been a flier in World War One, was old enough to be the father to most of the Assam Dragons. Between wars he had written *Squadron 95*—a book about the flying exploits of his comrades in France—and later worked on the film script for *Hell's Angels* and other air war epics of Hollywood.

Buckley knew about Maingkwan. He knew that although it had not been singled out as a recent target, the deadly results of persistent bombing and strafing by the Assam Dragons on their installations farther to the south had terrified the ground troops. Many Japanese detachments were under orders to hide out in the jungle all day, safe from possible lightning-like air strikes, and to return only at night. This was probably why Mel Kimball did not encounter any Japanese in the village. And luckily for him, his decision to return to the plane when he did, caused him to miss a face-to-face confrontation, which could have resulted in his capture or quick death.

At Maingkwan, as elsewhere in northern Burma, the local natives had cleared out long before. Even the best-camouflaged targets were being systematically chopped up and the disrupted Japanese dared not drive north to the Burma Road. Buckley suspected the enemy would not expose themselves in the daylight to rush the PT—especially with the angry swarm of warplanes waiting overhead; they were thoroughly shaken by the devastation that could be wreaked by American air power.

Back at Maingkwan, a tiring, frustrated Sussky had made a decision. "The P-40s were doing an outstanding job of keeping the Japanese off our necks," Sussky recalls, "and we were thankful they were up there. But our biggest problem was simply trying to taxi the PT.

"About sixty yards from where I'd stopped the trainer after landing was a bullock cart road that wandered through the field. Carts had flattened it out and hardened it and there were no large holes such as those in the paddy. I knew if we could get over to that smoother ground we could get rolling without danger of nosing over.

"We kept pushing and trying to taxi. Every time the plane stopped the wheels would sink into a hole and we had to dig it out. It threatened to go up on its nose several times; that would have meant the end for us. I lost track of the times we jumped out of the plane to free it, but I know it took us more than an hour to work the PT onto the road. It was beginning to get dark and I was getting concerned. Time was running out and although I couldn't distinguish any noticeable closing-in by the Japanese, when darkness fell the P-40s could no longer help us.

"It was now or never. I lined up the trainer as straight as

possible on the snake-like road and gave the engine full throttle. The engine performed perfectly and we slowly gained ground in the soft earth. It was something like the astronaut shots of today," Sussky reflects with a trace of humor, "when they first get liftoff. Our urging to the struggling old biplane was like the encouraging shouts of everyone in the control room: 'Go, baby, go!'"

The Stearman lifted, and with no choice in the direction of his takeoff climb, Sussky was forced to pass directly over the sniping Japanese. Miraculously, no slugs struck the highly vulnerable fuel and oil tanks, and the engine continued to roar away. Sussky looked back in time to see the Warhawks peel off and send withering strafing bursts into the abandoned P-40. It burst into flames as the gathering dusk closed on Maingkwan.

Sussky steered a reciprocal compass course for base, one eye cocked on the bobbing fuel floats in the wingtank sight gauges. The hour's return flight was going to cut the gasoline supply close. As the P-40s assembled and streaked northwest and out of sight, their leader radioed Dinjan that Sussky and his passenger were safely on the way, but he was unable to predict on which field they would land. Cheers shook the old plantation bungalow at Dinjan.

Darkness fell over the Naga Hills and the PT's fuel floats were now bouncing in the critical bottom quarter of the gauges. Sussky chose Sookerating because it was nearest; he dared not risk stretching his luck to Dinjan.

They landed in the darkness, without lights. With no radio, no one knew where they were until they got out of the airplane and walked into Sookerating Operations. It wasn't until to following morning, however, when everyone awakened, that it was fully realized what had taken place—and it now dawned on Kimball that he had indeed landed in Japanese-held Burma. Colonel Sussky recalls, "The day after the flight,

Colwell, Kimball, and I got together for official photographs beside the PT, then Kimball soon got a hop on to Karachi, where he took delivery of a new model P-40. I remember him as a quiet person—one couldn't get too much out of him in the way of conversation—but it was evident he was grateful for the rescue run. We never corresponded afterward and I never heard from him again, although I've often wondered what became of him. Several months afterward I received a very warm letter of thanks from his mother."

The man whose alert eyes first caught sight of his stranded countryman far below on that memorable afternoon, Charles H. Colwell, was promoted to major shortly thereafter and assigned to duty at the old American Volunteer Group Headquarters in China. A few months later the Japanese forced the withdrawal of the Americans to Assam, where Colwell was killed in an airplane accident in June 1943.

A short time after the Burma rescue, Ira Sussky was awarded the Distinguished Flying Cross, the first of three he would receive in addition to four Air Medals, the Bronze Star, and the Air Force Commendation Medal. His service to the Air Force and to his country has been active and distinguished. Into the nearly three decades of his action-filled flying years he has jam-packed an enviable and satisfying series of assignments, their pace set, perhaps, with his dramatic rescue of Mel Kimball twenty-eight years ago. From his home in San Antonio he filled in his career activities after the Burma rescue.

Lieutenant Sussky returned to the States late in 1943 to the bride he married on the day he graduated from flight school. He was assigned to the newly formed 2nd Air Commandos and trained for six months in Florida. He went directly back to the China-Burma-India theater as part of the team that were co-fighters with Colonel "Flip" Cochrane's 1st Air Commandos. His station was southeast of Calcutta along the coast at Chittagong and Cox's Bazar. When the bombs were dropped that ended World War Two, he was a major.

Following a break in service, Sussky was upgraded into F-84s at Langley Field in 1950 and his entire group, based at Itazuki, Japan, went into the Korean War. After this combat tour came Air Command and Staff School, Special Weapons, a NATO assignment in Europe with the 12th Air Force, transition into F-100 Super Sabres, a six-year assignment in the Pentagon and another NATO mission, this time in Norway. The end of his flying experiences came as a student in the final transition class of C-124s at Kelly Air Force Base, where he retired in August 1970.

Ira Sussky summed up his thoughts succinctly on the Burma rescue that late afternoon in March 1943: "I was glad to do it!"

8

Two Miles Down

ONE night in January 1944, Flight Lieutenant Thomas P. McGarry clasped the release ring of his chest parachute and tumbled from his burning bomber into the blackness over Germany. He spent the remainder of the war in captivity.

During World War Two, more than eight thousand applications found their way from P.O.W. camps to the Caterpillar Club, an exclusive organization whose sole qualification for membership is an emergency parachute jump from an aircraft. Thomas McGarry could not qualify; his parachute didn't open. Falling at 175 feet per second, 125 miles an hour, he decelerated to zero velocity with brutal suddenness—and survived. Thus he is a highly select member of an even more exceptional, though unrecognized group.

A career Royal Air Force officer, McGarry is now a Group Captain assigned to the Air War College at Maxwell Air Force Base. His decorations include the Distinguished Flying Cross and the Order of the British Empire. McGarry is a strikingly handsome man of middle age, erect, and well groomed. His straight blond hair is flecked with gray. He speaks softly, in a matter-of-fact manner. "I was born in Belfast in Northern Ireland and am in fact an Irishman," he said, smiling. "My home is in the south of Ireland now—at Cork . . ."

Here is the account he gave on the eve of the twenty-fifth anniversary of his escape.

In March 1942 I began aerial navigator training in the Union of South Africa, at Grahamstown, where the University is located. My air training was about eighty hours in Avro Ansons, Oxfords, and Boulton-Paul aircraft. Our operational training was in Whitleys.

I'd flown thirty-two missions prior to this particular one. On two of them there had been anxious moments when we were attacked by German fighters and took quite a number of flak hits, but nothing terribly near the bone. This raid began just like any other one; you had a queasy feeling about them all. I didn't experience anything that could be described as a premonition before takeoff.

Our pilot was Squadron Leader Jock Jagger, the other navigator was Flying Officer Frank Humberstone, the signaler was Flight Sergeant Don Smedley, the flight engineer was Flight Sergeant Bill Percival and one gunner was Flight Sergeant Eric Hie. There was another Flight Sergeant gunner who had been with our crew only a short time and whose name I can't recall. We left our base at Graveley, near Huntingdon, between 2200 and 2300 hours on the night of January 20, 1944. There were about six hundred aircraft on this raid altogether. Ours was with Number 35 Squadron and we flew Halifax IIIs. It was a Pathfinder squadron. Our task was to search out the target and identify it with colored markers for the main bomber force following behind us. Accompanying us were very few aircraft; between twenty and thirty bombers. We generally preceded the main force by about four minutes.

Our load consisted of pyrotechnics and colored markers. If

there was any weight to spare, we made it up with high explosives or incendiary bombs. The markers were a powerful magnet for the German night fighters when their communications with the ground were being jammed or otherwise interfered with.

The main target that night was Magdeburg and the bit we were engaged on was a "spoof" on Berlin. Most of the spoofers caught it that night. The loss on that particular raid was a fairly high one. We were then in a three to four month spell of high losses. Nürnberg for instance—two months afterward—had a hefty loss rate.

The general spoofing practice was to follow the route toward the main target, and then at a predetermined point along the course, the spoofing force would shoot off toward the false target. As we were in the van of the raid, and the first twenty aircraft shot off in the direction of Berlin—at that time the favorite and number one target—German radar, seeing us turn in this direction, would think Berlin was the target. The judicious use of "chaff"—a shower of thin metal strips—could add considerably to the delusion of the ground radars. If, for instance, we dispensed chaff heavily and the main force dispensed none at all, it was possible to convey the impression that the spoof was the real thing. The main force following behind, of course, continued straight on to Magdeburg. So our action was a diversionary tactic. Berlin was an odd place to go for a diversion, but that's what it was.

What the precise target was in Magdeburg we didn't know, because we didn't attend the briefing given to the crews of the main bomber force. For target areas within the towns there was no need for us to know what the targets were. All we were concerned about was our particular aiming point. The main force following on behind would be given their aiming point in terms of our marker. We had to be very accurate—quite positive of our accuracy—otherwise we didn't bomb. We just came home.

Our Halifax was one of the first model IIIs, equipped with air-cooled Bristol engines. Ceiling with our load was somewhere around eighteen thousand feet, a little lower than those with liquid-cooled engines. It was a particularly mild night and the aircraft wasn't climbing all that well anyhow. We weren't disturbed because we generally aimed to keep below the bulk of the bombers. Although those of us in the pathfinder force got a general briefing on the heights to fly, we were mainly concerned with flying the correct route and with getting to the target at the appointed time. Beyond that we didn't pay a great deal of attention to anything else and were inclined to pick our own heights to fly. On this night we were about fifteen thousand feet.

At this time the RAF Bomber Command carried out night bombing while the U. S. Army did day bombing. Fighter cover tactics varied between the services. We had no fighter cover in the sense the Americans used it. As the object of our fighters was to keep the German fighters on the ground, they operated in the area of the German fighter airfields and not in direct support of our bombers.

The weather en route to the target presented no problem. Our course was over a layer of medium cloud at around eight thousand to twelve thousand feet. If I recall correctly there were clear skies above. We had no moon.

We had come through a flak zone between Bremen and Hamburg, which was pretty intense—it usually was. But once we got through that, we could expect relatively little until we got into our target.

It happened about halfway between Hamburg and Magdeburg. We had veered off from the main bomber force on our spoof and were at a point about 120 miles from Berlin and 75 miles from Magdeburg, somewhere near Münster, when we were suddenly attacked by a fighter. I don't know what type it was; in the darkness it wasn't identified. He struck us from behind with quite a shower of stuff, which knocked out our gunners and virtually disabled the armament straight off. A second attack followed quickly and may have been from the same fighter or from a different one. He peppered the Halifax with gunfire which could have been either cannon or machine—probably a bit of both.

Shortly after the second attack, Jagger, our pilot, warned us the aircraft was on fire. He told us to get out. We had lost some altitude due to the attack and were about thirteen thousand feet when we began to leave the bomber. I was aware of an interval between the fighter damage and my leaving the bomber, but I didn't learn until later that the aircraft had, in fact, exploded. The next thing I knew I was clear of the aircraft. Two others escaped beside me, Humberstone and Smedley. Humberstone was first out—he had to be first out because he was sitting on the door. Smedley was second. My parachute was the standard chest type, and after falling a short distance I operated the parachute in the normal way and thought no more about it.

Strange as it may seem, I just don't have any recollection of sensations, thoughts, or anything else when I realized the parachute didn't open. In fact, I didn't realize it until I had gone through some cloud—the layer of cloud below us. I can remember going through this (and probably recalling from the briefing what the depth of the cloud was) and saying to myself: "That was damn fast!" In and out. It's the only recollection I have of the whole affair.

I didn't attempt to open the pack by any other means. I couldn't see the ground. I had no idea what my relative motion was. The absence of a moon meant I didn't have any reference point. The last thing I was conscious of before impact was hurtling toward the ground at a fair speed, but practically coincidental with that I hit something. I didn't know until afterward what it was.

It was a Monday night when I came down. My first recollection after that (by process of going back in time when I later determined what day it was) was some thirty hours later on Wednesday morning. I was lying on the floor of a fir forest. Above and around me were the splintered and broken tree branches that had broken my fall. Although I was barely conscious, I realized that I had painful injuries to my back, legs, and chest. As I slowly gained strength I made myself as comfortable as I could with the remains of my parachute. We had survival packs with water and high-energy foods such as block chocolate and condensed milk, so food or water didn't present any problem.

No single injury caused me any more suffering than another, certainly not that I can recall. I do remember having considerable trouble with my feet, but it was fairly general pain. I had quite a lot of trouble with my face because I had two beautiful black eyes. They were swollen and lacerated. As my senses returned I became aware that my feet were greatly swollen inside the boots, and this accounted for the dream I'd had, a dream I can still remember quite distinctly. In this dream I was visiting the factory that made the flying boots; while there I'd been made to ride bicycles and do exercises which had made my feet very sore. So very soon after I regained consciousness I took the boots off and used them to protect my hands in crawling.

Sometime after I became aware of my surroundings, I was able to get an estimate as to why my parachute malfunctioned. The pack itself didn't snag in any of the tree limbs because it was still attached to the harness, and to me. I knew that I had pulled the release pin—I must have—because it wasn't there when I got to the ground. A small flap protected the pin as well as the three little engaging grommets, each of which was fastened with a stud fastener. The fasteners were conical in shape. On the inside of the metal grommet hole was a small wire tension spring, which was intended to engage on the conical fasteners, but no more than that. I subsequently discovered that the three conical fasteners were grooved and the only conclusion I could come to was that the spring clips were caught in the grooves and that there wasn't sufficient power behind the spring to force the parachute flap open.

There was only one field between the forest and the nearest road, and in all, I crawled on my hands and knees for three days. I fainted several times due to pain. Later I realized that it was probably a mile from where I came down to the road.

All during this time the weather remained surprisingly mild. Some light rain—a drizzle—fell while I was there, but I didn't feel cold at all.

On Sunday morning I finally reached the road where I decided to wait for help. Eventually a German approached. I was lying face down on the left-hand side of the road as he came toward me. I lifted my head and bawled something at him. He looked at me, kept looking, and walked past. Just disappeared.

By the time the next one appeared I was over on the other side of the road, sitting propped up against a tree. His reaction was more or less the same as the first one. Of course it's quite conceivable that they might not have been Germans at all. They may have been foreign prisoners, a lot of whom were employed in Germany and who were allowed to walk around freely.

When the third one came along—he was riding a bicycle—I was determined that he wasn't going to get past. He did get off his bicycle but showed no inclination to come anywhere near me at all. It didn't appear to me that he intended to go for help. He was surprised to find me, probably a bit frightened and fearful for himself. This was in the middle of a country area and the Germans out there weren't going to be involved in this sort of thing unless they had to. But with a bit of cajoling and a bit of movement toward him I laid my hands on his bicycle and refused to let go. Eventually he took the point and somehow or another we got on the bicycle and he proceeded to wheel me into the town.

I came down near a town called Dannenburg. This, at least, is what my prisoner of war documents later said. Some years later I went to Dannenburg and tried to orient myself but couldn't, so I've got my doubts. Although I was able to identify a lot of points that did have some relevance, I couldn't really identify the area in which I came down or the place to which I was taken. Conceivably, it could have been a little township or village within a mile or two of Dannenburg.

As it was fairly early in the morning I didn't create any sensation when we arrived in the local village. The man who provided my transportation dropped me off at the first building, which happened to be a beer hall. It was managed by a large and rotund German who spoke English. He was a friendly character indeed and soon told me that he had spent some time in Chicago. He took me in, and his wife and daughter got to work on me and cleaned me up a little. They laid me on a settee in their parlor where I stayed most of the day. They gave me an occasional beer and fed me with what they had; it was probably as good as they were eating themselves. The proprietor went through my pockets, took out every scrap of paper he could find and promptly consigned each one to the fire. There wasn't anything significant among the papers because it was common practice for us to go through our pockets before we set out on a raid. I was certainly quite taken with this and it led me to think he was probably on our side.

While I was with him I didn't see any local Germans during the day. They came and went outside, in the drinking hall, but nobody came into the room other than the owner and his family. Later on in the morning, about an hour after I got there, a German civilian policeman arrived. He kept popping in and out during the day and was obviously going to stay there as long as I was. He didn't have too difficult a task as I was quite incapable of moving anyhow.

Around six o'clock that evening, after dark, a couple of young German officers arrived in a Volkswagen to pick me up. They treated me well and were friendly. As we drove back toward a base at Lüneburg, we stopped three or four times along the road for various reasons. On a couple of occasions we stopped outside beer halls and they went in and had their beer and quite obviously broke the news that they had a *kriegsgefangen*—prisoner of war—in the car outside. The beer hall emptied out each time to see what it was. They plied me with beer; whenever they had a beer I had one. At one stop a German gave me three apples. At the second stop a woman put her hand in with five cigarettes—which was again quite something, for someone to part company with cigarettes. But she did, and was determined that I was going to get them, too.

The next stop we made was to pick up Don Smedley, my signaler, who had been captured this same day. He hadn't been injured, though; he was perfectly all right and I rode to the hospital at Lüneburg with him. He was quite surprised to see me; he thought he had been the last out of the Halifax. Our conversation was guarded as we were under surveillance all the time and couldn't admit we were even acquainted. We didn't discuss his capture or survival. It was then, almost a week after we came down, that he told me our aircraft had, in fact, exploded. He said it happened immediately after he had jumped. It's quite conceivable that somehow or another

I was caught up by the explosion. I know I wasn't "helped out" the hatch by it because I can recall actually leaving the aircraft. I think it may well be that before I got clear of the aircraft I may have been caught up by it.

That night on the way to Lüneburg the weather changed abruptly. It was freezing—and freezing jolly hard.

At Lüneburg the German Air Force put me into sick bay where I was treated quite well. I got exactly the same treatment, I think, as one of their people would have got. I only stayed there overnight and the following morning was taken to Lüneburg station in a horse-drawn hansom and put aboard the train under guard. From there onwards I was regarded as a prisoner of war.

I was taken to a place called Stade and to a Stalag at Sandbostel which was between Hamburg and Bremen. It was a prisoner of war camp for Yugoslavs, Frenchmen, and Belgians. The small hospital there was maintained by the prisoners and I got into the hands of two Serbian doctors. One was Colonel Kiminkovich and the other was Major Lazarovich. It so happened that one of these was an orthopedics surgeon. They didn't have any real medical equipment, no X-ray. They were very short of materials and had to work with what they had. The injury that was most obvious was to my right leg and foot, which they put in a plaster. I don't think they ever recognized that I had any other injuries there. As I was pretty sore anyhow I wasn't in any position to determine whether one part of me hurt more than any other. Later I was to learn that I had fractured vertebrae, ribs, and both feet.

Communication between myself and these two doctors was limited. They didn't speak English and I didn't speak Serbian. I did learn, however, that they had voluntarily become prisoners to look after other prisoners of war. Quite clearly they weren't content with me because after three or four weeks I was removed to a regular German Air Force hospital up at Wismar, on the Baltic between Lübeck and Rostock. I was treated precisely the same as a German patient; got exactly the same food, the same medical attention. I might have got a little more because the nurse on my ward was married to a German Army major who was a prisoner of war in Canada. She kept telling me how well her husband was being treated so I feel I did all right there. The German doctors who came round certainly didn't differentiate between me and any of the other patients.

I stayed at Wismar until the end of April. Then I was taken down to Frankfurt for interrogation by German Intelligence. By that time the cast on my leg had been removed but I wasn't very ambulatory. When I arrived at Frankfurt I was cold from an intelligence point of view. They weren't interested in me, just sufficiently to let me know they knew who I was, who my girl friend was, who my parents were, what squadron I came from, and they as much as intimated: "There's not very much you can tell us anyhow."

After three or four days at Frankfurt we set out for the POW camp, Stalag Luft 1 at Barth up near Stettin. It was primarily a USAAF camp. There were, I judge, about fourteen thousand USAF prisoners and a thousand British, Canadians, Australians, and New Zealanders. On the whole, my treatment at Barth was more or less what a prisoner of war would expect it to be. There was the odd incident of untoward treatment toward other individuals, but generally speaking I think it accorded fairly well with what you would expect.

There was very little medical treatment there, although I had a few visits to hospitals outside. On two occasions I went to Neu Brandenburg near Berlin, a POW hospital with mostly Dutchmen. Then, six or seven months after my arrival at Stalag Luft 1, they commenced screening prisoners for repatriation on medical grounds. The German medical organization thought I was okay for repatriation. They took me around again to a number of hospitals, including the local hospital at Barth and the German Naval Hospital at Sassnitz, east of Barth, the terminal of a Swedish ferry service. There was another civilian hospital at Rostock. At each I met a German medical screening board to see whether I was eligible. After getting through them all I appeared before the Red Cross Commission composed of Swiss doctors who met at Barth. But unfortunately they weren't convinced that I should be repatriated and they left me there. I was of course surprised that the Germans were quite content to let me go home, but the Swiss weren't. By that time it was getting along toward Christmas and I don't think anybody was greatly concerned about his ultimate release. We knew it was only a matter of some months.

We were liberated eventually by the Russians and then promptly incarcerated again. There was a big hassle about how we were going to come out. The Russians fell back on a long-term agreement we had; apparently they hadn't caught up with the times. They insisted we were to go out through Odessa. Our spokesman said no, we weren't, that we were to be liberated through Barth, and there we sat. We were evacuated finally by B-17s and brought back to Ford, an airfield on the south coast of England, several days after V-E Day.

I have no personal philosophy as to why I was spared. The way I look at it is that there were thousands who hit the silk during the war, and it would have been nothing short of a miracle if there hadn't been one or two incidents like this. There have been much more extraordinary events than mine. After all, if you look at the country where I came down, the possibilities of someone hitting in the trees there and surviving it must have been pretty high. There are certainly enough trees there and all you had to do was hit one in the right place and you get away with it; if you were six inches one way or the other you wouldn't.

The circumstances were right for my survival. I came down through a fir tree, and the weather was mild in spite of its being January. There was no snow, and at that time of year a mild spell in that part of Germany probably happens only once in ten years—but I got it.

9

The Girl Who Rode the Buzz Bomb

SHE was the most celebrated and admired aviatrix in Hitler's Luftwaffe. As a child, she had wandered in the open sunlit meadows around Hirschberg, watched hawks circle lazily ever higher in the summer thermals and knew she wanted to fly. Her strongest wish was to become, like her father, a doctor. Not an ordinary doctor, but a flying missionary doctor in Africa. Her name is Hanna Reitsch.

Before she began her medical studies, her father allowed her to take glider lessons at the nearby Grunau School of Gliding. The young girl progressed to increasingly longer flights down the Silesian slopes in simple primary gliders. In a short time she excelled in the art and became a soaring instructor. It was then she knew flying would become her life's pursuit.

During her first year as a medical student in Berlin she graduated to powered flight in a 20-hp Mercedes-Klemm and in the summer of 1933, at the conclusion of the Rhon Soaring Contest, she was invited by Professor Georgii, Europe's "Professor of Soaring," to join his South American expedition to study thermal conditions. To earn money for the trip she flew stunt gliding scenes for the film *Rivals of the Air,* in which she crashed a glider squarely into a lake and nosed it over.

After months of research flying along the mountainous slopes of Argentina and Brazil, she returned to Germany and accepted membership in the German Institute for Glider Research. Shortly afterward she set a new women's world record on long-distance soaring. Another expedition, this time to Finland, was offered the slender, attractive twenty-two-year-old girl. She accepted eagerly and taught Finnish military personnel and civilians the art of gliding. The Finnish expedition ended, Hanna Reitsch learned she was to be decorated for her dedicated work. The aviatrix was not one to place great stock in awards and, thinking quickly, she asked instead to be allowed to train at the Civil Airways Training School at Stettin. The request was granted, and she became the first woman to match her skills with men in the rigid, semi-military air academy. She came through the training well, graduated to twin-engine aircraft and advanced aerobatics.

In 1935 she tested gliders for the Institute of Glider Research in their development of dive brakes and spoilers to control the descent of soaring planes. Glide-diving from heights between fourteen thousand and nineteen thousand feet, she pulled out of the headlong plunge at six hundred feet —and never exceeded 125 miles per hour with the new devices. The test results led to the use of dive brakes on powered aircraft, an important milestone in aeronautics.

In 1937 the energetic aviatrix repeated the tests before Ernst Udet, Professor Georgii, General von Greim and other Luftwaffe generals at Darmstadt-Griesheim. Udet afterward conferred on Hanna the title of *Flugkapitan,* a rank previously reserved exclusively for pilot officers of Lufthansa, the German Civil Airways. At the ceremony she met Adolf Hitler for the first time.

That May she was one of five glider pilots who were the

first to cross the Alps by sailplane, and in September she was instructed by Udet to report to Rechlin as a test pilot for Luftwaffe airplanes. She flew, and tested, every type of military airplane in the Luftwaffe inventory.

Professor Focke of Bremen had developed the first helicopter, and Hanna Reitsch tested it in competition with Udet, who flew a Fieseler Storch, a short-takeoff machine. Later she demonstrated the helicopter inside a huge building, the Deutschlandhalle, to thousands of enthusiastic, air-minded countrymen.

During her visit to the United States in 1938 she participated in the International Air Races at Cleveland. The adventurous young woman became enthralled with America —its cities, its people, their humor and spontaneity. And the people loved "Germany's Amelia Earhart." Wherever she spoke in her halting, imperfect English, the trim, fair aviatrix was met with loud applause and complete acceptance.

There followed a gliding tour of Africa, Tunis, and Tripoli; and after winning greater laurels in World Distance Flights, she became a wartime test pilot soon after the invasion of Poland. One of her first assignments was the flight testing of a new idea, a troop-carrying glider. It became a weapon of great strategic value along with the parachute troops and the Blitzkrieg.

As a test pilot she came increasingly in contact with the Services, and because she was a woman, she fought an uphill struggle against proud male pilots whose obstructive prejudices cost her many battles. Often her vital work would have been delayed were it not for the timely intervention of generals like Ernst Udet and Ritter von Greim, whose minds were more intent on the greater struggle than on the battle of the sexes. They were able to smooth Hanna's path, and the arrogant attitudes of her detractors could never turn her from her duty throughout the war years.

A few of her test projects—one of which was the flying gasoline tanker—did not win acceptance. The flying tanker was a pilotless glider to be towed behind a parent machine which would be refueled from storage tanks carried inside the glider. To succeed, the glider had to be a small and efficient design, and it had to have the greatest possible inherent stability. This was because, being uncontrolled, it would have to settle into level flight of its own accord after passing through rough air. The testing sorely tried the patience Hanna gained in her years of gliding experience. Seated in the glider she had to lock its controls in neutral, deliberately allow it to get into trouble, and observe its reactions. Time after time the glider turned turtle when its stability became unbalanced. It was finally abandoned, as an impractical effort.

Another experiment that failed was an effort to find a way for a small observation plane to take off and land on the limited deck space of a warship. A series of parallel hundred-foot-ropes were stretched on an inclined plane twenty feet above the deck. The plane was to pancake on this netlike arrestor and brake smoothly to a stop due to its friction against the arresting ropes. But problem after problem arose until the idea was abandoned.

The Battle of Britain was now at its height, and daily, German bombers collided with the cables that tethered the barrage balloons floating over southern England. The task of finding a means to cut the balloon cables in flight fell to her, and she undertook the assignment with enthusiasm. A fender was designed to fit the leading edges of bomber wings and to divert the balloon cable to the wingtips where a sharp cutting blade severed the line. In one test run a cable struck a propeller, sheared away part of the blade and caused the engine to vibrate off the airframe. Too low to bail out, Hanna flew the badly crippled bomber to a controlled crash and emerged unhurt. That the device became a success was reflected in the letters of thanks she received later from pilots whose lives had been saved in action. In March 1941, in the presence of Udet and other high-ranking generals, Hermann Goering awarded the diminutive flying fraulein the Gold Medal for Military Flying, with diamond. The next day Hitler, in the Reichs Chancellery, conferred upon her the Iron Cross, Second Class. Four years later she was to meet the Führer here again—for the last time—under vastly different circumstances.

Hanna's most demanding project to that time came in October 1942. She was assigned to test-fly the Me-163—a rocket plane designed by Willi Messerschmitt. It was a small, tailless plane with a powerful rocket power unit. Purely an interceptor, it was designed solely to split apart high-altitude Allied bomber formations, then turn and pass back down through the groups, attacking the bombers individually with its two 30-mm cannon. Here was clearly a giant step into the realm of speed and power that far surpassed anything with wings to that time. One moment the fat rocket plane took off with a flash of white-hot flame and a roar of thunderous power, and the next moment the pilot was vaulted into the very heart of the stratosphere. Within five minutes the Me-163 would burn its entire 336 gallons of special rocket fuel, a mixture of concentrated hydrogen peroxide and hydrazinc hydrate in methanol. These liquids, pumped separately into a combustion chamber, ignited spontaneously. The superheated gases were forced through twelve jets to produce 4500 thrust horsepower. Within seconds after breaking free of the earth, caught in the grip of raw, savage, rumbling power, the stubby little machine with its sweptback wings accelerated to two hundred fifty miles per hour. Now the undercarriage launch skid was released. A few more seconds and the plane was flying at more than 500 mph. If the pilot held a climbing angle of seventy degrees, he would reach thirty-thousand feet

—the height of the bomber formation—in one and one-half minutes.

Hanna Reitsch discovered that the Me-163 had superb flying qualities. Because it became a glider as soon as the fuel was exhausted, she was confident she would have no trouble in controlling it, even at its high landing speed of 145 mph. To her bitter disappointment she was never given the opportunity to fly the craft under rocket power. Fate intervened.

First flights in the rocket plane called for towing by a twin-engine Me-110, an air release, followed with several gliding turns to a landing. On Hanna's fifth towed flight the undercarriage failed to fall free when she operated the release lever. The only alternative was to cut loose from the tow plane and, during the glide, to try to shake it loose.

She released from the 110 at 10,500 feet and, despite several sharp pull-ups, the undercarriage remained hanging at an awkward angle. Rather than bail out, she decided to risk landing the plane. Coming in intentionally high, she sideslipped toward the field. The dangling undercarriage blocked off the airflow around one wing and, despite the high gliding speed, she got into serious trouble quickly. It all happened so rapidly she had little time to think. As the earth loomed up she continued to struggle until the last second, but she could not bring the streaking plane under control. Just before the machine hit, she huddled her small figure tightly together.

Crash! There was a cracking and tearing as the tiny monoplane tumbled over and rocked to a dusty stop. She escaped death, but barely. Four skull fractures, a concussion, and several broken facial bones spelled serious damage. For the next three months she was on the verge of death, and it was not until March 1943 that she was discharged from the hospital. With her release came the award of the Iron Cross, First Class. She was the first woman to receive this decoration.

Her return to flying was slow. Although she regained her

confidence quickly, she gained strength more slowly. She was ready to resume testing the Me-163 when she received a call from her long-time friend General von Greim to come to the Eastern Front as his pilot. There she experienced front-line bombings, attended to the wounded, and by her mere presence uplifted the sagging morale of the Luftwaffe's fighting men. The experience haunted her, and she found herself pondering more and more about the probable outcome of the war.

In August 1943, at the Flying Club in Berlin, a plan was born that might well have altered the course of the war. Over lunch with two old friends, one a highly skilled glider pilot and the other an aviation medical specialist, Hanna discussed the questionable future of the war. The disaster of Stalingrad was months behind them, and there was much uneasiness everywhere. Germany was surrounded, and the noose was growing tighter. The trio agreed that time was definitely not on Germany's side. Every passing day her resources were drained further, and there was no replenishment. For the first time, the Third Reich was on the defensive. Allied bombers were systematically pounding her towns, industry, and transportation system to pieces. Raw imports were down to a trickle. The death lists, military and civilian, continued to mount.

As the three at the Flying Club conversed solemnly, it became apparent the very thoughts Hanna had pondered for months were also in the minds of her companions. They agreed that Germany still had the power to determine the course of the war, but they believed, erroneously, that their nation could only be saved from disaster by a negotiated peace. If they could considerably weaken the enemy's military strength, they thought the Allies would negotiate. The means by which they proposed to bring about a widespread and sudden destruction of the enemy's resources was a masterpiece of sound planning that, at any other time, could have succeeded.

They knew their proposal could be carried out only by a scientific and technical weapon of absolute accuracy and telling destructivness. The three agreed that the only way to deliver the weapon was by air, and that it must be delivered in such a rapid succession of devastating and staggering blows that it would—in a matter of hours—stagger the enemy. It would have to zero in on generating plants, waterworks, petroleum dumps, industrial complexes, and warships. Destruction would have to be decisive or total; repair impossible. The weapon: piloted projectiles manned by volunteers for certain death.

Oddly, none of those at the table had heard of the Japanese suicide pilots—the *kamikaze*—of the Pacific war. At first, they wondered whether volunteers could be found, for it was not a task for daredevils, for men totally indifferent to the significance of their act. It was not for the blind fanatic or those who would use the weapon to make a dramatic exit from a disenchanted life. Nor was it enough that these volunteers be motivated only by idealism. Their self-sacrifice was not the objective; it was only the means to reach their Fatherland's objective. They would have to act with calm and deliberate calculation, in the conviction that their sacrifice was the only way they could save their nation.

To their astonishment, the concept of using suicide pilots was more widespread throughout the military than they realized. A quiet probe for volunteers brought them from everywhere in surprising numbers. Most were married, and fathers. They were hardy, uncomplicated, matter-of-fact individuals who faced up to this simple truth: their lives would mean nothing when compared with the millions of countrymen who would die if the war continued to a bitter finish. Not unexpectedly, many voiced a conviction that their sacrifice was mandatory if their wives, children, and country were to be preserved.

At first, the idea was confined to a limited circle, but as other associates were taken in, the plan gained impetus. There was some outright rejection by those who would gain no fame in its adoption, but this was minor.

The proposal was organized on sufficient scale (on paper) to prove its implementation could destroy Allied war concentrations in one fell swoop. Hanna Reitsch prepared to submit a concise plan to those in authority, in order for all technical details to be worked out before it was presented to Hitler. Filled with hope, and with scant inkling of the resistance she would encounter, she approached Field Marshal Milche, Goering's second in command. He flatly refused to entertain any thought of the idea. She tried, at her own peril, to persuade him to change his mind, but he was adamant.

Next came a conference with the Aeronautical Research Institute. Here she found encouragement. The assembly of tacticians—all specialists on weapons, explosives, aircraft, electronics, naval affairs, medicine—listened carefully as she outlined the plan. They declared it to be sound, both technically and operationally. With officers representing fighter and bomber groups, the conference first considered adopting the V-1 as the vehicle, but rejected it in favor of the Messerschmitt 328, a converted glider bomb adapted for powered flight and already in production.

There now remained only Hitler's approval, and Hanna arranged to meet with him at the Berghof, his mountain chalet at Berchtesgaden. After the usual amenities, she launched immediately into the scheme. At first Hitler was opposed to the idea of suicide missions. He did not believe the war situation was serious enough even to consider the plan. If it were necessary, he said, he would order it and decide on the proper time to use it. In their exchange of comments, during which Hanna Reitsch tried to convince Hitler the time was indeed critical, she became aware from his lengthy monologues that he was living in a world of his own making. Risking his anger, she pleaded for permission to at least start experimentation so that when—or if—the proper moment arrived, he could make the decision. Hitler reflected for a moment, agreed this could be done, but with the strict understanding that she and her workers were not to bother him further during its development. She had won the fight—for the moment.

The project was given to General Korten, Chief of Staff of the Luftwaffe. Of the thousands who had volunteered to pilot the suicide bombs, only seventy were initially called up for training. All volunteers, including Hanna Reitsch, signed this statement:

I hereby voluntarily apply to be enrolled in the suicide group as pilot of a human glider bomb. I fully understand that employment in this capacity will entail my own death.

Responsible, with Hanna, for the testing of the prototype planes was a pilot whose skill she highly respected, Heinz Kensche. At Horsching, near Linz, they conducted the first tests, using the Messerschmitt 328. The plane had been designed originally as a long-range fighter or light bomber. It was a single-seater with a very short fifteen-foot wingspan and could reach a speed of 470 mph. Two Argus-Schmitt jet engines were used to power the aircraft, but after two flights the Reich Air Ministry realized progress with this combination was useless. Experimentation was abandoned.

The project leaders decided to try flights using it without the power unit—as a human glider bomb. The powerless Me-328 was carried pickaback to height between nine thousand and eighteen thousand feet for launching. When ready for lift-away, the Me-328 pilot released a lever and was separated from the bomber's back. As the testing progressed, the pilots became increasingly aware that here was the plane that would more than meet their requirements for a glider bomb. It had superior maneuverability, strength, good visibility, and, above all, ease of navigation. The tests were completed in April 1944, and an aircraft factory in Thuringia was given a contract to go into immediate production. They awaited the first modified plane, but it never came. For some reason, unknown to Hanna Reitsch to this day, production never began. When the truth finally dawned that there would be no production of the Me-328 gliders, the pilots bitterly regretted their failure to carry out V-1 experiments simultaneously with the Me-328 tests. The war was worsening steadily, and there was diminishing hope that at this late stage they would find the support needed to continue their last-ditch effort.

Then came a break. Fraulein Reitsch was called to the telephone one spring day in 1944, and Otto Skorzeny introduced himself over the wire. Skorzeny was the pilot who had rescued Mussolini by helicopter from a hotel in the Abruzzi Mountains where he was held by the Badoglio government. Here was renewed hope, for the daring flier had formed the same concept about piloted glide bombs. After appraising the discouraging state of affairs, he set directly to work. Whenever he met objections or resistance he told the obstructionists calmly and bluntly: "The Führer has vested me with full powers in this matter. And he has expressly called for a daily progress report." There were no further delays.

Under the code name "Reichenberg," several V-1 flying bombs were set aside for modifications. So secret was the project that none of those working on the regular V-1 guided missile project was aware of their intended use.

The V-1 had its beginning in 1930, when a Munich engineer, Paul Schmidt, patented a simplified jet propulsion device called an intermittent pulse duct. The Argus Engine Works developed the crude engine prototype, and after considerable modification it became fairly dependable. Aircraft designers looked with encouragement on this revolutionary new power source as a break-through to propellerless flight. They experimented with its installation in conventional airplanes. But the engine vibrated so badly this adaptation was abandoned. The engineers discovered something else during their testing. The peculiar principle of intermittent pulses upon which it produced its powerful thrust, gave its fluttering valves a life of only three hours—much too short for prolonged flights in aircraft. Although limited experimentation continued in an effort to lengthen its operating life, little improvement was made in the basic engine. The war came in 1939 and while Hitler's armies were spreading over Europe, *der Führer* was looking ahead to the culmination of a secret weapon—a guided, long-range, self-propelled projectile. By 1941 the experiments by the German Army had encountered so many snags, the project appeared hopeless. Hitler turned his attention from the testing laboratories of Peenemünde and ordered the Luftwaffe to develop a weapon that would put England under continuous bombardment. When his staff decided a small, preset robot plane—or flying bomb—would do the job, Goering called on the aircraft industry for designs. The pulse jet came into prominence again as the *Vergeltungswaffe eins,* or V-1, took shape.

A futuristic design was submitted to the Luftwaffe by the Fiesler Aircraft Works, to be powered with the intermittent pulse jet. The proposal was approved and testing began with enthusiastic fervor. Unlike the military-directed rocket experiments at Peenemünde, the responsibility to produce a workable weapon fell to the aircraft manufacturers.

There were technical problems and frustrating delays as the first engines fell short of expectations. Many of them developed only a fraction of the required thrust or erratic power. Those engines that burst into their ear-splitting crescendo vibrated so greatly they threatened to fly apart in the air. To solve the problem, one V-1 was mounted intact in a giant wind tunnel and tested with the engine running, but the results were still inconclusive.

The standard production line V-1 was 25.4 feet long and carried a 2200-pound warhead. Behind the high explosive was the 80-octane fuel tank. Its wingspan was 17.6 feet—barely large enough to keep it airborne. In the machine's tail was a gyroscope that operated on compressed air that was bled from a steel tank. This instrument kept the V-1 on a fixed course and altitude. In short, the V-1 was a blending of aerodynamics and engineering that was typical of Teutonic ingenuity.

In less than five days, Hanna and Otto Skorzeny had the first V-1 converted. It had a pilot's seat immediately behind the wing, and cushioned landing skids. Because it would be used to train the suicide pilots, it had a jet power unit and a landing flap to reduce its touchdown speed.

The second V-1 was modified differently. A two-seater with one cockpit forward of the wing and the other directly behind it, it had dual controls. Also intended for training—as a glider—it was unpowered.

The third model was a fully operational V-1 with its standard jet engine. Its only alterations were a single-seat cockpit and primary flight controls. No skids, no landing flap. Once airborne, it would not be landed; it would be deliberately crashed, exploding, into a critical target. Operation Suicide.

When the first V-1 was ready for testing, Hanna immediately volunteered, but the Rechlin experiment group decided to use its pilots instead.

The Allied Air Forces had already pulverized the Pas de Calais launching sites on the French and Belgian coasts and the regular pilotless V-1s could no longer be launched from there by catapults. Their range was too short to allow them to be launched from catapults in Germany and, in any case, a catapult launch for a manned V-1 was unthinkable due to its high 17G acceleration. The buzz bombs were now launched from mother planes—Heinkel 111s—and carried nearer their targets before release. Slung under the medium bomber, the guided missile's pulse jet engine could be started by the He-111's pilot before release, or by the V-1's pilot after separation.

This was how Hanna and Otto Skorzeny found the first V-1 awaiting its test when they arrived at Larz on a balmy summer day. As they watched, the bomber took off with its underslung "baby" and circled higher. Finally came the release and slowly, for the first time, a man-carrying missile was under human guidance. It dropped down swiftly, like a tiny swallow. The pilot banked right and left in tight circles, testing, probing, sensing for the flight pressures needed to control the sensitive metal bird.

Then the missile settled on a straight course—momentarily. Suddenly it nosed down, its dive angle growing ever steeper. Hanna and her companion sensed this was not the pilot's doing. Down . . . down . . . In seconds the machine disappeared behind the trees on the horizon and a muffled explosion rumbled across the distance. A thin column of black smoke curled upward in the summer sky. They waited, anxious, as rescue crews raced to the spot. Thirty minutes later the news came back. The pilot was still alive, but seriously injured. Later they learned he had accidentally touched the release to the cockpit canopy. It had opened suddenly, directing a blast of wind against the pilot. Momentarily dazed, he lost control.

The following day another pilot was launched in a V-1. He crashed during landing but fared better than the first test pilot. After this, it was decided that *Flugkapitan* Reitsch and Heinz Kensche would conduct the flight tests of the suicide planes. Hanna's first flight was harrowing. The green fields and lush fir forests dropped slowly away as the Heinkel rose in the warm updrafts. She tensed, then forced herself to relax. She knew this was the most challenging test flight she had yet encountered. In the next ten minutes she would experience sights and sensations no aviatrix before her had ever known.

Directly behind her head was the intake duct for the pulse jet engine that would thrust her through the air at speeds faster than any propeller plane she had flown. Between her knees was a stubby control stick by which she would direct the torpedo-shaped flying bomb.

As they approached the release altitude of eighteen thousand feet, the bomber pilot called out their altitude and airspeed. The release stage neared and Hanna heard over the communication set: *"Prepare for release . . . release . . ."* There was a gentle tug . . . and she was free.

Within seconds the missile's stubby wings caught a cushion of air and became buoyant. It sliced through the air at better than 350 miles per hour, its engine bellowing in her ears. She was tempted again and again to tighten her grip on the controls but, realizing the other pilots probably tried this and to their sorrow overcontrolled and crashed, she moved the control stick carefully. She tested the aircraft under different power settings and learned that if she allowed the pulse jet to run at full power it operated more smoothly. She recalled now the early Argus engine tests she had seen at the military testing center long before the aeronautical engineers dreamed a person could fly in such a tiny machine. The rocketing, vibrating powerplant shook out its deafening din just inches away from her head. Carefully, she put the speeding V-1 into graceful turns and spirals. When at last the bedlam of sound ended, she knew the 156-gallon fuel cell was empty. Now began the glide to a landing. She made a wide, gentle turn, kept a safe margin of flying speed, and glided the missile to a skidding, ninety-mile-per-hour landing. There was a wild ovation as fellow pilots—many of them Luftwaffe-experienced—crowded around. She was able to report in detail on the handling characteristics of the sensitive machine and today she recalls:

Altogether I made about ten flights; how many were powered flights is difficult to say because several began under power with the pulse-jet operating but had to be stopped soon because of engine trouble or other malfunctions. We were in the beginning of testing the V-1 for our "special task" and we were trying to overcome the many, many difficulties, even those with the unpowered glider V-1 and the two seater training V-1.

The remaining flights in the series went without mishap except for one awkward and near-fatal moment. The Heinkel pilot had just released her when the bomber grazed the back of the missile. Hanna heard a loud tearing sound and thought the V-1's tail had been riped off. Her plane suddenly became difficult to control, for it vibrated fiercely, slewed right and left, and lagged dangerously in its control responses. The craft was buffeted and seemed on the verge of going berserk. Mustering every bit of flying skill at her command, she struggled with the machine and herself until she could maneuver it to a miraculous landing. On inspection of the tail surfaces she discovered the fin had been smashed and twisted thirty degrees to the right. She marveled that it held together in her descent.

Soon afterward she narrowly missed death in the two-seater V-1 when a bag of sand used as ballast in the front seat shifted its position in the critically balanced plane. The V-1 would not come out of its dive and she was already too low to bail out. She thought quickly and, instead of continuing to tug on the control stick, nosed the plane down more steeply and gained even greater speed . . . 370 . . . 380 . . . Then, at the last instant, she pulled back on the control stick. The elevators responded, and she pancaked hard. Dust flew as the skids splintered and the metal hull ripped open. She emerged without a scratch.

The final phase of testing called for gliding an unpowered V-1 at high speeds with a full load. This was to confirm the flight characteristics of the fully operational suicide plane which would be loaded down with high explosives. To simulate the weight of the warhead, water was used. The V-1 could not be landed in its loaded condition, for its improvised landing skid did not have sufficient spring suspension to withstand the landing shock; the plane would crash and break up. A quick-drain valve was fitted into the bottom of the tank. When the flight test was ended, the pilot would move a lever to open the valve and drain the water. Lightened, the plane would be landed normally.

She was launched in the crisp, cold air at eighteen thousand feet, flew through the tests quickly and recorded the results. At forty-five hundred feet she pushed against the lever that would open the drain. It refused to move. Frozen shut. The plane continued to glide steeply and to gain speed. Without power to keep it airborne, it was only a matter of minutes before it would plunge into the ground. She clawed feverishly at the small handle until her scratched fingers were bloody. Over the pointed nose of the missile the green-brown landscape patchwork moved steadily upward. Time was running out. With only a few hundred feet remaining, the lever broke free at last—in time to spill most of the water and permit a safe, but hard, landing.

Tests completed, pilot training began immediately. None of the instructors, test pilots, or trainees deceived themselves about the risk of surviving the training phase itself. The entire operation could easily fail here if the fatality rate among instructors and trainees was high. Landing the V-1 was always a touchy business. Pilots of average flying skill, even though specially trained for this work, could never be sure of surviving the training flights. For this reason the instructors were carefully selected from among the best of the pilot volunteers. They were the first to be trained, using the two-seater glider version. The training operation put a heavy strain on everyone. Although an average pilot could fly the missile without difficulty on the air, its high landing speed demanded outstanding skill and experience to put it down in one piece, time after time. There was simply no margin for error.

"Of the seven pilots flying the V-1, four were killed and three were injured," Hanna recalls. "I remained the only pilot untouched. The accidents were caused either by the difficulty of the pilots in making a spot landing—the V-1 had a very bad gliding angle—or by structural failures caused by the pounding vibrations that weakened parts of the wing."

Meanwhile, the first catapulted buzz bomb had exploded in southern England, fifteen minutes after it was launched from the French coast. It happened during the night of June 12–13, 1944, six days after D-Day.

As early as June 1942, British Intelligence had puzzled over aerial photos that showed small airplanes resting on inclined ramps at Peenemünde. There were scorch marks, as though from a huge blowtorch. Secret agents had already suggested the Germans were building a long-range bombardment weapon of unusual design. The French coast, from Cherbourg to Calais, was photographed, revealing more than a hundred concrete launch ramps, all pointed toward southern England. Late in December 1943, British and American bomber commands pounded these sites relentlessly until they were destroyed. By March 1944 the Germans had repaired them, and again they were bombed. The Germans then built a new series of launching points. They were of such simple design and so extremely difficult to see from the air, they went undetected for a time.

D-Day spurred the Germans to launch their "vengeance weapon one" in great numbers. Salvos were sent over in cloudy and rainy weather that limited British and American fighter operations. On some days two hundred flying bombs smashed into England in twenty-four hours. Barrage balloons, antiaircraft rockets and guns, and fighter planes formed the defense systems. In the first weeks of V-1 attacks, fighters shot down over a thousand flying bombs—thirty per cent of the total launched.

Though most V-1s flew in at two thousand feet, there were many that skimmed along lower—at a thousand feet—and became difficult targets for British antiaircraft batteries. After a predetermined time, the fuel flow ended and the bomb plummeted indiscriminately into the ground. A manned flying projectile would have struck a specific target with more deadly results.

The German technicians knew, from tests, that the V-1's constant 360-mph airspeed had a slight edge on the Spitfires flown late in 1943. With Hitler himself as an onlooker, a captured Spitfire was flown in a demonstration dash with a V-1 and failed to keep pace with it. But by the time the V-1 was launched in numbers, new British fighters and late-model pursuit planes had the speed edge. When the early model fighters encountered a V-1 over the Channel, they compensated for their slower speed by diving on the flying bomb. A few daring pilots even edged up to the thundering monsters and, with their wing, gently tipped up the stubby airfoil of the V-1 to set its directional gyros off course and turn the missile back to its launch point. Often the V-1 would spiral into the Channel.

Although the speed, size, and sturdy construction made the missile a formidable target, several fighter pilots became skilled at shooting them down. A few British pilots shot down more than fifty each. In all, 1847 were shot down by fighters,

232 were lost to balloon cables, and 1878 to antiaircraft guns and "Z" rockets.

There are some who say the V-1 program was not a success, that because of its inaccuracies, misfirings, and faulty steerings it was premature. Yet for a weapon that was a "failure" it left a record of devastation. Of the 8070 launched against England, 2420 got through to the London area. They killed 5864 persons, injured 17,197, and gave minor injuries to 23,174. They destroyed 24,491 buildings and made 52,293 more uninhabitable. Allied bombing of the launch sites cost 450 aircraft and 2900 airmen. Because the weapon was not sufficiently perfected due to lack of time, the conventional countermeasures were enough to check it. It could not stop the scheduled invasion of Europe. Hitler had made a "too little, too late" gamble with the weapon that could have—a year earlier—altered the course of the war.

Hanna Reitsch remembers the end of "Reichenberg" this way: "We had to follow the government order to stop our testing; it was too late now for the purpose of being used with any real hope of success as a 'self-sacrifice' weapon."

Thus, all the feverish labors, struggles, and heartbreaking frustrations to build the first operational suicide squadron was for nothing. Time, not lack of perseverance, defeated them. With enemy infantry fanning across Europe the personnel of Operation Reichenberg knew they had lost the decisive moment.

Late in April 1945, Hanna received a message from Colonel-General von Greim to report to Hitler at the Reichs Chancellery in Berlin at once. The beleaguered city was even then surrounded and awaiting its final hour. Flying in a Fieseler Storch observation plane, von Greim and Hanna landed at the Brandenburg Gate, but not before the General was wounded by Russian ground fire. In the Reichs Chancellery, Hitler, pale and resigned to the inevitable, appointed von Greim as Chief of the Luftwaffe, replacing Goering, whom he believed had betrayed him.

Hanna Reitsch remained three nights in the bunker, where she told bedtime stories to the six little Goebbels children to calm them as thundering Russian shells shook the underground quarters.

During the night of April 28 Hitler ordered von Greim and Fraulein Reitsch to make their escape. An Arado 96 awaited them nearby. Two days later, in Lübeck, they learned of Hitler's death.

Taken into custody by the American army, Hanna was regarded mistakenly as a high criminal personage and confined in an internment camp until August 1946.

As soon as conditions permitted, she returned to gliding, powered flying, and helicopter piloting. In 1952 she won the bronze medal in the World's Gliding Championship meet held in Spain. In 1955 she became the German National Champion. At both competitions she was the only woman contestant. Pandit Nehru asked her to come to India in 1959 to help improve that country's high performance gliding program. Then, in 1962, she accepted a position in Ghana, where, as director, she built a civilian gliding academy and trained Ghanaians to become gliding instructors. "My work was not with the Ghana Air Force," she says. "It was one of our tasks to train officer cadets—Air Force aspirants—and we proved that those with glider training and experience had less difficulty in learning powered flight."

With the 1966 *coup d'état* in Ghana, Fraulein Reitsch returned to Germany, earned her helicopter license, and, again as the only woman contestant, participated in her country's 1969 National Helicopter Championship. Today she is engaged in research gliding—high mountain soaring—and working toward her commercial helicopter license.

Gliding and soaring remain her first love. From her years of discerning observations with this type of flying, she has formed a striking conclusion on flight training in general: "Gliding is excellent training—even for those who already fly powered planes. Learning to glide first makes one familiar with the air, with moving around the airplane's three pivotal axes, with navigation and learning the effect of the controls.

"Gliding will be a great help in training pilots for powered flight in those countries where technology—and aviation especially—has no tradition and is experienced for the first time by this generation. I am convinced, because of my experiences in Ghana, that gliding is an excellent tool with which to form the character of youth in a developing nation, for teaching them to think for themselves, make their own decisions, and above all become reliable, responsible, disciplined personalities."

Fortunately, through all her hazardous test flying she was never forced to parachute to safety. "I had good luck," she asserts, but to young men and women who seek a flying career today she offers these words: "Enjoy your flying, but remain careful! Never forget, as an old German proverb says: 'Carefulness is not cowardice and carelessness is not courage.' "

Looking back to the time when she test flew the V-1 twenty-seven years ago. Hanna Reitsch speaks of her motivation for this highly dangerous mission:

"I didn't do it for the adventure of it, nor for the sake of sensation. I was only trying to find a valuable tool that would help my country through a very bad situation."

10

Sixty-six Sorties in a Marauder

THE amassed power of the Army Air Forces and the fighting strength of its individual units in the Second World War were built upon the accomplishments of the individual crewman. Every combat move was vital to the operation of the aircraft, for aircraft were useless without men to operate them—men who willingly put their lives on the line when the situation demanded it.

Chester P. Klier was one crewman in that two-and-a-half-million-member service. Young and alert, he was well trained in his job. Like every member of his crew, he had to be. There was no war effort where the lives of the men were as interdependent as in a bomber over enemy ground.

Staff Sergeant Klier was a flight engineer-gunner on a Martin B-26 Marauder, then the fastest and highest-powered air weapon in its class. In those days it was considered a "hot bird." It landed at 120 miles an hour.

Despite its early reputation as a crew killer, the Marauder's loss-in-combat ratio was less than one half of one per cent—the lowest of any Allied bomber. Over 250 of them completed more than a hundred missions each. Records show they flew 110,000 sorties and dropped 150,000 tons of bombs. As a part of that record, Chet Klier says that the Marauder was one of the finest tactical bombers of the war—and this from the only man in the A.A.F. who had to depart its top turret with the aid of a screwdriver.

Klier won the Distinguished Flying Cross twice, the Air Medal eleven times, and the Purple Heart. Here is his own story:

I was nineteen when I left my native St. Paul and joined the Air Corps. My basic training began on a hot, sticky August day in 1942, at Sheppard Field, Texas. After mechanic training I was sent to the Martin factory in Maryland with other aircrew trainees to learn the systems of the new B-26 Marauder. A month later I was taking six weeks of air-to-air gunnery at Buckingham Army Airfield in Florida. From the rear cockpit of drafty AT-6 trainers we practiced firing 30-caliber Browning machine guns at air-towed sleeve targets.

A newly activated Bomb Group, the 386th, was my ultimate assignment. At Barksdale, Louisiana, I began air training for flight engineer in March 1943 and eventually became engineer-gunner as part of a combat crew. Except for the career gunner, all enlisted aircrewmen doubled as gunners during attacks.

Few aircraft attracted as much adverse, and unwarranted, criticism as the Marauder. Because its short wingspan made it appear to have little means of support it was nicknamed the flying prostitute. It was also called the widow-maker and the killer. I flew in the early models with the 1850-horsepower Pratt and Whitney engines and sixty-five-foot wingspan. We lost nine planes in a very short time. Fast, but unforgiving at low airspeeds, the Marauder, with its steep glide angle, made power approaches practical. It was as maneuverable as a pursuit and certainly no plane for Grandma to fly, but in the hands of a capable pilot it was the hottest, hardest-hitting thing with wings. During combat training, one pilot made a belly landing on an airfield in England with both engines out and thirty bombs aboard. The plane was torn up but the crew walked away unhurt. Despite the crashes, we liked the Marauder and most of us seemed to think that this sort of thing would happen to the other guy.

After graduation I was given a seven-day leave, but on my first day at home I was suddenly recalled. Our orders had arrived; we were going overseas immediately. We were given the newest model B-26s with seventy-one-foot wingspans and 2000-horsepower engines. We named our ship *Buzz-n-Bitch* and painted a picture of a diving girl on the nose. Our crew left Barksdale on June 28 and what a trip we had! Eight hops and fifteen days later we rolled our wheels onto the air base at Prestwick, Scotland. Here we left our plane, took a train to London and then to Colchester.

Our group commander was the famous air pioneer, Colonel Lester J. Maitland. As a young second lieutenant in 1927 he and navigator Albert Hegenberger made the first successful flight from California to Hawaii. Both became generals in the war.

Ours was a typical medium bomber group made up of four squadrons of sixteen planes each. In all, the group was supported with about 293 officers and 1297 enlisted men.

On July 31, 1943, I flew my first combat mission. Our pilot was First Lieutenant George Howard. Preparations for that morning sortie set a fair pattern for the hundreds that were to follow. On the night of the twenty-ninth we received our first telegraphed field order from Eighth Air Force Headquarters. They had awaited the latest weather reports over the target and made the decision to go. Operations and Intelligence began working backward from the zero hour—take off —to set times for awakening the crews, feeding them, getting them to the briefing, a time to start engines, takeoff, and rendezvous with the British fighters.

Photographs and maps were broken out and flak data from every source were gathered and posted on the 1:500,000 scale map used to plot the bomb run. Every gun from German 88s down to small automatic weapons was pinpointed.

In the predawn, armorers loaded the guns and put bombs in the B-26s' bellies. Ordnance men followed to fuse them. The photographic officer saw that one of every four or six planes had loaded cameras to record the strikes. We carried our personal equipment. Parachutes, Mae Wests, and flak vests were dropped off at each bomber by a truck. The bombardiers checked out their Norden sights from the bombsight vault.

At nine o'clock the briefing room was almost filled. As crews entered they were checked off by Security and some of the men emptied their pockets dramatically. The room was heavy with smoke, and every man was wide awake now. We got all available information bearing on the mission: weather, target information, opposition. We were to hit the German airfield at Abbeville, France. An hour in and an hour back. Intelligence gave us the latest on flak and fighters, communications ciphers and procedure orders. As we filed outside to the waiting trucks that were to carry us to our planes, each man was handed an escape kit and escape money.

Half an hour later engines were started. The Marauders rumbled from their dispersal pads and grouped together along the taxiways and end of the runway. A short wait, then a green light flashed from the control tower and the lead ship rolled forward. Others followed at thirty-second intervals. We were among the last to take off.

As soon as we were airborne, base area controls at scores of base operations offices went into effect. They had tactical plans for fighter escort rendezvous and diversionary missions

—all designed to keep the Luftwaffe guessing about our actual target.

We made the bomb run from twelve thousand feet. The flak came up; ugly black puffs. It *cracked* and *whuffed!* We dropped our bombs on target, turned and headed home. Despite the hazards it was comforting to know everything possible had been arranged for our survival. In the briefing the signal officers supplied our radiomen with a schedule of communications ciphers on edible rice paper. If one of our bombers were forced to drop out of formation with battle damage, the radio operator could tune to a timed series of signals from stations all over our base area. Each station transmitted a specific signal for homing in. If we had to ditch in the Channel, the British air-sea rescue boats would pick us up.

While at Boxted we had several air raid alerts. At first no one took them seriously; a few sauntered outside to look up. But one morning a German bomber planted a 500-pounder midway between Headquarters and the 76th Air Service Squadron. Two men were killed outright and twenty-nine were wounded. This made us believers. That afternoon every man had his personal slit trench and when the sirens sounded the Nissen huts emptied fast. A few days later the Jerries dropped "butterfly" bombs—canisters of small land mines. No casualties.

Our first missions proved we were a good, stable crew that could work well together. Tight-knit. Our pilot was First Lieutenant Don Vincent, and the co-pilot was Flight Officer Robert Gragg. The bombardier was First Lieutenant Anthony Popovici, Staff Sergeant Robert O'Kane handled the radio, and Staff Sergeant James Wilkie was the tail gunner. There was a fine camaraderie among us; whether on leave or in combat we were like a family. After a few missions crew gunners were usually reluctant to change positions because each felt he had the most secure place in the plane. With all the trouble I had, no one cared to exchange positions with me.

We flew our fifth mission against the marshaling yards at Courtrai, in Belgium. On the way back German fighters jumped our escort Spitfires over Dunkerque, and the dogfighting became savage. Just out of our gun range two ME-109s got on the tail of a Spitfire and sent it down burning. Then they came after us. My search zone was from three to six o'clock, and overhead. Wilkie called out: "Three fighters at six o'clock level, twelve hundred yards!" I snapped my head in that direction and there they were. Two fighters were flying in echelon and a single plane was ahead by about three hundred yards. Suddenly, when the lead plane, an ME-109, was at thirty degrees elevation and five o'clock, it erupted in a big ball of flame. I assumed the two trailing planes were Spits and they had got it. I felt relieved. But the two fighters came around in a fairly flat left turn and flew level about a thousand yards back and five hundred yards to the right of our heading—still at a thirty-degree elevation. They held their distance for at least a minute. I was tracking the leader in my gunsight and thinking: They must be Spitfires to hang around this long. Then, in an instant, the wings of both fighters lit up with belching cannon fire. I remember saying aloud, "No friend of mine!" and squeezed both triggers of my twin fifties. As Jerry cannon fire sprayed our flight of six bombers both 109s appeared bracketed by my tracers. We could sense their machine-gun bullets striking remote parts of the plane, but a 20-mm cannon shell would make an unmistakable "smart rap" on contact. They had closed to seven hundred yards and slipped from the four to the five o'clock position. Now they were at four hundred yards. Smoke out there; the leader quit firing but I let my guns yammer on. The trailing fighter dropped below our tail and out of sight. Wilkie picked him up with his tail guns and I heard him call out: "I got him! I got him!" The German fell right on down and across to our nine o'clock low position. I stopped firing because my target dipped below my line of sight, then he pulled up vertically about rudder-high at seven o'clock—not more than twenty-five yards out. Man! Those black crosses looked big! Smoke poured from all around his engine cowl and for an instant he wallowed there before he fell off on his left wing. He slowly rotated about ninety degrees with his belly toward us and slanted down at a steep angle, trailing a greasy black plume. He didn't bail out that I could tell. I reasoned he must have been dead or dying at the controls—for what other reason would he pull up and hang on his propeller just a few yards from enemy guns?

Back at base we went into debriefing. Claims were filed for enemy fighters destroyed. The S-2 officer asked whether anyone else on our crew saw the fighters shot down. Lieutenant Vincent said Gragg was flying our plane during the attack, and he was free to watch both go down under the left wing. That confirmed it; we were a happy lot that night.

The Germans bombed Boxted three times while we were there—and we bombed it once. In some ways we were a SNAFU crew so we did it the hard way—parked on the hardstand thirty minutes before engine start time.

I'd just completed the preflight check and was still sitting in the pilot's seat. Lieutenant Vincent was in the co-pilot's seat at my right and the bombardier was in the nose. Our radio operator was at his station behind us and Bob Gragg was standing outside in front of the left engine with Jim Wilkie. The bombardier—not our regular man on this mission—had closed the bomb bay doors, but for some reason he decided to open them again. They wouldn't budge.

This wasn't our regular plane—it was grounded for repairs. The bombardier told me an "experimental" bomb door opening device had been installed on this plane, part of which was inside a small box mounted on the floor in front of the pilot's seat. I found it and he said: "Pull out the long pin with the chain attached." I leaned forward and started to pull it out. Unknown to me, he was depressing the thumb button on the bomb bay door handle and was trying to push the handle forward to the *Open* position at the same time. When I pulled the lock pin free in the cockpit, his lever slammed full forward past the *Door Open* position and into *Bomb Salvo*. The doors flew open and *Crash!*—the plane emptied two tons of five-hundred-pound demolition bombs onto the hardstand. The sudden release of all that weight made the B-26 jiggle violently on its tires and chocks. Bombs rolled all over the pavement. Within seconds every man, ashen-pale, was out of the plane and running to get at least a hundred yards away. We weren't the only ones making tracks. The crews parked on each side of us saw the bombs hit the ground and were sprinting with us. In a few minutes our operations officer, Major Charles V. Thornton, who saw the entire fiasco, roared up in his jeep. He was pale too, very angry and so "shook" all he could blurt out was: "You've got to be more careful with those things or somebody will get hurt!"

The time was rapidly approaching for the start of the mission. We thought we'd sit this one out but the operations officer told us otherwise. "Bombs or no bombs, you'll fly this mission," Major Thornton growled. "We need your firepower in the formation." So we flew merrily off to war with an empty bomb bay. As it turned out, when our group was almost across the Channel, we were recalled because of cloud cover over the target. In those early operations, when the mission was canceled en route, our orders were to drop the bombs into the water and return to base. As we watched one bomb load after another fall from the swarm of Marauders and splash into the English Channel, we all knew our eight eggs were still very dry on the hardstand at Boxted.

Almost from the beginning we had flak vests and flak helmets. The vests were made in three pieces; back, chest, and lower front, but in the top turret of a Maurader there simply wasn't very much room to wear one. I put the back piece behind me, sat on the lower front piece, placed the chest piece on the floor near the hot side of the airplane, and hoped for the best.

We tangled with both the ME-109s and the Focke-Wulfe 190s. Because we usually bombed at altitudes between ten thousand and thirteen thousand feet the ME-109 proved the deadlier. It was excellent from eighteen thousand feet and lower, and would stay with us to mix it up. The FW-190s were designed as high-altitude fighters to knock down B-17s and B-24s at the upper levels. If they attacked us, they usually made one dive on our formation and kept going.

Jerry fighter pilots demonstrated superb skill in combat. After all, they got their training from the best aerial gunners in the A.A.F. They were either good or they were dead; it was that simple.

On the bomb runs, the initial point was about fifteen to twenty miles from the target. Flak usually became frantically intense, and our evasive action developed into an upwind run to the aiming point. This was the most suspense-packed period of the mission, when we were on a steady, straight-line path for twenty to thirty seconds. The enemy antiaircraft gunners knew this and redoubled their efforts to zero in. When the bomb load was released in salvo, there was the welcome lurch of the aircraft that told us it was "bombs away!" The big bird seemed to give a sigh of relief and so did we. A steep turn out of the target area followed immediately.

Our respect for flak was complete when we saw it break an eighteen-ton bomber in half. We'd taken another plane, *Hazzard,* on its maiden bombing mission, and I remember the comment of the squadron photographer who snapped our picture as we stood beside it. "It's brand-new and we want a picture while it's still in one piece," he quipped. We brought it back without a scratch.

On this particular mission its regular crew was flying it in the number three position of our six-plane formation. We were in the "tail-end Charlie" spot—the number six position of the high flight. It was on September 9 and we were raiding Boulogne. As we crossed the shoreline, the coastal guns opened up with a murderous barrage. It happened on the bomb run, seconds away from the release point. A 155-mm burst caught the *Hazzard* directly under its belly, and it broke apart at the aft bomb bay, just behind the wing. The tail section fell open-end down at a slight angle, and the rudder and elevators kept it sailing straight. The front half rolled lazily into a spin and because the door in the radio compartment was open I saw all the way through the length of the fuselage to the pilot's pedestal and instrument panel. It was a sickening sight to watch the bomber die and realize its crew was dying with it. It had been parked next to ours on the hardstand, and we'd chatted with the crew just prior to takeoff. No one got out, and when the bomb strike photos were developed they showed the forward half of the plane where it had crashed just fifty yards short of our bomb craters.

I had flown eleven missions when the 386th moved to Easton Lodge, Great Dunmow, Essex. Colonel Kenneth Martin's 354th Fighter Group of P-51s took over our field at Colchester. Dunmow was twenty-five miles farther inland and, like most English airfields, was close to town. Our B-26s were parked in the open, three or four to a hardstand, and it seemed that almost every English airfield had a dip in the runway. The engineers didn't bother—or didn't have time— to level them; they simply paved over hill and dale. I recall Dunmow especially, because halfway down the runway a bomber on takeoff disappeared from view. In a few seconds it lifted out of the depression and took to the air. We hit the dip at 130 miles an hour and became unstuck at 145 with a full bomb load.

Not having a superstitious attachment to numbers, I didn't look with any particular sense of foreboding on my upcoming thirteenth mission. Certainly an hour and a half after our departure, at twelve thousand feet over occupied France, I had other things to think about. It was on September 27 and our target, the German airfield at Conches, was coming up. When we rolled steep to the left, our initial point had been reached and from here on, everyone sweated it out. We felt like a flock of sitting ducks for the Messerschmitts and that dirty word, *flak*. Within minutes the bomb bay doors would open and our two-hundred-mile-per-hour bomb run would begin.

The chatter of machine-gun fire was the first warning that Jerries had slipped through our Spitfire cover. Almost everything can be seen from the top turret; front, back, both sides, and overhead. In other gunnery zones the overall visibility isn't as good and one had to imagine what was happening in those areas. I couldn't decide which case was the more nerve-racking.

Wilkie, in the tail, had an ME-109 lined up at six o'clock level and was pumping lead. As the German sailed past he trailed whiffs of black smoke. It didn't necessarily mean a hit had been scored; the German pilot may merely have poured on the coal to get out of range fast. Below, two more ME-109s tore into the low flight and the tracers flew freely now. Most of the action was on the other side of the formation. I could hear the crew spot the enemy fighters and shout out intercom warnings. And there I sat, out of range, fidgeting with my twin-fifty Brownings, nursing eight hundred rounds of ammunition. I couldn't get in one lousy shot! Frustration at its worst!

Our position also limited my zone of fire from three to six o'clock and overhead. The fighters attacked from six o'clock low and were breaking clear at nine o'clock high. Their tracers preceded them and zipped over my turret about rudder-high. I looked down over my shoulder and saw an ME-109 about two hundred yards out. It was literally hanging on its propeller and both wing cannons were belching orange flame. My thought at the time was: What's wrong with the waist gunner in the opposite ship? He can almost hit that fighter with a baseball bat! It turned out that Sergeant Hadley had exhausted his ammunition just before this joker turned up.

Lieutenant Popovici's voice came over the intercom: "Bomb bay doors open." Almost at once the fighters broke off their attack. They had good reason; ugly black puffs of 88-mm shells began to burst all around us. The fighters wanted no part of the heavy flak.

We all wanted to shrink when the flak came up—the smaller the target the better. My buddies heard me say a dozen times that if they'd look into my turret during the flak barrage all they'd see on the seat would be a pair of G.I. shoes covered with a flak helmet.

The intercom crackled again and the bombardier called out, "Bombs away!" The plane lurched as two tons fell clear. That called for a sigh of relief, and as we swung away we saw the bombs hit the target squarely, two miles below. They walked through aircraft hangars, barracks, and runways, bursting into ugly mushrooms of dirt and smoke.

We seemed to be in the clear now. The flak subsided and there were no Messerschmitts in sight. Even our fighter escort had disappeared. The Spits would leave the bombers only to do battle with enemy fighters trying to close on us.

A fighter appeared at three o'clock level, making our exact speed. I estimated his range at fifteen-hundred yards. Friendly fighters never pointed their noses at our bomber formations; they made wide, sweeping turns when they joined up with us. A gunner couldn't mistake that beautiful elliptical wing of the Spitfire so there was no need to worry until the stranger turned a wing up—that meant he was going to make a pass on us.

This fellow seemed to edge in slowly, in a sort of side-sliding horizontal fashion. He was at twelve-hundred yards now, still too far out for positive identification. Was it a Spitfire or an ME-109? At that distance, flying straight and level, they were much alike. I tracked him in my gunsight and moved my thumb to the mike switch to alert the crew, then decided to wait. Unknown to me, Lieutenant Gragg was watching him and O'Kane was tracking him with the waist gun. It had all the markings of a Jerry trick: fly parallel for several minutes, out of range, to simulate a flank escort fighter, then, after the gunners become accustomed to seeing him and turn their attention elsewhere, come barreling in.

He edged closer, still flying at our speed. In a flash, it happened! A quarter roll and quick up-elevator brought the ME-109 in on a beam attack. It was a straight-away shot for me; I didn't have to allow for lead. He zeroed squarely into my gunsight and I squeezed both triggers. The turret shuddered as the two streams of tracers poured from the guns. An acrid odor of burning cordite filled my nostrils as I heard Gragg shout over the intercom: "Get that so and so!" O'Kane was firing a few degrees up, I was firing a few degrees down, and we had him cold in our crossfire at eight hundred yards. Empty shell cases clattered to the floor of the plane in a brass blur. As the tracers whizzed all around him, the enemy pilot maneuvered desperately to dodge the deadly hail from our three guns. Then, suddenly, like a rock he dropped from view—straight down. He wasn't burning and he didn't explode. Maybe we got him and maybe we didn't. At any rate, he knew he'd been in a fight; we hadn't given him the chance to fire one shot. In the waist, O'Kane kicked the empty shell cases from under his feet.

Our box of eighteen was still intact as we neared the French coast. I relaxed a little with the thought that another mission was almost wrapped up and soon we'd all be back on Dunmow. In our tin hut, "Section Eight," I'd paint another bomb on my well-worn jacket. The thirteenth.

It was late afternoon when St. Valéry came into view. I remembered we were supposed to stay off to one side of it going out. At the briefing our intelligence officer reminded us of the German flak school there. We didn't like the idea of graduating any of their students.

Somehow our formation passed too close to the concentration of ack-ack guns and all hell broke with sudden fury. Flak bursts saturated our formation, and it was deadly accurate. Close bursts jolted and rocked our bomber. We could hear them. *Whoooomph! Shooom!* A flak fragment slammed through my turret dome and I felt a hot sting as the jagged metal slashed the left side of my face. Instinctively my hands covered up! Everything turned red! My first horrifying thought was that my eyes had been hit and I was blind. Faintly, I heard my shaky voice over the intercom: "Engineer to crew . . . I've been hit!" My leather gloves were slippery with blood as I tried to wipe my eyes. They cleared—and I saw a horrifying sight. The Marauder perched in the number three position a hundred feet ahead and slightly above us caught a direct hit in its left engine. A sheet of flame shot two hundred feet backward and burned off most of its tail surfaces. Lieutenant Stephen Danforth did a heroic job of maneuvering the flaming hulk clear of the other planes. It was his last act. None of the crew had the faintest chance to bail out as the bomber plummeted to earth like a flaming meteor.

Then, in our flight, the number four plane suddenly

zoomed upward at a crazy angle. Its pilot, John Albers, was struck with a piece of shrapnel. The bomber wallowed and staggered as co-pilot Jim Engels struggled to regain control and rejoin the flight. I heard myself shouting at the top of my lungs: "Stop shooting, stop shooting! You got one—that's enough!" Aerial combat was a strange, unreal experience. Everything happened so fast it accelerated emotions at a fantastic rate. Aircrewmen found themselves praying in one breath and swearing in the next. While they cringed with fear, they were defiant with anger.

The ack-ack barrage lifted as quickly as it began; we were over the English Channel now. I slumped down in the turret, emotionally drained. Faces looked up at me from the fuselage interior. Don Vincent had turned the plane over to Gragg and hurried aft, Bob O'Kane left his gun, and Jim Wilkie moved back from the tail turret. I gave them a weak smile and a thumbs-up wave that I'd be okay. Bob wanted me to get out of the turret for first aid. I said no, I'd stay where I was because we were still over enemy ground. The wound must have looked serious; they told me my face was pretty well smeared with blood. They gave me a reassuring pat and returned to their positions.

Thirty minutes later we were gliding on the final approach. Ambulances and fire trucks waited at the far end of the runway. Doctors were there when the planes rolled to a stop, and the more critically wounded were rushed to the hospital. On my way to surgery in a jeep I reflected that it had been a rough mission; eight men in our eighteen-plane formation were wounded, some seriously, and six had been killed in the downed B-26.

The flight surgeon held up the sliver of flak he had fished from my face. "You're lucky," he remarked. "It was a clean, glancing slice instead of a gouge."

As I settled back in bed and slowly began to unwind, the

entire mission drifted past in hazy perspective. I thought of my crew. They had been rushed from the plane to the briefing room and interrogated while details were still fresh in their minds. Over hot coffee, doughnuts, and cigarettes the intelligence personnel were getting firsthand details from every man. "How many fighters did you see? What type? Did the Germans attack singly or in pairs? How many did you see go down? How heavy was the antiaircraft fire? What was the extent of direct hits on the target?" And so on. When the questioning was finished, the mission was officially ended and the long-sustained suspense was over. In the photo lab wet films were being studied. Mechanics were securing the bombers on their dispersal hardstands.

Some of the men in my truck had joked about this being mission number thirteen. "Let's call it 12-B," one fellow suggested. I said, "I'm not worried and I'm not superstitious." Now, as I drifted off to sleep I wasn't so sure. . . .

Seven days later I was back in action. We were now part of the Ninth Air Force and continued to hit targets in northern France: Beauvis-Tilles, Martinvast, Bois-Urench, and Cherbourg. Cherbourg was my twenty-sixth mission—my second thirteenth—on January 7, 1944. It was very nearly my last.

We took off on a cold morning at eight-thirty, climbed into a brilliantly clear sky, and headed for the Channel. When we reached twelve thousand feet the temperature was down to thirty-five degrees below zero. By the time we started over the target at ten-thirty, I was huddled in my fleece-lined leather flying suit trying to keep warm. Then all the flak started up and cracked and huffed around us. Suddenly it didn't seem nearly so cold! I began my usual bobbing and weaving act in the turret, watching for shrapnel damage and trying to see everything that was happening. In leaning over I accidentally breathed on my rear gunsight and it immediately frosted over. To allow it to clear I cocked my head over the receiver section of the right-hand gun and waited about a minute. I'd no sooner moved my head back to the gunsight when a great chunk of flak slammed into my right-hand gun barrel and sliced off the right side of my turret with a crash and a howl of wind. My head was there just seconds earlier—and when the shrapnel struck I was halfway through a Hail Mary.

On January 11 we made the first of three strikes against St. Omer, near where a launch site for V-1 robot bombs was under construction. The 386th pounded these sites for six months before the Germans launched the first one against England. After our first strike we were grounded for a week to patch the holes in our aircraft. Our box of eighteen was divided into three six-plane flights. The lead flight flew ahead, usually at twelve thousand feet. The low flight trailed to the left at 11,500 feet, and above and to the right at 12,500 was the high flight. Our crew flew most of their missions in the high flight as a "tail-end Charlie." Fighters usually hit us first because their diving speed carried them on down to hit the low flight on the way out—all in one pass. Intelligence warned us St. Omer had 125 guns that could reach us on the bomb run. Their report was dead accurate. I never saw as much flak before or afterward.

At the start of the bomb run Lieutenant Popovici cut in on the intercom: "They're off the target line!" Seconds later the bomb bay doors clacked shut as our box started a steep 360-degree turn to the right. The flak never let up. We began a second bomb run. The doors opened. Popovici cut in again: "They're still off!" Bomb bay doors closed again for another right turn off, heavy flak all the way. Someone gave an anguished moan over the radio: "My God . . . we're going around for a third run!" Popovici cut in with: "They're lined up perfectly this time!" Man, that flak was close; the German gunners had a field day with their 88s and 155s.

Aircrewmen had a favorite phrase, one I know was uttered more than once that day as the ugly black puffs rocked and pounded the formations. "God, please help me through this mission and I'll gladly go through the next two by myself!" I think it helped to pray. Reflecting on some of the scrapes I came through, I don't see how it could be explained any other way. I can only speak for myself, but I strongly doubt an upper gun turret was ever manned by an atheist.

It seemed a year passed before the bombardier called out: "Bombs away!" We'd been flying in steady, dense shrapnel for twenty-five minutes, yet not one plane was shot down. Several limped across the Channel and crash-landed at various places, from the coast on inland. Most of these planes had heavy battle damage and some brought back dead and wounded. Our six-plane flight lost an engineer-gunner; he died in the hospital with a piece of flak in his back.

Our fuel was very low so we landed at an R.A.F. Lancaster base with several other B-26s. We stayed two days. Others had to remain longer for repairs. We inspected the Lancaster bombers inside and out and came away with the typical expression most everyone said when they looked over another type of bomber: "I wouldn't be caught dead flying in that thing!" We knew what other aircrewmen thought of our wonderful Martin B-26, but those of us who took her into battle knew she was a good ship and deserves a better place in the history of World War Two aerial combat.

My thirty-ninth mission—the third thirteenth for me—was another near hit. We were bombing the airfield at Deelen, Holland, on February 24 when a piece of flak slapped against the plexiglas dome and merely cracked it. Things were looking up. When my fourth thirteenth mission, the fifty-second, passed without incident I began to think there was nothing to the misfortunes of my missions whose numbers were multiples of thirteen.

I had yet to fly mission sixty-five.

On February 4, when the orders that awarded me the D.F.C. were received, it was discovered that Headquarters of the Ninth Bomber Command had misspelled my name as Sergeant *Flier*. It stuck, and from that day I was hailed as "Klier the Flier."

Fifty missions in medium bombers normally constituted a tour, after which an aircrewman was eligible for a thirty-day leave in the States. I chalked up fifty-seven sorties before I got orders to board the S.S. *Mauretania* for home. On D-Day morning I was sound asleep when my father awakened me. "Chet, the invasion is on!" He showed me the headlines in the morning paper. I mumbled, "Great," and turned over for some more sleep. It was an easy invasion for me, but I made up for it later. I knew within a few weeks I'd be on my way to the combat zone. In August I was back with my squadron.

The launching platforms for the robot bombs in the Pas de Calais area across the Channel and at Abbeville and Boulogne were given special attention by the 386's Marauders. We hit experimental stations where development was under way on multiple artillery, jet fighters, and radar, and kept the enemy production continuously behind schedule.

February 20 to 25 went down in Air Corps history as "Big Week." On February 20, 21, and 22, we flew three consecutive strikes against the German airfield at Gilze Rijen in Holland. During the bomb run of the third raid I saw our lead ship lose an engine to flak and collide with his left wing man. The bombers locked together and passed three hundred feet directly under us. Thirteen men bailed out. Then we saw our bombs walk down the runway and blow up several German fighters trying to get airborne to intercept us. Hangars disintegrated. Entire flak batteries were wiped out. As we left the target, several flights of Spitfires roared in and strafed the place. It was a thorough job and we learned later many high-ranking Luftwaffe officers were killed.

The pilot of the lead ship was Major Thornton—of our snafu bombing at Boxted. I knew him well. One of the men who bailed out after the collision—another gunner—told me Thornton stayed with the bomber and bellied it in. He did a remarkable job, but during the slide his left wing tip struck a tree. The bomber spun around and Thornton was struck a fatal blow on his head. The next day the gunner saw the officer's body still seated in the plane a short distance from the target. Major Thornton and I were written up for our second D.F.C. in the same general order, but he died for his.

A few months later in London, I met a tail gunner from Brooklyn who had bailed out of a B-26 in our box that day. He landed in a pine forest near the target and spent all day and part of the next huddled under a tree, wrapped in his parachute. Intense cold and hunger got the better of him and he finally said: "To hell with it!" He started to walk down a road. After traveling a short distance he was recognized by a Dutch farmer, who called cautiously to him. From then on he was in the hands of the Underground. They slipped him out of Holland and into Belgium, where he lived with a family until they could move him all the way across France, over the Pyrénées and into Spain. From there he made it back to England. He told me that after the war he was going back to Belgium and marry the girl whose family hid him from the Germans.

While returning from one mission we saw the crew bail out of their burning B-26 over the English Channel. All six chutes opened. The plane spun down and we heard it scream until it crashed into the water. The crew dropped into the water one by one and were picked up by the Germans near the French coast.

All spring and summer the V-1s came over. I've never experienced a weapon as frightening as the robot bombs. They fell as near as four blocks—much too close. Before they came into view you could hear a throbbing sensation like a turbine generator. They were always easy to see. Once I saw three simultaneously, and one of them, traveling at least three hundred miles an hour, passed over my head at no more than a hundred feet. It sounded like a faulty air compressor gone ape and trailed a bluish-white smoke from its tailpipe. It crashed half a mile beyond our airfield and the earth shook when its 2200-pound warhead exploded. At night the V-1 exhausts glowed a brilliant orange-red and spouted fire six feet to the rear. In the daytime the flame was invisible. By the end of the war, 2420 got through to the London area to kill 5864 persons.

In September 1944, General Patton made his headlong thrust toward Germany, and on the eleventh we were ordered to locate his armored spearhead. We found it near Metz, unable to get through the concrete dragon-teeth fortifications of the Siegfried Line. Our job was to blast a hole for it. There was heavy flak on the bomb run, but it was "bombs away." The doors had just closed when I heard three separate flak bursts right under our belly. The plane lurched out of control and I thought: This is it! I started to scramble out of the turret for bail-out but I'd barely moved when . . . *Whooomph!* another one hit under me. The bomber seemed to stand still, buoy up, then drop. I flew off the turret seat, my head slid along the contour of the turret dome and jammed between the gunsight cradle and the inside of the turret dome. The co-pilot yelled over the intercom: "They got us! Get out! Get out!" I tried to do just that but my feet were still on the turret footrests and my flak helmet remained firmly caught between the dome and the sight cradle. The airplane seemed to be flying at an odd angle. I pressed the mike switch. "Engineer to crew . . . I'm caught in the turret!" No answer. The intercom was dead.

This was my sixty-fifth mission—my fifth "thirteenth."

I had watched many bombers go down. Some fell burning, wings gone. A few had collided; others exploded in midair. Was it our turn? *My* turn? The thought flashed through my mind: This thing's going to crash . . . and I'm trapped in it! I went weak and numb.

Then a flash of bright metal caught my eye—the brass tip of my headset cord. In my frantic scrambling I must have accidently disconnected it with my arm. I plugged it in and heard wonderful sounds—the voices of my crew. We were in a shallow diving turn and I cut in on the intercom. Our co-pilot said, "We're okay now . . . settle down . . . we're going to make it." The whole chilling ordeal lasted less than a minute; it seemed like an hour.

I was finally able to unhook the chin strap on my flak helmet and pull my head from the trap. I slumped down in the turret seat, reached under it and pulled the cable release that would lower the seat and enable me to pull my flak helmet free. It was jammed! I was still trapped in the turret. O'Kane was on the waist gun and I called to him for help. He tried to pull the seat latch but no luck. I asked him to take the tools from the leg pocket of my flight suit, and after ten minutes' work he freed me. By now we were across the bomb line and well on our way back to Dunmow.

Nineteen days later I flew my last combat sortie and the following week we relocated in France at a former target, Beaumont-sur-Oise, near Paris. After seeing tons of high explosives fall on French cities, I was surprised to find Paris was spared and practically undamaged. My first visit was on a forty-eight-hour pass. Gragg was stateside for treatment of battery acid burns on his hands. Wilkie was also stateside for an eye operation due to wounds. The remainder of us got rooms in the Grand Hotel at 2, Rue Scribe, and had a great time at the Lido. Champagne and cognac flowed. After two days on that diet we were feeling no pain—except for Popovici who showed signs of weakening. He said, "Fellows, we'd better find a place to eat soon . . . all these perfumed women on an empty stomach is making me feel sick!"

One night in the village bistro at the edge of our airfield one of the 386's intelligence officers, Captain R. R. Meservey, bought then Captain Vincent, O'Kane, and me a drink. He had debriefed our crew on occasion. Most people wouldn't connect his legal name with the motion picture star Robert Preston.

In late October our squadron C.O., Captain George Howard, told me: "I think you've had enough combat flying, Klier—I'd like to see you go home to stay." It seemed almost appropriate that he was the one to tell me this; I'd flown my first combat sortie with him almost a year and a half earlier.

Several of us were to catch a C-47 flight from Paris to London and then go on to Liverpool for the ocean voyage home. As luck would have it, the weather turned bad and the flight was delayed for a day at LeBourget. In their hasty retreat, the Germans left many aircraft behind and I had a fine time exploring the Dorniers, Ju-88s, and Condors. The next afternoon we caught the C-47 to London. It was my last flight with the A.A.F.

The war, I soon learned, wasn't over for me just yet. Once in London, several of us went to Piccadilly Circus and got a room in the Regent Palace Hotel. It was Number 753—I'll never forget it. I was relaxing on the bed and thinking about boarding the S.S. *Argentina* next morning when the Germans opened up with V-2 rockets and very nearly canceled my stateside leave. One landed four blocks away. Everything vibrated from the heavy ground shock and concussion. One of the crewmen expressed the solitary thought in every man's mind at that moment: "My God! I came through my missions all right . . . and now they might get me sitting in a hotel!"

Back in the States I married the day after Christmas, 1944. My combat service was ended, but I followed the action of the 386th through their bombing of Germany, and the Battle of the Bulge. They converted to Douglas A-26s shortly after the Ardennes Campaign and never let up their bombing raids until V-E Day. I ended my service at Fort Snelling, where it had all started for me.

In the years that followed I lost contact with Gragg and Popovici. I got back in touch with O'Kane in 1970 where he lives in Massachusetts. Jim Wilkie went into business in California and we exchanged letters. I visited him in 1955. Don Vincent remained with the Air Force and flew on the Berlin Airlift. We exchanged visits several times until he died of a heart attack in 1963. He was still in the service and jet qualified. This was a deep, personal loss to me for I regarded him as a brother. Another heartbreaking loss was Jim Wilkie, who died in 1967.

After the war I became a private pilot, got active in the Experimental Aircraft Association, homebuilt airplanes, and wrote a bit for the aviation magazines. I've never lost my love for flying. Today I'm a design engineer with McDonnell-Douglas, working on the F-15 fighter. In looking back twenty-five years I can only reflect that we six were just a handful out of the millions. During our long months in battle we shared a great common experience that put a brand on our type of air fighting. The war I helped wage with other members of the A.A.F. didn't bring the lasting peace we'd hoped for; we're still living in a turbulent world and it appears as though the sons and daughters of World War Two veterans must still decide the future for America. Each of our sons have served overseas with the Air Force.

The tyranny that threatens us can never win as long as brave young men are willing to challenge it. Violet and I are proud of our sons and of their service to our country. They did not seek the responsibility, but it was theirs, because they are Americans.

Part Three

Danger and Endurance

11

England to Australia—the Hard Way

THE great London-to-Australia air derby proved to be as grueling a flying adventure as ever to try the mettle of two daredevil fliers. In March 1919 Australian Prime Minister William Morris Hughes offered ten thousand pounds—fifty thousand dollars—for a still-to-be-pioneered flight from England to the land down under. He wanted the airplane to prove its worth in the undeveloped island continent, where many had denounced it as good for nothing but carnival exhibitions and the killing of innocent passengers.

The air race, which Hughes believed would bind the Commonwealth closer to the mother country, had a rigid list of rules for the contestants. Every plane had to be of British manufacture and every man on board had to be an Australian citizen. The flight had to be completed within thirty days of departure and no one could start before September 8, 1919.

It would not be an easy course. Oceans and seas had to be crossed, as well as the rugged peaks of Europe and the blistering deserts of the Middle East. Beyond these lay the jungles of Southeast Asia, and island-hops along the Malay Peninsula. There were other perils: rain and fog over Europe, desert sandstorms, tropical heat, and monsoons. But there was no shortage of contenders. By October five teams were assembling at the starting point, Hounslow aerodrome in a London suburb. An odd internationad twist was added to the rivalry when two French noncontenders, Étienne Poulet and his mechanic, M. Benoist, left Paris on October 12. Flying a twin-engine Caudron, they hoped to be the first to link Europe with Australia.

On November 12 a twin-engine Vickers-Vimy biplane thundered off Hounslow with Captain Ross Smith, his brother Keith, Sergeant J. M. Bennett, and civilian W. H. Shiers. First stop Lyon, France.

The next day another team of Australians, Lieutenants Roger Douglas and Leslie Ross departed from the aerodrome in their Alliance P-2. Shortly after they were airborne, the plane was seen to dive from a low cloud bank over Surbiton and crash. Both men were killed instantly.

On November 21 the third Aussie team bumped down the runway and pulled their twin-engine Blackburn Kangaroo into the misting air. The flight commander and navigator was George Hubert Wilkins. Lieutenant Valdemar Rendle was the pilot and Lieutenants Garnsey Potts and Reg Williams were co-pilots.

Then, for a second time, disaster struck the air race. Flying a lumbering, single-engine Martinsyde, Captain Cedric Howell and his mechanic, Henry Fraser, left England early in December. They reached the Italian port of Taranto without mishap. As they neared the island of Corfu the plane crashed into the Ionian Sea and both airmen were drowned.

The remaining contestants, scattered over the untried air route between the Mediterranean and the Netherlands, droned on.

The Frenchmen retained their early lead, but their hopes were dashed a thousand feet over the peaks east of Moulmein, Burma. A huge vulture soaring overhead dived, and crashed head-on into the plane's starboard propeller, shattering it. Luckily a mountain plateau was below them, and Poulet was able to set the crippled plane down safely.

The Wilkins flight was plagued with engine and control trouble all the way. After the airmen took off from Crete for Cairo, one engine sprang an oil leak. They turned back and crash-landed without personal injury. Wilkins reluctantly decided it was futile to continue.

The Vickers-Vimy flew steadily on with a minimum of delay. On December 10 it touched down at Darwin, twenty-seven days out of Hounslow. But oddly, the Great England-to-Australia Air Derby is remembered in aviation annals because of the flight of the last team, who hadn't as yet left England. Lieutenants Raymond Parer and John McIntosh knew the Vimy won the contest fair and square, but they decided to race anyway. Termed by some as the world's wackiest flight, their planned thirty-day hop became instead a seven-month, fifteen-thousand-mile aerial odyssey of two vagabonds. For decades this cockeyed pioneering flight has been buried in the back pages of aviation history.

The planning for one of the most adventurous distance flights of all time began shortly after Prime Minister Hughes announced the race. Outside a hut in their camp on Salisbury Plain in England, two Australian officers sat in the sun and talked. One was Lieutenant Raymond Parer, a twenty-five-year-old A.F.C. pilot from Melbourne. The other was Lieutenant Edgar Briggs of Tasmania. The war over, both were impatient, footloose. They felt stranded as they waited, with thousands of other Australians, for transportation back to their homeland. Parer was small of stature and quiet by nature. Something of a mechanical wizard, he had designed planes, engines, and gliders before the war. He had entered the A.F.C. as a mechanic, but his officers learned that he was also a skilled pilot—of the caliber sorely needed at the front.

To his disappointment he was turned down. A doctor said he had a weak heart so he was given a job testing new combat types, an occupation with a one in two mortality rate.

Parer had been thinking of the London-to-Australia race for several weeks. "I'm going to fly home, Ed," the young flier said, and with a stick he scratched his proposed route in the sand to show his fellow officer just how he intended to do it.

"I didn't think much of the idea," Briggs recently remarked. "Parer didn't have an airplane."

But in June 1919 Parer notified the officials of his entry. When November came, and the other contestants were departing, Parer still didn't have an airplane. Meanwhile Briggs had left for home by boat.

The flying officer wanted desperately to fly home and pick up the prize money, but he was unsuccessful in his attempts to get a plane and financial backing. As he leaned dejectedly on the bar in a London pub, he struck up a conversation with a tall, amiable Scot, Lieutenant John Crowe McIntosh, an R.F.C. veteran who had been wounded during the Gallipoli Campaign. A woodcutter in Western Australia before the war, he had enlisted with the Aussies and transferred to the Royal Flying Corps. Imaginative and intelligent, though with limited flying experience, he had developed an aerial bomb that was accepted by the War Office. McIntosh listened as Parer poured out his disappointment. Then the young Scot put his hand on Parer's shoulder. "Look, if I can get the backing, what do you say to taking on a partner?"

"Of course," Parer said, wondering whether his drinking companion had downed one too many.

On his ancestral home ground of Scotland, McIntosh arranged to meet the distiller millionaire of Glasgow, Peter Dawson. Not only was this sports-minded Scot agreeable to buying their plane and financing the flight, he promised them more money if needed. "I think I can risk a few thousand pounds," he said, "if you fellows can risk your lives on a flight like that."

They lost little time in purchasing a surplus DeHavilland-9 biplane with a 230-hp 6-cylinder Siddeley-Puma engine, a powerplant that did not have a reputation for dependability. On the biplane's sides in huge block letters they painted the initials "P.D." for their backer Peter Dawson. The DH-9 had been used for long-range bombing during the war and despite its ungainliness it could carry a heavy load at a steady 112-mph cruise. There was a heavy silence when Parer and McIntosh heard the news of the arrival of Ross Smith and his crew at Port Darwin. It was all over. But their flight was still on. Dawson was in full accord with their attempt to set a flying record to Australia; their plane was fast, they could travel light.

The first of a long series of mishaps began when they ferried their newly purchased machine from the aircraft disposals depot to Hounslow. They left at dusk and became lost in the semidarkness. McIntosh made out a clearing ringed by trees and pancaked the big biplane, narrowly missing a fence.

They prepared to depart from Hounslow on a dismal, gray-leaden day, January 8, 1920. Wet fog mists swirled lazily over the grass and from France came the weather wire:

Heavy winds all the way to Paris, visibility decreasing rapidly, all cross-Channel flying suspended.

In the drab wartime administration hut, a reporter for the London *Times* picked up his camera and prepared to leave. "Guess I'll probably see you chaps again tomorrow." Parer, who rarely commented, stared at the midmorning murk outside and downed his last cup of tea in England. "If you do," he said quietly, "you'll be seeing things." It was this spirit, shared by each flier, that set the tone for the entire trip. They droned skyward into the beginning of the winter's worst storm.

In minutes they rose into the gray-milky overcast and were flying blind. The wind at five thousand feet buffeted their cumbersome machine, threatening to rip it apart. Interplane wires thwanged and vibrated as the plane pitched and bucked in the 40-mph gale. Fighting the elements, McIntosh applied full rudder and aileron to remain upright.

Below them, the freezing waters of the Channel frothed and churned, but they never saw it. As they crossed into France the cloud density worsened and they had to descend lower and lower. They were forced to make a hard landing at Conteville, where they broke a wheel. Parer left McIntosh with the plane and begged a slow, rainy, forty-five-mile ride to Paris in a peasant's cart to find a replacement. At LeBourget two days later he got the loan of a wheel, but when he returned to the plane it wouldn't fit. There was another snail-like journey to Paris and back, this time with the proper part. The delay seriously reduced their slender budget. After the short flight to Paris, they left LeBourget for Lyon, battling dense clouds and near-gale winds all the way. Their engine threatened to quit several times because of contaminated fuel they had received at LeBourget. Only an unmistakable landmark—the brilliant white peak of Mont Blanc—saved them from becoming hopelessly lost in the foul weather. At Lyon they were delayed two days because of a faulty fuel pump. When they were ready to go on January 17, French officials tried to talk them out of leaving the fogged-in airfield. Parer and McIntosh shook their heads, climbed aboard and gunned the engine.

They bored above the clouds, down the Rhône Valley to St. Raphael, a Riviera resort. Here they had to repair a broken exhaust pipe. Their money dwindled quickly, and between their frivolous chats with the local girls they barnstormed to earn badly needed cash.

On January 21 they took off on a course that roughly paralleled the Italian coast. The weather was much improved but within minutes trouble appeared in another form. McIntosh noticed the engine oil pressure was steadily dropping, and without lubrication the six-cylinder Puma would soon burn up. They needed a place to land, but the nearest field was at Sarzana, one hundred miles distant. McIntosh turned toward it. For the next hour the two lighthearted fliers were unusually quiet, for it was touch and go all the way. Parer knew that if the engine began to smoke the trip was ended—and the oil pressure was touching on zero.

To their amazement and relief, the Siddeley-Puma continued to pound away and, despite the blistering invectives they heaped upon it, carried them safely to the airfield. After a two-day delay for repairs they decided on a direct flight to Rome. They had settled on course scarcely ten minutes when the engine backfired violently and caught fire—a carburetor fuel leak caused by a badly jammed needle valve. The orange-blue flame speared backward toward McIntosh, who had survived the air war without mishap. Later he said his only thought was: "Now we'll know what it's like to go down burning!" But Parer, at the controls, closed the throttle, gave hard right rudder and left stick. The DH-9 creaked, groaned, and went into a breathtaking sideslip for several hundred feet. The violent maneuver did the trick; the flame was snuffed out. Parer landed "P.D." at Forte di Marmi, an abandoned seaside aerodrome, where he made repairs.

By the time Rome came over the southern horizon, they had been on the way for nearly a month. Finances were again depleted, so they sent the first of a series of telegrams to Peter Dawson, requesting money. It always came and, while they waited, they found work stunt flying and scattering advertising handbills over the city.

On February 2 they departed from Celli aerodrome for Naples. Sweeping wide around the city, they saw Mount

Vesuvius loom nearby. McIntosh motioned to Parer to fly closer for a look into the boiling crater of poisonous sulfur-laden steam and molten lava. Parer obliged by flying directly over the gaping opening. As they peered into the seething depths, the DeHavilland suddenly fell as though pushed toward the crater. Then the engine cut out. Parer feverishly yanked throttle and mixture levers. An inferno yawned at them as they dropped. A hundred feet down . . . two hundred feet . . . five hundred . . . Then the engine caught and they pulled up and over the edge in time.

The next morning they left Naples and cruised along the craggy Apennines that run the length of the Italian boot. The day was gray and cold; low-hanging clouds reduced the visibility. Parer decided to climb above the dreary scene to fourteen thousand feet. At that height the temperature fell below zero, and the cold became intensely painful. They were not dressed for extreme cold-weather flying, and though they shivered uncontrollably in the raw, thin air, they realized their movements were becoming increasingly sluggish. They slapped their faces and stamped their feet on the floorboards to restore circulation, but they could almost sense the blood congealing in their veins. Parer leaned toward McIntosh to shout a message. The sound was a croak; his words would not come out. Their dulled senses told them that they were steadily freezing to death. The aircraft slowed, grew less controllable. The engine labored, and again the oil pressure began to fall.

Added to the already perilous situation was yet another danger. Looming ahead was a dense, dark cloud bank that extended north and south above them. It was too high to climb above, and they could not descend into the overcast that shrouded the snow-tipped Apennine peaks. Their only hope was to veer toward the southwest.

They held fourteen thousand feet and slowly the cold diminished. After two and a half hours of numbing inactivity, they sighted a hole in the cloud layer below. As they spiraled through it, they identified the smoking volcano and dark sands of Stromboli. They turned toward the mainland where there was sunlight, safety, warmth. They glided down, out of fuel, and landed in a hay field fourteen miles from Nicastro. After they had walked into town a footsore McIntosh decided to wait while Parer took a train back to Naples. There, the British Consul arranged for gasoline, and a few days later a train delivered a two-hundred-liter drum to a point five miles from their stranded DH-9. The fliers rolled the heavy drum awkwardly along the dusty roads, tugging and sweating for hours until it came to a stop beside their plane.

They refueled and departed on the morning of February 10 for Taranto, where they landed at the Italian dirigible station. Here Parer and McIntosh tallied their air time from London. It was twenty hours and twenty minutes.

Again, Fate disrupted their flight plan. Their intention was to fly from the Gulf of Taranto directly across the Ionian Sea to Athens, but shortly after takeoff a fuel pump failed, then they lost their charts overboard in a blast of wind. After an emergency landing for repairs at Brindisi's St. Vito aerodrome on the Adriatic, they proceeded to Athens. The next leg was a hazardous one, a long over-water flight to Africa with one stop at Suda Bay on the island of Crete. The remaining two hundred and twenty miles of open water proved to be a tense ordeal. A valve spring failed and, as the clattering valve stuck intermittently, the weary DH-9's engine backfired and lost power. They dropped toward the water until they were only five hundred feet above the surface, expecting every minute to be their last as the backfiring engine sputtered away. Three hours later they crossed the African coast after setting one bona-fide record: the first flight across the

LONDON
PARIS
LYON
ST. RAPHAEL
SARZANA
ROME
NAPLES
TARANTO
ATHENS
CRETE
MARSA MATRUK
CAIRO
RAMLA
BAGHDAD
BASRA
BUSHEHR
BANDAR ABBAS

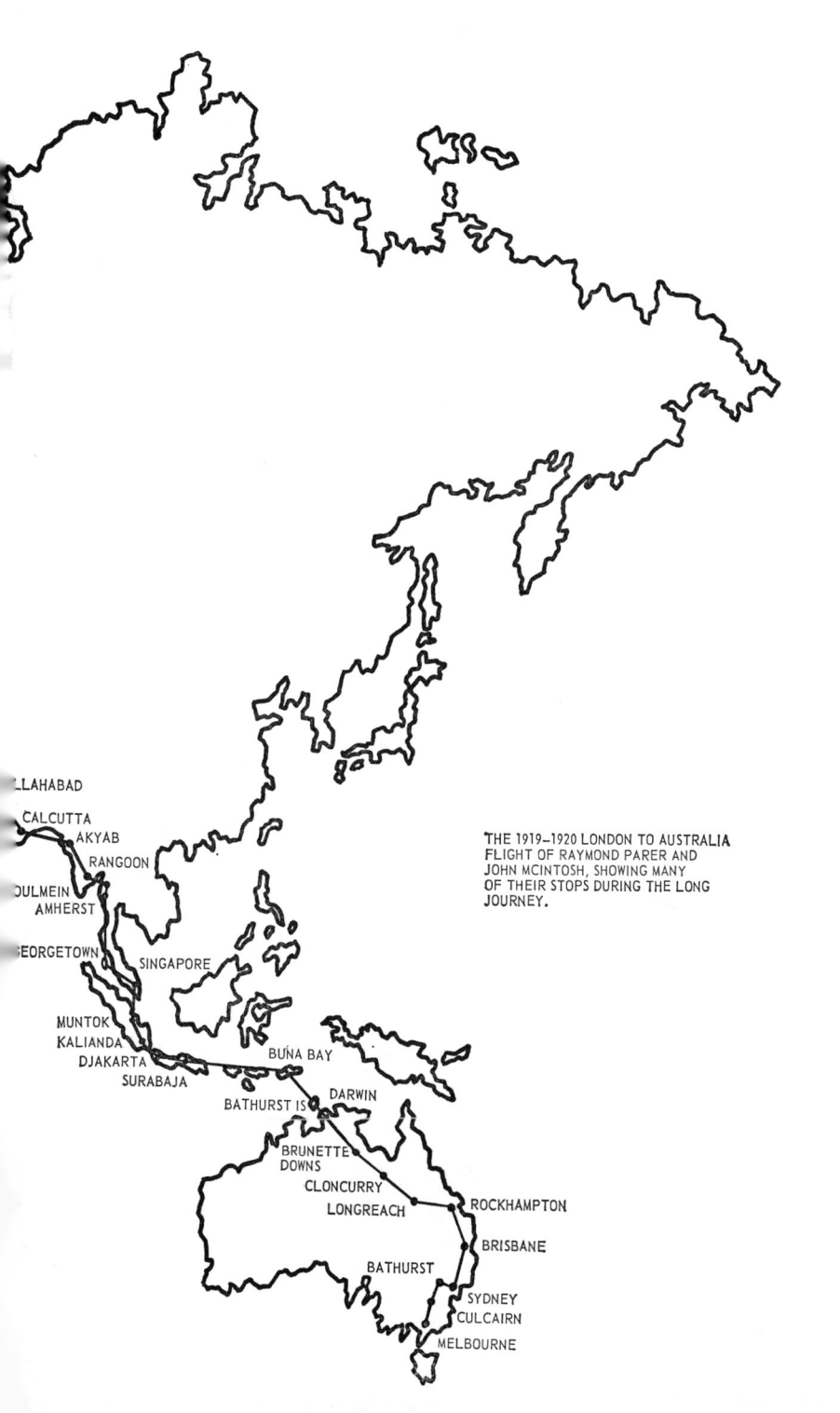

THE 1919–1920 LONDON TO AUSTRALIA FLIGHT OF RAYMOND PARER AND JOHN MCINTOSH, SHOWING MANY OF THEIR STOPS DURING THE LONG JOURNEY.

Mediterranean in a single-engine airplane. They landed at Marsa Matruk.

When they arrived at Cairo's Heliopolis airfield on February 21, they agreed that old, battered and tattered "P.D." needed an overhaul before braving the arid deserts of the Middle East. But British maintenance crews were reluctant to help and told them to fly on to Helouan. There they met Lord Milner, a high British pro-consul who, as chance would have it, had just landed at Helouan. He became greatly interested in their venture and directed the R.A.F. to give the Aussies full assistance. The next day a mechanic told McIntosh and Parer if they had flown another thirty minutes, the entire tail assembly would have separated. With the plane out of control, they would likely have fallen to their deaths.

British fliers at Helouan urged them to abandon their flight. The gist of their comments was that the pair were insane to push across El Hamid desert. They told the two men it was virtually impossible to cross the desert from Palestine to Baghdad, but Parer and McIntosh laughed. When the army officers realized they could not dissuade them, Ordnance supplied them with Mills bombs—grenades—and a supply of ammunition for their service revolvers.

On February 26 the DeHavilland lifted from Helouan aerodrome, skimmed over the Suez Canal and across the Sinai desert for Palestine. They landed at Ramla, on the Plain of Esdraelon, the jumping-off point for Baghdad. Again, flying officers who knew the desert advised them to call it off. "Look," one pilot argued, "it's almost six hundred forty miles to Baghdad over the El Hamid. Your machine only has a range of five hundred miles. There are no landing fields. How in heaven's name can you make it?"

McIntosh grinned. "Tailwinds," he quipped, adding they would carry extra cans of petrol. Early in the morning of February 27 they topped the tanks, took on two flasks of brandy, some tins of bully beef, and a container of biscuits, and waved "cheerio."

The flight went smoothly until they were three hours into the sandswept wasteland, where the temperamental engine coughed and backfired. Again flames licked backward from the faulty carburetor. They selected a none-too-smooth spot strewn with boulders, and gingerly settled the sputtering machine down. Before it rolled to a slewing stop, it threatened to nose over in the soft sand holes.

Parer adjusted the engine again and within an hour flew on. The delay, however, was enough to prevent them from reaching Baghdad that night. After darkness closed around them they made a moonlight landing at Lake Habbaniya in the desert, refueled from the containers, and bedded down under the plane's broad tail for a miserably cold night. When they awoke shortly after dawn, a fierce-looking Arab tribesman was standing nearby, scowling and scrutinizing their airplane. The Aussies scanned the horizon and saw more Arabs rise threateningly from behind the sand dunes.

"Visitors," Parer said grimly.

"Not very friendly looking chaps, are they?" McIntosh observed sleepily. They drew their revolvers cautiously, aware they might have to fight for their lives. McIntosh found the sack of grenades. Without waiting to see what the intentions of the hostile-looking band were, he pulled a pin from a Mills bomb and lobbed it toward them. The explosion spewed a geyser of sand upward and the Arab marauders retreated in disorder, shouting fiercely. Before the tribesmen could recover from the surprise welcome, Parer had leaped into the cockpit. McIntosh yelled, "Switch on!" and pulled the huge nine-and-a-half-foot mahogany propeller through compression. The Puma caught immediately and McIntosh scrambled for the rear cockpit as Parer gunned the engine to full throttle.

At eleven the magic city of Baghdad was reached; the adventuring Aussies were the first to cross the desert by air. Again they took stock of their progress and discovered, of their eighteen stops thus far, four had been forced landings.

On March 2 they struck out for Basra. They arrived in Bushire on March 4 and on the fifth departed for the small Persian city of Bandar Abbas. The Tigris and Euphrates slipped beneath their wings. Ahead, the sky threatened as a blinding sandstorm swirled upward to their altitude of eighty-five hundred feet. Their only alternative was to detour far over the Persian Gulf. Without parachutes or flotation gear, an engine failure would have left them to the sharks, but Charbar was reached without mishap. Nasratabad was next, then a hop across the barren Baluchistan to Karachi, gateway to India.

Despite the pressures of grueling hours in the air over uncharted regions and with poor maps to guide them, the two never lost their sense of humor or the pleasure of one another's companionship. Little mechanical trouble was encountered as they flew over the Thar desert to Delhi, from which they followed the Jumna River to Allahabad. They pushed on to Calcutta on March 14 where they landed at Ellenborough aerodrome, very tired, very hot, and very broke.

They had the good fortune to meet a former major of the Indian Army who offered to become their agent in finding work. In a few hours the man had several business firms interested in a startling new idea—aerial advertising. For the next two weeks the flying team scattered leaflets over the city and gave flying exhibitions for their enthusiastic sponsors. They were two thousand pounds richer and ready to head out for Akyab and Rangoon by way of the Bay of Bengal when a cable from Peter Dawson caught up with them. It was a credit for a thousand pounds. Their Scottish friend had not forgotten them.

From Akyab on the Burma coast they headed over and past Sandoway, by way of which they tried to reach Rangoon. Again engine trouble forced them to land—this time on a sand bar in the Upper Irrawaddy. A few hundred friendly natives materialized from the humid jungles and, grinning and jabbering, helped them push their plane across the shallow water to a firm bank. The next morning they appeared with hundreds of bamboo mats. These they spread on the muddy ground for a runway, and the fliers were able to take off safely and reach Rangoon.

The Oriental city proved to be a memorable stopover. They remained ten days to overhaul the engine and patch the aircraft. Officials, genuinely concerned about the oil-streaked, patchwork quilt of a flying machine, urged them to take a boat the remainder of the way. It was then the usually reticent Parer, annoyed by the houndings of government men, reportedly made the most celebrated comment of their entire venture: "We're going to fly this bloody crate until it falls apart!" Their delay wasn't all frustration however; a Chinese millionaire offered Parer and McIntosh thirty thousand rupees each if they would marry two of his daughters. Parer later quipped: "The girls were beautiful, but we figured we were having too many aeronautical problems to take on matrimonial ones." They left the Chinese beauties behind and winged across the Gulf of Martaban. It was at Moulmein their intrepid journey nearly came to a complete finish.

It was the ninety-third day of their flight—Easter Sunday— when, on the approach to the landing field, their "faithful" Siddeley-Puma let them down again. To make matters worse, a large throng had gathered on the field outside the town and Parer was obliged to land the plane on rough ground. Old "P.D." kangarooed all over the terrain in a crescendo of buckling metal and tearing fabric. When it came to a standstill, the undercarriage had been wiped off, fuel tanks crumpled, radiator smashed, and the propeller shattered. Miraculously, McIntosh and Parer were unhurt, but as they examined the wrecked machine their spirits fell to rock bottom. It would take a long time to patch the plane. Their flying time now stood at ninety-five hours, and the distance covered was 8343 miles. They were tempted to take that slow boat to Australia, but instead found the courage and patience to try again.

Heavy-hearted, they set to work. The biggest problem was finding a new propeller. They ordered one from an aircraft supply company in Lahore, India, but it never arrived. They modified a huge Caproni propeller that had been used on a more powerful Fiat engine and fitted it to their Siddeley-Puma. It worked, but barely.

A small crowd of mechanics arrived from Rangoon to lend a hand, and slowly the bits and pieces of their broken machine were fitted together. Any makeshift part that could be adapted was used, including a crudely designed cooling system composed of two Overland car radiators bolted back-to-back. Burmese elephants helped move the heavier parts. Finally, after six weeks in the steaming jungle, old "P.D." was again in one piece. In celebration, the Burmese gave the Australians a night-long farewell party.

They left Moulmein late in May and headed south into Malaysia. After sixty miles they landed at Amherst, now aware their makeshift propeller was going to cause trouble. It was out of balance and seriously vibrated the plane and engine. Over Georgetown their laboring powerplant threatened to quit again and they hurriedly landed in the middle of an afternoon polo game. The polo club's presiding officer rode jauntily up to the mud-spattered war plane with its smoking engine and indignantly demanded of the pilots what right they had to land there.

The next day they arrived in Singapore, where they were

able to replace their troublesome makeshift propeller. They left in the teeth of a bad storm that forced them back. Muntok, on the island of Bangka, was their next stop, then Kalidiati. They crossed Batavia at two thousand feet, flying due east for Surabaja. As their cantankerous engine pulled them across the islands of the East Indies, it frequently gave them several anxious moments over the open water. There was another forced landing on a river flat at Samarang and they were taken into a Dutch homestead for the night.

Coming into Gruse at Surabaja, they saw the landing ground was level and smooth, but someone had laid an earth-colored wooden beam on the strip. The DH-9 touched down, rolled squarely into it and nosed over with a splintering crunch. The fliers were bruised, but were more concerned about the condition of "P.D."

Now, so near their goal, the determined young men cast aside all thoughts of quitting and set to work again. Miracle of miracles, they located a propeller that would fit their engine and in just four days were again airborne, heading for Buna Bay, Atambua, and the island of Timor. From here they would jump off for their homeland on a five-hundred-mile overwater flight across the Arafura Sea.

To have a fighting chance for survival should they be forced down in the dangerous waters, they lashed a crude bamboo raft to one wing. It had wire netting underneath to protect their feet from the sharks and two automobile inner tubes for flotation. On August 2 the DeHavilland rose into the air and headed south toward Koepang. Over the brilliant blue sea at eight hundred feet they set a course of 118 degrees for Bathurst Island.

Alone over the monotonous stretch of sparkling water, they lost their bearings and milled about using precious fuel before settling back on course. The crossing was another first for a single-engine plane. When their wheels touched the ground at Port Darwin, the engine sputtered and quit cold; there was not enough fuel to taxi. They were astonished to be met by what appeared to be the entire populace, who gave them an enthusiastic welcome.

Home at last—but not quite. They had to cross the continent to Melbourne, which was then the capital, to fulfill a special mission for Peter Dawson. With the tired engine still sputtering away, they continued their flight east and south to be welcomed warmly at every landing stop. It was understandable. Although Ross Smith and his men made the trip from London in twenty-seven days, the people down under had almost seven months to follow Parer and McIntosh's trials and misfortunes as reported almost daily in Australian newspapers. Their determination to complete the flight against all odds set them apart from the rather cut-and-dried Smith flight in a twin-engine bomber.

They flew on in short hops, landing at isolated ranches and small towns for the night. At Anthony Lagoon they slept under the wings. At Brunette Downs they nailed steel strips to wing ribs and repaired a damaged tire. Rankins River, Avondowns Station, Cloncurry, Longreach, Rockhampton. By the time they reached Brisbane, the plane's fabric had deteriorated so badly that it had to be patched. Flying south from Brisbane they had to land again to repair rotted fabric that threatened to separate from the wings.

Newcastle, Sydney. Parer and McIntosh were feted at great receptions, parties and banquets. While little Raymond Parer stool by quietly, John McIntosh kept audiences in an uproar with his accounts of the more humorous and incredible events of the long flight.

An Australian who had recently returned to his homeland after the Armistice, and who is now retired in California following a long career of film scripting, retains a vivid recollection of the plane's arrival in Sydney.

The Parer-McIntosh flight was, in my eyes, one of the most extraordinary flights in all of aviation history. I had the good luck and complete incredulity of personally examining the plane on its landing on Australian soil. It was both astounding and unbelievable that this weird contraption, this fantastic collection of emergency substitute junk could get off the ground—least of all stay in flight for fifty feet without disintegrating in the process . . . I clearly recall the remark that I made to a companion following an examination of this flying scarecrow. It was: "The two chaps who flew this wreck had three things in common: doggedness, ingenuity, and an overabundance of plain guts!"

The aircraft looked like a Heath Robinson grotesque cartoon of some comic, do-it-yourself creation. There seemed little of the original plane remaining. What parts had been damaged, or just dropped off during the long and tardy flight from "Blighty," had been replaced by a strange assortment of odds and ends that had no relation whatever to the original construction. One had to see it to believe it. How this broken and bent caricature of a plane ever flew those some twelve thousand miles of uncharted—and previously unflown—course was . . . and still is to me . . . a dark mystery.

Many of the details may have escaped me over the years, but I remember that most of the fabric covering both wings and fuselage had rotted away during the long months of tropical heat, humidity, and pelting rainstorms. The missing fabric had been replaced with patches of canvas tents, old shirts, and even newspapers. Layers and layers of these had been shellacked together and used to cover sections of the fuselage and even parts of the wings. It was an experience to read, or attempt to read, the stained pages of Chinese, Siamese, Javan, or Malayan newspapers pasted as fabric on this amazing plane.

Where the wire braces between the struts had been carried away or deteriorated, ordinary fencing wire had been rigged as a substitute . . . Half of the struts had evidently fractured, and been reinforced with splints of bamboo wrapped with bits of rope or rawhide.

258   **Wings of Adventure**

With Sydney behind them, they took off on the last leg of their flight to Melbourne. Now, close to their ultimate goal, the engine pounded its last beat and the propeller made its last revolution. Parer told about it later:

On the way to Melbourne we landed at Bathurst . . . the engine running very badly, rigging in shocking condition. The other magneto cut out before we reached Culcairn, so we had to land. The ground was very soft after the rains and when the wheels sank six inches into the ground it was too late to open up the engine. The plane turned over completely, petrol pouring over us from the tanks. The propeller was broken and it was a great disappointment.

Again the adventuring Aussies walked away from the wreck, but this time "P.D." had made its last landing. It was disassembled, strapped to a car, and taken to the nearest railway. A fast passenger train took it to Melbourne where it was reassembled at the Flemington Racecourse for an official reception. The tattered old airplane formed a fitting backdrop for the hero's welcome that was led by Prime Minister Hughes. In recognition of their pioneering spirit, he presented the fliers with a purse for a thousand pounds. Then Parer and McIntosh presented Mr. Hughes with a surprise gift from Peter Dawson—a bottle of his finest Scotch that had somehow remained unbroken through their many crashes—the first air freight to Australia.

Among the hundreds of congratulatory telegrams and cables was one from Geoffrey DeHavilland, the DH-9's designer. He praised their flight as one of the finest distance endurance records ever made. The DH-9 that had carried them fifteen thousand miles was restored and housed in the War Memorial at Canberra and in 1966 arrangements were begun to provide a separate memorial to house the famous machine.

For John Crowe McIntosh, there is a sad postscript. The long flight depleted his quota of good fortune. The man who was an accomplished and much-admired after-dinner speaker, who had kept up his flying companion's spirits when things seemed hopeless, went into the flying business. On Easter Monday, 1921, a drunken passenger caused him to plunge to his death near the Kalgoorlie gold fields in the southwestern desert. Parer told of his friend's death in these words:

> Mac left for Western Australia and I later heard he'd purchased Major Brearly's two Avro aeroplanes and all accessories. It was while flying one of these machines that the crash occurred which caused his death and that of one of his passengers. It is thought he got into a spin and was not able to recover. This was at Pithara, 1921. His death came as a great blow. It took me some time to realize he had gone, and it is only since his death that I fully realized what a fine chap he was. I never expect to find so intimate a friend again as I had in Mac during this trip.

Ray Parer flew on. In 1920 he won Victoria's first Air Derby with an average speed of 142 miles per hour—a record that held until the famous Bristol Bulldogs came ten years later. "The only race I ever won," he commented with his shy grin. With his brother, Kevin, he went on to carve a career in aerial trail-blazing throughout New Guinea—one of the most untamed places on earth. In 1927 they formed Bulolo Aerial Transport Services to operate between the coast and the interior gold fields. In 1934 Ray entered the second England-to-Australia air derby—the Centenary Air Race. He was the only person to have competed in both the distance dashes. He flew a Fairy Fox and when he learned the race had been won by Sir Ross and Campbell Black he came home leisurely. To him the race was a holiday from his pioneering of air routes in New Guinea between the wars.

Odd incidents never stopped happening. On one New

Guinea run in an old Fokker, he was transporting a cow into the isolated town of Wau. As he droned along peacefully he heard a crash behind him and felt himself being shoved firmly out of his seat. Somehow the cow had broken free in her compartment and, on the verge of panic, had shoved her horns through the plywood partition behind the cockpit. As usual, Parer handled the emergency with his natural aplomb and landed his cargo safely.

He established five airlines in the islands before the Japanese scorched-earth policy ended them. When he was told he was too old to fly in the Pacific War, he joined the American small ships, salvaged many of the sunken craft, and still managed to get in some personal combat with the Japanese. Some years after the war he retired at Mount Nebo in Queensland. In July 1967 he died in Brisbane at seventy-three. Just six months earlier, the airman visited his sister, Mrs. Mary Shiel, in Brisbane and reminisced about his flying years. She made notes of this and passed them on as a fitting commentary from a famous flier:

In 1919 when Ross Smith left England for Australia he was fortunate to have the best-type engine procurable at the time—two Rolls-Royce engines. But it must not be forgotten that the later flights had all the advantages of those years of research and improvement in the engines. At the time of the "Early Birds"—who were out to try their wings—we were insufficiently experienced and the instruments were inadequate to navigate over such stretches of water.

In 1926 I offered to fly Lebius Hordern's flying boat with two Rolls-Royce engines to New Zealand, not knowing the plane would not do the journey. The flight was discouraged by the authorities. The plane was new but had not flown. But then in 1928 Kingsford-Smith with American engines made the wonderful flight from San Francisco to Australia in the *Southern Cross*. The navigation was a wonderful feat for that early date.

The Dole flights to Honolulu, before the Kingsford-Smith flight, ended in disaster, for most of the planes failed to reach their destination because of the pilots' inexperience. Aircraft are now equipped with directional navigation instruments and very reliable engines. Now housewives have flown from America to Australia—across the Pacific—doing their own navigation without any trouble.

Now that I am older I can make comparisons and better evaluate and understand the chances of those early flights. Planes have been getting better at an amazing speed and now man has orbited the earth. Although it is a wonderful thing, man himself seems to be immune from surprise and just accepts these new discoveries and accomplishments as they come along.

Call it what you will, the series of short hops of the kangaroo kids was an accomplishment in 1919. It might seem humorous today—especially when we realize that Edgar Briggs arrived home by boat long before the "P.D." touched down at Darwin—but the two adventuring Aussies really set a different record of sorts—for the *longest* flying time from England to Australia. And that record stands unbroken today.

12

"Get the Mad Trapper!"

AIR adventuring has all but disappeared from Canada's raw northern skies, replaced with the comfortable acceptance of modern-day jetliners. As descendants of the fabled era of the first bush pilots, they whine steadily over the vast hinterlands of the Canadian Northwest. In our preoccupation with the new air age we tend to forget the heritage of those early air blazers, many of whom opened the sky trails that still serve the barren outposts of the Royal Canadian Mounted Police.

Among the fliers who brought air commerce to the Yukon and Northwest Territories was "Wop" May. Wartime ace, airmail pilot, mercy flier, and later airline executive, Wilfred Reid May's flying years were a test of human skill and ingenuity against the bitter elements and lawlessness of the North.

His nickname belied his appearance; May was tall, blond, and muscular. A little girl once tried to pronounce *Wilfred* and lisped "Wop" instead. There was a round of laughter and the name stuck. He was a restless youth, sometimes reserved and moody, but his friends remembered best his outgoing traits.

"He was about five feet eleven," recalls Major Francis Riddell, formerly of the Royal Canadian Signals, who worked with May in the early thirties, "well built and good-looking with a very friendly personality. He had a great interest in everything about him, had lots to say, and liked a good party, stag or mixed."

Major Earl Franklyn Hersey, also with the Royal Canadian Signals, remembers that May was not a clever man, but that he was considerate, kind, well mannered and liked by all associates with whom he came in contact.

May grew up in Edmonton at frontier trading posts, with their meandering mud streets, squat, ugly buildings, and harness shops—all pungent with the odor of fat, new-cut lumber. Several whitewashed lodges stood aloof and dignified amidst the gray-weathered, square-fronted stores. They were the barracks of N Division of the Royal Northwest Mounted Police, a "man's outfit" held in high esteem by the young Canadian.

From childhood, May nourished two ambitions. One was to explore the unoccupied lands of the Northwest. He watched the pioneer settlers head northward in their covered wagons into hope and hardship; he had read McKitterich's tales of the Peace River and Grand Prairie, and he talked with the bronzed, grizzled prospectors who had returned from the mysterious Yukon. To his brother, Wilfred once vowed: "I'm going there some day, Court—and discover why it's so fascinating."

His other ambition was to fly. In school he was a close friend of Roy Brown from Ontario. Like May, Brown too wanted to fly and they often talked of the latest Wright and Curtiss flights.

The war in Europe began the chain of events that caught up the dreams of both men and brought them to realization. In 1916 May joined the "Sportsman's Battalion" in hopes of finding his way into the Royal Flying Corps. A year and a half later Sergeant May, slogging through the mud of France as a machine-gunner, finally got his orders to report for pilot training. Short weeks later at St. Omer, while awaiting his combat assignment at the front, he met several compatriots who later flew with him through the frigid skies of their homeland.

May's endless drive for adventure began over the battlefields of Europe. He was posted to Number 209 Squadron at Bertangles, where he met his flight leader, his old friend Roy Brown.

On May's first patrol over the enemy lines, 209 clashed with von Richthofen's deadly Jagdgeschwader Nr. 1. The famed Red Baron himself, with his uncanny ability to spot a novice, fastened himself on the tail of May's Camel. At treetop height he chased the young officer almost two miles behind the Australian lines. Of that chase May later said: "It looked like the end."

Roy Brown dived to his friend's help, directed a burst at the weaving all-red Fokker triplane, and veered away. Richthofen took evasive action but almost immediately settled once again onto May's tail. The Canadian maneuvered frantically now, swept up the side of the Morlancourt Ridge with Richthofen close behind, firing hotly. At the brow of the ridge, less than fifty feet in the air, the red triplane ran squarely into the combined fire of two Lewis guns and fell to earth. May was spared. A controversy raged for years over who rightfully deserved the credit for the kill—Australians or Brown—but that's another story.

When the Great War ended, May had thirteen victories, a captaincy, two wounds, and the Distinguished Flying Cross. In 1920, with other wartime pilots, he introduced the airplane to the bush country.

On New Year's Day, 1929, news reached Peace River Crossing by dog sled that Red River, fifty miles beyond Fort Vermilion, was ravaged by a diphtheria epidemic that threatened to spread to the Indian camps throughout the territory. From Peace River the telegraph flashed the news to Edmonton. Twelve days of travel separated the fort and Peace River, and if the antitoxin were to reach Fort Vermilion by return dog sled it meant two more weeks on the snow trail. By that time the entire community could be wiped out.

At Edmonton, Wop and Vic Horner were asked to help. They prepared their tiny open-cockpit Avro Avian immediately for the 650-mile mercy mission. "Captain May made many mercy flights," Major Riddell recalls today. "He would never see anyone stuck."

Early next morning, with 600,000 units of diphtheria antitoxin buried in rugs in the fuselage, the men pointed their 90-horsepower biplane into the wilderness and were swallowed up. Buffeted by winds and snow, fighting the subzero cold, the pilots stopped only to refuel. They reached Fort Vermilion the next day, where a crack dog team rushed the serum on to Red River. May and Horner were so stiff from their long exposure they had to be lifted from their cockpits, but they were smiling; the early delivery meant hundreds would be saved.

This was not May's only mercy mission in his years of bush flying, nor was it—by his own admission—his most exciting adventure. It was while pioneering Canada's airmail plunge into the Yukon that he experienced his most harrowing encounter. His opponents were time, the elements, and a cold-blooded criminal so vicious that he is remembered to this day in the annals of the Royal Canadian Mounted as the Mad Trapper of Rat River.

Fort McPherson is fifty miles above the Arctic Circle. Its summers are short. In July 1931 the settlement was balmy with its brief period of warmth, and the air carried the faint rhythm of a Loucheux tom-tom mingled with the ever-constant buzz of swarming mosquitoes. Constable Edgar Millen of the Mounted Police leaned on the rough counter of the trading post and passed the time of day with gray-bearded John Firth. "Spike" Millen was not the happiest man in the Northwest Territory; he had been recently transferred from Cambridge Bay to a daily beat at Arctic Red River, a few miles south. A handsome, strapping officer, Millen was described by fellow Constable Alfred W. King as, "Over six feet tall, very friendly, good-natured and full of fun . . . a man liked by everyone who knew him."

Millen pushed his wide-brimmed Stetson back on his brow, sighed, and gazed at the few late Loucheux trappers who squatted on the floor, waiting their turn to barter their lynx and bear skins. He shook his head. In this God-forsaken outpost, his job was certain to be uneventful.

The Constable was mistaken. Half a day's journey to the west, a dramatic incident was unfolding. It would climax in gunshots, murder, and a grueling chase. On a curve in the Peel River, three Loucheux bucks watched silently as a lone trapper on a flimsy raft swung around the bend. Their black eyes took in the slightly stooped, wiry figure with a pole, and they observed his light brown hair, rough, unshaven face, and slightly upturned nose. He maneuvered his raft like a veteran. When he was almost abreast of the Indians, the trapper's steel-blue eyes caught sight of them through the willow thicket.

"Hey you—copper-nose!" came a surly shout. "This the Porcupine River?" It was a demand; the arrogant stranger didn't smile. The Indians stared in silence for a moment, their reddish-brown faces twisted into scowls. Then one snapped back. "No! Him not Porcupine—him Peel Ribber!"

"Damnation!" the stranger spat. Irritated, he jammed his pole against the rocks and pushed for the curve ahead with renewed vigor. The natives watched as he disappeared around the bend and, muttering their contempt for him, headed for the fort. Indians despised an unfriendly stranger and this ill-mannered white man gave them good cause to remember him.

A month passed. At Arctic Red River, with its strong scent of drying fish and the view of tumble-down dwellings that made up the ugly little settlement, Constable Millen gazed through the barracks window, watching the lush greenery sway in the slight breeze. The rising drone of a gasoline engine—the Eskimo schooner from Aklavik—drowned out the buzzing mosquitoes. Down the river dock a grinning Nunatagmuit handed him a confidential directive from Inspector A. M. Eames.

It is reported that a strange white man, going by the name of Johnson, landed near Fort McPherson on July 9. Apparently he came down-river on a raft, tying up below the settlement, and walking into the post. He had neither outfit, rifle, nor dogs, but appeared to be amply supplied with money. Please make inquiries in the district and submit a report, but do not make a special patrol.

Millen, glad to have something to do at last, took a quick trip to the fort and made inquiries. Yes, Albert Johnson was thereabouts; he was a particularly nasty chap who carried a large sum of money in neat rolls that were tucked in every pocket. He was surly to everyone and became angry when questioned about his business, but thus far he hadn't made trouble. "Says he's not staying, so we don't need to know his business." Firth told Millen. "He pays for what he wants and doesn't trouble anyone."

Millen nodded but decided to judge Johnson for himself. He learned the stranger had bought a canoe and was stocking it with provisions, probably intending to proceed to the Yukon by way of Rat River. The Constable decided to maneuver about and "accidently" cross Johnson's path at the river.

"Hello!" Millen greeted the man, smiling. The stranger before him stood about five feet nine, had a receding hairline, and was about forty years old. Johnson glared at the uniform in sullen silence.

"Haven't seen you here before," Millen went on, his voice unconcerned but friendly. "What's your name?"

"Johnson!" the rough one growled. "Albert Johnson—if it's anybody's business."

"Where'd you come from?"

"Arctic Red River!"

Millen's smile faded. "No you didn't," he challenged. "That's my outfit and I know every man in the district. Now," he repeated coldly, "where are you from?"

"From the prairie country—down the Mackenzie!" Johnson spat, clearly angered.

It was another lie. Millen met Johnson's defiant glare. "Where-are-you-going?" he demanded evenly.

"None of your damned business," the bristling man shot back. "You police are always trouble!" He spun on his heel and stalked away.

As Millen watched him disappear toward the willow flats he could sense trouble. Back at the store he told Firth: "Johnson's going to cause distress for someone. I know it."

Months later those who overheard the Constable's prophecy reflected on its deadly truth.

May landed at Aklavik on his regular mail run and heard of the irascible fellow's activities from Inspector Eames and [then] Quartermaster Sergeant Riddell. The trapper had settled in a shack on the Rat River, much to the concern of local natives.

Snow and ice covered the Arctic northland again, and dog teams mushed through the purple twilight between Aklavik, Arctic Red River, and Fort McPherson. Their jingling bells echoed in the clear, cold air, across the ice-dipped willows deep in snow, and over the many-fingered frozen Mackenzie. In their webbed snowshoes, Loucheux hunters shuffled along the frozen lakes and hammocks to follow the fur trails and set their traps. The ill-tempered trapper was almost forgotten by the fur-clad Mounties who drove their dog sleds on the rounds through the white wilderness.

On Christmas Day the snug log barracks at Arctic Red River resounded with merriment as Constable Alfred W. King and Spike Millen entertained a group of traders. Outside a blizzard raged. Toward evening, as the celebration reached a tumultuous roar, the door flew open. A misty cloud of frost swept into the warm room and from it the fur-hooded figure of a snow-covered Loucheux emerged. The crowd stilled.

"Dat white trapper . . . come from Yukon las' summer!" the Indian growled to Millen, his features pinched in fury. "Him take traps and throw in trees. Say *him* trapline . . . not Injun. Say Injun no trap dere!" In excited bursts of broken English, the Loucheux told how the stranger threatened the villagers until they were too terrified to hunt or trap. Now, with no pelts to trade for supplies and ammunition, the Indian families were nearing starvation.

Millen turned to King. "It's Johnson," he said. "Don't like to ask you to go out in weather like this, but there's no choice. Find him and see if he has a license to trap. If not, bring him in. Take Joe Bernard with you and hit the trail in the morning."

It was three days by dog sled. King and Special Constable Bernard carried rifles, hardtack biscuits and beans, dried fish for the dogs, and stopped only to eat and sleep on the trail.

The lower reaches of the Rat run through a large canyon over a thousand yards wide in most places with banks varying in height from two hundred to six hundred feet. The river itself is narrow, the valley well timbered and covered with brush. In the bitter cold of a brief Arctic daylight, the officers stopped their slant-eyed huskies at Johnson's place. "Now that's an odd-looking cabin," King said. Flat, ugly, and windowless, it stood in a small clearing on the north bank of the Rat, a few miles from its junction with Driftwood Creek. The Mounties scanned the odd structure. It was unlike any trapper's cabin they had ever seen, designed along the lines of an early frontier blockhouse fort. Johnson had obviously built it of thick logs with loopholes at each corner.

"When we first arrived," King said later, "I saw Johnson looking at us through a small opening, which he immediately covered when he realized I'd seen him." They walked to the heavy door and King pounded with his gloved fist. "Halloo," he shouted over the sharp wind. "It's the police, Mr. Johnson. Open up!" Nothing stirred from within. They circled the cabin on snowshoes but saw no fresh tracks. Johnson had not left since the storm began.

"He's in there," King said grimly, again pounding on the door. "We know you're in there, Johnson!" he bellowed. "Open the door!"

Again, nothing.

After twenty minutes King spoke angrily. "We'll have to hit it for Aklavik, get a warrant and break in." He grabbed the team's harness. "Let's go."

On New Year's Eve a patrol of rifle-bearing Mounties returned, this time four strong and with two dog sleds. With King and Bernard were Constable McDowell and Special Constable Lazarus Sittichiulis. The squat cabin stood dimly outlined in the gloomy light. With the others, King strode the twenty yards from the river bank to the cabin door. Inside his fur *ahtegi* [parka] was a warrant for entry and search; in his hand was an axe. The Constable rapped on the door. "Are you there, Mr. Johnson?" As before, nothing stirred.

"Open this door, Johnson. It's the police!" the Mountie called.

Nothing moved.

Constable King tells what happened next:

The door was made of double boards two inches thick. I had just raised the axe to strike down the door when *crack!* Johnson fired blindly through the door. Splinters flew. I was hit in the chest with a .30 calibre hard-nosed bullet from Johnson's Remington. It entered my left side through the lower rib and came out the right side. I reeled backward and fell, and called to McDowell to draw the trapper's fire so I could crawl away.

McDowell drew his pistol and fired repeatedly through a loophole to distract Johnson. "Get to cover!" he shouted while King crawled painfully toward the underbrush, trailing a red line in the snow. While the trapper fired again and again from alternate loopholes, Sittichiulis crawled to the wounded man, who had regained his feet and had managed to stagger around the gunfire to the shelter of the river bank. He was fast going into shock. When McDowell reached his friend and pulled the *ahtegi* aside, he saw the growing stain below King's heart. He stared at the half-closed eyes of his stricken comrade. Aklavik—eighty miles over grueling terrain—had the nearest doctor and their panting huskies were already bone-weary. With scarcely a word, McDowell and Sittichiulis carried King to a dog sled. In a minute he was lashed to the seat and they were off in a spray of snow. For twenty hours McDowell urged the dogs on. Constable King, weak but fully rational, recalls today: "McDowell didn't interfere with the wound, having decided it was better to leave it alone rather than perhaps start the bleeding again—if it had stopped. I remember all of the trip . . . it was a run with few stops."

The withering pace ended at the steps of All Saints Anglican Mission Hospital where King was put in the care of Surgeon J. A. Urquhart. "The doctor was a fine fellow," King reflects. "Friendly and well liked. He was a rather stout man and always clean-shaven.

"This was the extent of my near-fatal encounter with Albert Johnson. I was under treatment for a month, then spent three months convalescing in my home town of Ottawa. There was no doubt in my mind that Johnson was desperate and was not going to be taken alive. He must have had a reason for this, though no one knows what it was."

News of the cold-blooded shooting spread quickly. Tempers flared and men assembled at the police barracks, rifles in hand, ready to avenge the gunning down of a mounted policeman. Inspector Eames knew what now had to be done. By radiotelegraph he put out a call for all trappers in the Delta to join the Force in tracking down the mad dog. Mounties were drawn from Fort McPherson and Arctic Red River. When Eames inspected his determined posse, he confronted a grim-faced assembly of constables, Loucheux guides, and veteran trappers. Aside from officers Eames, McDowell, and Millen, there were Special Constables Sittichiulis and Bernard as guides, and trappers Ernest Sutherland, Karl Garlund, and Knud Lang. Their sleds, loaded with twenty pounds of dynamite, caps, fuses, ammunition, and provisions, required forty-two dogs. As they were about to begin the trek, welcome news came from the hospital. Thanks to McDowell's dash, King would live.

The party was hampered by the intense cold—at times forty-five degrees below zero—and short supplies, particularly dog feed. The trip was longer than usual because Inspector Eames would not travel along the river itself for fear the wily Johnson would take this opportunity to ambush them.

They approached the cabin site by a trapping trail through the woods, and at noon, January 9, about an hour and a half after daybreak at that time of year, stopped a half mile from the shack. They tied the dogs to the timber and moved forward. The cabin lay sinister and silent as the men partially surrounded it. In the interim, Johnson had added more loopholes; there were now eight. "By listening from our position under the river bank," Eames reported, "we learned that Johnson was at home, and I called to him to come out and said we were determined to arrest him."

The mad trapper answered. *Crack! Queee!* A bullet narrowly missed Eames fur hood and ricocheted into the wilderness. Siege.

With less than two nights' supply of dog feed, Eames decided to storm the cabin. But Johnson was ready and began firing as soon as they clambered over the top of the bank. The posse sent a blistering hail of lead against the log walls but Johnson, passing quickly from one loophole to another, was able to hold all eight men at bay. As the exchange of lead progressed, Eames sensed Johnson was tiring. "Rush him!" the Inspector called. "Break the door!" Under cover of fire from .30-caliber rifles, Knud Lang, Millen, and McDowell dashed across the clearing and slammed their rifle butts against the door. When a rapid fusillade of gunfire from Johnson's Remington forced them back to cover, Lang stumbled breathlessly over the river bank, fell beside Eames, and, gasping for air, told the Inspector: "I saw him . . . through the broken door. It's filled with smoke . . . and he's dug the floor below ground level! He was crouching there with two automatic pistols . . . That's no cabin, Inspector . . . it's a damned fort! Let's dynamite!"

Eames nodded. The men dug in for the long night and made shelters for protection from the raging blizzard and driven snow. A numbing cold and lack of sleep made their job difficult and all through the night until 3 A.M. the siege continued. Johnson seemed to have an unlimited supply of ammunition. The Inspector planned to catch Johnson napping before dawn and about 9 P.M. small charges of dynamite had been thawed, capped, and fused. The sinister cabin lay black against the purple snow. Stars blinked coldly against a sky now glimmering in the spectral sheen of the aurora. The blizzard calmed.

"Now!" Eames called quietly. Charges in hand, the Mounties moved forward in a crouch, shuffled to the cabin and heaved their explosives against the log walls. Several charges failed to detonate; those that exploded had no effect. The rushes continued between hot, intermittent exchanges of gunfire. One officer lobbed a large charge onto the roof but it blew only a small hole and failed to stun Johnson.

Noel Verville, a member of the posse, rose from behind a snow-covered log, rushed several yards and heaved a bundle of sticks against the weakened door. The detonation shook the ground as the squat square of logs was illuminated in the red burst of flame. As the clearing plunged into darkness again, the posse rushed forward, rifles ready.

Knud Lang reached the splintered doorway and squinted through the billowing smoke. He saw Johnson on the floor, stunned, bewildered, and motionless, his wild eyes trying to see through the thick, suffocating smoke. Lang drew a bead on Johnson's head, then lowered his rifle slowly. "Hell," he was heard to mutter, "I can't shoot a man with his eyes open like that!" A moment later Lang sprang backward as the man whose life he had just spared regained his senses and fired at him through the shattered opening.

The men withdrew and planned another assault. When the light came briefly to the sky, they saw a ragged hole in the cabin's roof. The ridge pole had also been knocked upward.

At 3 A.M. the following morning the last of the dynamite—four pounds—was prepared. Karl Garlund arced the parcel squarely toward the door, where it exploded with a shattering crash. Logs and splinters flew. Revolver in hand, Eames ran across the clearing, Garlund beside him with a rifle and flashlight. Eames later told what followed.

We intended to throw the rays of the spotlight on Johnson and endeavor to disable him by revolver fire. Johnson evidently saw or heard us when we were within a few yards of the shack and commenced to shoot. Garlund succeeded in switching on his light, only to have it shot from his hand shortly afterward, whereupon we retired to the safety of the river bank.

As the nearby trees rang with the resounding *smack!* of bullets, one round flicked the Inspector's hat through the air. Again the posse dug in for a council of war.

"Let's hang on," Verville argued. "He's in as bad a condition as we are." But Eames, after sizing up the situation, said, "No, it's back to Aklavik for us. Our dynamite's exhausted. We've no more food for the dogs. And it's getting colder by the hour." As the sleds moved off over the frozen river, Noel Verville shook his fist at the cabin and shouted, "We'll be back, Johnson—and next time we'll get you!"

Refreshed by a stay at Aklavik, a few days later Eames sent Millen and Garlund back to the Rat with orders to camp two miles from the cabin and determine whether Johnson was still there. On January 16, 1932, Eames set out again to apprehend the desperate trapper. Aside from Sittichiulis, Verville, and Sutherland, this party had new men: John Parsons, Frank Carmichael, and two members of the Royal Canadian Signals, Staff Sergeant Earl F. Hersey and Quartermaster Sergeant Robert F. Riddell. When the party reached the mouth of the Rat, an Indian messenger brought news from Millen. Johnson had fled.

At the cabin, the men inspected the inside of Johnson's stronghold. The odor of gunpowder still hung heavy in the air. After one look the men understood why the trapper's fort was invulnerable. On the side facing the river bank the walls were double-logged, reinforced with frozen sod for two feet above ground level—and bullet proof. The floor was thirty-eight inches below ground level. Scattered underfoot and around the loopholes were dozens of empty cartridges. Johnson could see on all sides. The dirt floor was littered with cookery, flour, beans, and dried meat—all scattered by the concussions of the dynamite blasts.

"Look here," exclaimed Hersey, pointing to a shadowy corner of the cabin.

"So that's how he survived the dynamite," Millen said. "He dug a tunnel . . . and was ready for anything."

A few hundred yards from the cabin one of the trappers found a cleverly concealed store of food. Millen frowned. "Johnson's an odd kind of trapper," he said. "Why did he go to all the trouble to dig the trench and double-wall the cabin? There isn't a single pelt or stretcher anywhere. And why did he add to his work by hiding his food store three hundred yards from his cabin?" He shook his head. "It's senseless—it's all crazy."

As insane as it may have appeared, the cabin and outbuilding were constructed with forethought, built to meet the climate of the northern woods.

Rat River country to this day is a land of winding streams, heavy undergrowth, snow-drifted ravines, and rough mountains. For fugitive Albert Johnson it was home. An excellent woodsman with great stamina, he was deadly with a rifle. Eames knew the odds that confronted his men. While his posse was burdened with supplies and feed for the dog teams, Albert Johnson was traveling light.

Inspector Eames recruited eleven Loucheux, among whom were the three Indians Johnson had insulted on the Peel River. Then he set up a base camp, and for days the party fanned out along the entire Rat River Canyon to the Bear

River, searched old cabins and followed the trap lines. But a severe windstorm had obliterated all tracks.

Provisions dwindled again. The Inspector estimated supplies on hand would keep four men going for nine days. Millen, Riddell, Verville, and Garlund were selected to remain and scout as far as the Yukon if necessary. The others returned to Aklavik, made plans to haul supplies to the mouth of the Rat and replace the four men after nine days.

Sergeant Riddell carried a portable short-wave transceiver in his toboggan, a set of his own design. Using his ham operator's call letters, he was able to receive messages from Aklavik and, despite his limited power, occasionally reply by key.

For days Spike Millen led his posse back and forth through the canyons, deep in drifted snow, along the frozen streams, and headlong into the howling, cutting winds of the icebound summits. The elusive fugitive had left no snowshoe tracks.

Leading his party into a previously unsearched hill area beyond the junction of the Bear and Rat rivers, Millen was overtaken on the twenty-eighth by an Indian who reported that two shots were heard the previous day near the mouth of the Bear. The scouts backtracked and found Johnson's tracks, leading into a thick patch of timber.

On the afternoon of January 30, the eleventh day since they had left the cabin site, they urged their tired huskies past the mouth of the frozen Barrier River. Shortly before, Noel Verville had looked up at the rocky, nearby cover and remarked to the others: "I hope we don't run into him here. We're a perfect target against this frozen creek bed!" The others grunted and trudged on. When the red sky of the short Arctic day faded into purple, they knew in another hour the long, frigid night would come again. Today Riddell remembers: "At this time of year the sun never comes over the horizon. The only daylight is a twilight from 10 A.M. till

2 P.M. It was between 1 and 2 P.M. when we had the encounter . . ."

They were crossing a wide bend when Garlund stopped suddenly and crouched. "Look!" he whispered hoarsely, pointing to a clump of spruce on the high bank. "There he is!" The others stopped and saw, behind a log barricade four hundred yards across the frozen ice, the huddled figure of a man. Riddell focused his glasses. "It's Johnson." Turning to Millen he said, "It's getting dark fast. Do we tackle him now or wait till morning?"

In low tones they made their plans, decided to retreat to creek cover behind them. As the hidden sun tinted the rugged peaks with deep purple, they closed in, slipping cautiously from one snow-covered bush to another. When they were three hundred yards from the barricade, Johnson's animal sixth sense warned him danger was afoot. He rose up for an instant, silhouetted against the drifts.

In the words of Riddell:

Mr. Garlund and I went to a point on the opposite side of the creek, where we could see Johnson's camp. Constable Millen and Noel Verville came down the hill into the creek close to Johnson's camp. We could hear Johnson in his camp coughing; we could also hear Millen and Verville coming down the hill from where we were. We heard Johnson rattling his rifle, and as Millen came past an opening in the timber Johnson fired a shot at him . . . Johnson could not be seen by any of us.

We made several calls to Johnson to surrender. For more than a half hour it was explained to him that he had not killed the police officer he shot at the cabin. He was advised to come out from where he was hiding. He never spoke to anyone at any time.

Some shots were fired blindly into the timber and no more shots came from there. We thought Johnson had been hurt. Millen and I went up the bank into the path of timber and a shot was fired at a very short range. I went over the bank into cover. Millen, who was right behind me, remained on the bank. I do not know if he knew where the shot had come from or not. He fired two shots to my knowledge—I could tell by the sound of his rifle—and Johnson fired three. When I got to the top of the bank again, at another point, Millen had been shot.

I was less than ten feet from him when he was hit and was the first to reach him. He had been fatally struck in the left chest by Johnson's .30-.30. Death was instant. My emotion was great sorrow at the loss of a good friend whom I'd known for quite a few years.

Verville and Garlund crawled through the snow. Verville's eyes were wide with anger; Garlund had a shocked expression. "He's dead," Riddell said grimly, his face granite-hard and livid with fury. He vowed to get the madman or "die in the attempt!"

The small group huddled around the Mountie's still body. Riddell was silent for several moments, then he said: "We can't rush the barricade; he can hold off a small army as well as he's dug in. But we'll get him. We'll stay out of gunshot and dog the heels of that killer until we wear him down. This chase has just started!"

Leaving the others to shadow Johnson, Riddell struck out for Aklavik to report Millen's death. En route he met Hersey and Sittichiulis on their way to bolster the party. On Sunday afternoon, January 31, Riddell brought the sad news to Aklavik.

Eames broadcast another appeal for volunteers throughout the Yukon. "Get the Mad Trapper!" was the call and woodsmen hit the trail from all directions to converge on Aklavik. The Inspector noted, "The report of Constable Millen's death brought men from all parts of the Mackenzie River delta to offer their services, some traveling over one hundred miles to do so."

With the hunt spreading, Eames knew the supplying of

search parties was going to be a difficult task. Dogs and men had to be fed to keep going. With heavy snows covering the long trails, the task appeared insurmountable. Then the Inspector thought of using a supply plane. Although the Mounted Police had not yet become aware of the advantages of the airplane in their work, Eames recognized its usefulness in supplying the searchers by air. Too, Eames reasoned, if rifle fire failed to flush Johnson again, he could be bombed. Although extended northern flying at that time of year was largely experimental, he decided to give it a try. He telegraphed Edmonton shortly before he left Aklavik with a fresh party of ten men.

On February 2 Wop May received a wire from "Punch" Dickens, Superintendent of Canadian Airways at Edmonton, asking him to fly to Aklavik and join in the search for Johnson. May was then based at Fort McMurray and the following morning he met Dickens, who arrived with Constable W. S. Carter, replacement for the murdered Millen. As soon as tear gas bombs and supplies were loaded, May, Jack Bowen (Wop's mechanic), and Carter boarded the six-place, ski-equipped Bellanca Pacemaker and turned north on a 1500-mile flight into thirty-degree-below-zero weather. The plane was a workhorse, ideally suited for bush flying. Its nine-cylinder, 300-horsepower Wright J6 pulled it along at an airspeed of 120 miles an hour. Its landing speed was low, 50 miles an hour, which enabled it to get in and out of small clearings. It could carry almost a ton of supplies.

At Fort Smith a blinding blizzard grounded them for the night. They pushed on when it subsided, into the teeth of a blinding snowstorm, the ground completely obscured. When they finally reached Arctic Red River, they got instructions to meet Eames' posse at the junction of the Peel and Rat. May droned back and forth over the rendezvous point but saw nothing of the men below. He turned for Aklavik.

Meanwhile Eames' party reached the barricade where Millen was shot and discovered Johnson had fled to the high ground. It took a day to pick up his trail on the Barrier river. It was only a few hours old but they lost it when it went up to the tundra.

On the morning of the seventh the Bellanca was buried under drifted snow. It was noon before Indians and Eskimos dug the plane free, and with Dr. Urquhart, Constable Carter, and Jack Bowen, May set out again to locate the ground patrol. When they reached the V junction of the Peel and Rat rivers there was still no sign of Eames' party. May flew on and a few minutes later, over the Barrier River, Bowen pounded May's shoulder and pointed below. The scouting party.

May curved back, zoomed low over the waving men. Through his binoculars he could faintly see the single snowshoe track the searchers were following. The windswept drifts eradicated it in places, but skimming the Bellanca monoplane low over the trees, they followed the trail for five miles up the Barrier. They discovered the fugitive had doubled back on his tracks, swung from the river across the rock-ribbed ridge, descended into a valley, and headed west into the rugged mountains that divide the Mackenzie from the Yukon. There they disappeared into thin air! May landed on the frozen tundra two miles from the posse and Constable Carter joined the searchers.

"Johnson's been doubling back on his trail and might try to ambush you," May told Eames. "Keep a close watch; he's tricky."

Eames nodded. "We know. He's been crossing the tundra from creek to creek, probably at night, and circling eight to ten miles back on his own track." After May flew Millen's frozen body to Aklavik, he began ferrying provisions and dog feed. Before each landing he scouted ahead of the party in the hopes of sighting the lone trapper.

For the next ten days the Bellanca flew back and forth between Aklavik and the camps, shuttling men, supplies, and doing occasional advance scouting for the posse. Quartermaster Sergeant Earl Hersey comments: "Captain May was an outstanding natural-instinct flier. When freighting supplies to our posse, he landed and took off from places another pilot wouldn't attempt." Hersey worked tirelessly with the searchers. Today, a retired major of the Royal Canadian Signals, he lives in Barrie, Ontario, and recalls those grueling days in the white, numbing wilderness.

Inspector Eames requested and obtained permission from Ottawa for me to continue as a member of the posse. I owned a powerful, fast dog team with which I usually traveled and hunted extensively in the winter. It carried the big tent in which the posse slept and usually led the search patrol. We were on the move most of the time but sleep was not a problem; usually we got six to eight hours a day. I used a Woods Arctic Eiderdown sleeping bag, slept naked and used a flannelette sheet inside the sleeping bag. Personally, I slept near a canvas tent wall with one of my dogs at my back on the outside of the canvas. He would warn me of the approach of animal or man.

Our staple diet was frozen fresh meat or canned meat, and bannock—a flat, baked oatmeal or barley-meal cake. Johnson, we found, was a very good traveler. He had a much smaller burden and carried all his essentials on his back.

The Mounted Police in Dawson had earlier requested a broadcast from radio station UZK at Anchorage, Alaska, which reached the isolated Yukon post of Old Crow. Constable Sidney W. May was in charge of the post. With Special Constable John Moses, two trappers, the great gray-haired giant Frank Jackson, Frank Hogg, and two Indians, he set out for Eames' camp by way of La Pierre House, Bell River, Loon Lake, and Rat River. They reached Inspector Eames on February 8 with news of seeing a recent track headed for the Yukon Divide. On the tenth there came an encouraging break in the chase. Johnson's tracks were found farther up on the mountain range—a desperate course and a clear sign that he was weakening. Inspector Eames recalled the Indians had declared in the early stages of the search that neither white man nor Indian could cross that divide alone, but to Wop May he now said: "It looks as though he's trying for Alaska. As soon as you can fly in larger snowshoes for us, I'd like you to take Riddell on a flight across the divide again, as low as possible."

On the twelfth, Constable May and Indian Peter Alexi arrived at the Rat River base camp. The Kutchin Indian drove the dog sled into the clearing at a furious pace and the panting huskies had barely stopped when Alexi shouted, "Dat man Johnson—him cross mountains! Injun find track on Bell Ribber two days 'go!" The excited man told how the native trappers, terrified at the prospect of encountering the mad killer, had deserted their traps and fled to the posts for protection. A hunting party, he added, almost bumped into the man.

The news that Johnson's track had been seen near La Pierre House in the Yukon changed plans drastically. "So he made it across the Divide," Eames said grimly. "He *is* trying to reach Alaska—and we could lose him forever." The Inspector shook his head. "You have to give the devil credit. He's certainly traveled—ninety miles in three days without a dog sled in this bitter weather. But I think he's nearing the end of his rope." Eames ordered Constable Sidney May, Sergeant Hersey, and six others to make the passage through the mountains.

Back in the air on February 14, Wop May swept low beyond the lands from which Alexi had come, picked up the fugitive trapper's tracks and followed them as they looped for almost thirty miles around the bend of the frozen Bell River.

They vanished again after ten miles on the Eagle River, where Johnson took advantage of a hard-packed trail made by thousands of caribou. He had removed his snowshoes and lost his tracks in theirs.

On the seventeenth, Inspector Eames sensed the gap was narrowing.

> . . . his track was again picked up and appeared to be not more than twenty-four hours old. We had broken camp before daylight, intending to travel a long distance and if possible catch up with Johnson before he could reach the cabin of a trapper named Barnstrum, though none of the party knew where the cabin was located. Barnstrum's position gave us great anxiety, as it was known that he knew nothing of Johnson's murderous acts in the Northwest Territories. Captain May would have flown a message to this man on February 16 but was unable to leave La Pierre House through the fog.

May's Bellanca had, in fact, been grounded until noon of the seventeenth because of blowing snow and mist. When the storm subsided, Wop, Constable May, and Jack Bowen headed north for the Eagle. Unknown to them, the hunt for the Mad Trapper was moving quickly toward a violent climax.

Shortly before noon, the patrol of eight men with dog teams, three of whom were on foot, was approaching a sharp bend in the Eagle River. Sergeant Hersey recalls that moment.

> I was leading the posse with the teams following my trail at various intervals. We were moving quietly, for sled dogs used on the trap line or for hunting purposes in the western Arctic do not bark while working. I was fairly well alone at that moment, following a trail twelve hours old when, 250 yards ahead, slogging toward me, came Albert Johnson. Unaware that we were so near, he was back-tracking on his trail of the day before.

Johnson saw us at the same instant and paused only long enough to lace on his snowshoes. Then he dashed for the river bank, rifle on his back.

While he hurried to the bank I procured my rifle from the toboggan. Verville, driving the team behind me, stopped and drew his rifle also, with Riddell close behind him. Johnson attempted to climb the river bank behind the protection of the Point. I set my sights for 300 yards (the distance was later measured and found to be 270-280 yards).

I could see his pack at intervals. I hit his gear (carried on his back) each of the three times I fired, and down he would slide. Obviously he became fed up and I saw him reach over his shoulder for his rifle. I knew he carried a .30-.30, which I did not consider accurate at 300 yards. In order to shoot he had to expose part of his body. By now the others in the party split, and half climbed one bank and half the other, moving upstream.

I was a qualified marksman and planned to hit Johnson in the shoulder. I was on one knee, taking careful aim. He squeezed the trigger first and I fell backward, shot in the left knee, left elbow, and chest with a dum-dum bullet. My lower body and legs were paralyzed but I saw him continue and now take careful aim at me.

When struck, my only thoughts and actions were for self-preservation—to dig a hole in the snow as fast as I could for protection. (My comrades kid me about the speed I achieved in removing the snow from under my body. They say they never saw or expect to see a hole dug in the snow at a faster rate.) After this was accomplished I didn't like the sound of air going in and out the hole in the left side of my chest.

Johnson hit me with his first round but missed with his next two carefully aimed rounds. He was a good shot at short distances; there was small game in his pack, shot in the head for food.

Johnson fired rapidly at his pursuers, then, suddenly, stopped firing and made a run back up the river. Verville went back to care for Hersey, lying in the blood-stained snow. Inspector Eames saw the encounter turn into a running gunfight. "Johnson," Eames reported, "was running in his own track and occasionally stopped to fire. He was actually drawing away from the posse and appeared to be making for the opposite bank, which was not as steep as the one he had vacated.

"He was called upon to surrender, but he continued his flight, whereupon rifle fire was concentrated on him and apparently caused him to throw himself down and dig down in the deep snow after placing his large sack for cover—though it's probable he had just been wounded in the leg.

"Having entrenched himself in the deep soft snow, Johnson resumed firing at the men on the river."

Coming over the river at two thousand feet, the Bellanca was hitting a good speed when Wop May sat bolt upright and focused his eyes on a black form in the middle of the frozen river. Then he saw, to the south, half a dozen other black objects spread out along the eastern bank. On the opposite bank more dark figures contrasted against the white cover. May throttled the engine to an idle and rolled into a quick gliding turn. From the east bank a flash of reddish-orange flame leaped from a rifle barrel and over the muffled engine he could hear the shot reverberate through the cold air. At that moment they all understood: the black speck in the center was the mad trapper! The other specks were Eames' posse and the cornered fugitive was returning their fire.

Bowen yelled above the rushing slipstream: "They're closing in on Johnson! They're fighting it out!" May opened the throttle and tightened the turn.

"We came roaring down the river," May said later, "and once again I peered down at Johnson in his snow trench. Then, as I circled over the posse, I saw a figure lying on a bedroll near the west bank and realized, with a sick feeling, that one of our party had been hit.

"I circled back upriver, passing over the posse and Johnson. As I flew over the fugitive's lair it seemed as though he was lying in an unnatural position. Swinging back, I nosed the Bellanca down till our skis were tickling the snow."

The forty-eight-day "Arctic Circle War," which began as a routine investigation and mushroomed into the merciless death of one man and the serious wounding of two others, climaxed quickly. Inspector Eames said, "Gradually . . . the men who had gone up the banks of the river made their way through the deep snow and brush, and from their positions on the high ground quickly stopped Johnson's fire, and a few moments later, at 12:10 p.m., it was found that Johnson was dead, having desperately resisted to the last."

May flew slowly past the inert figure and banked gently. "I could plainly see, as I flashed past, that Johnson was lying face down in the snow, his right arm outflung, still grasping his rifle. And I knew as I looked that he was dead. The Mounted Police had got their man. The chase was over."

May rocked the Bellanca's wings to signify Johnson's death, landed on the frozen river and taxiied to where he had seen the wounded man lying on a bedroll. "Who's hit?" he called as he jumped from the plane with Bowen and Carter. Sergeant Riddell bent over his stricken companion. "Sergeant Hersey," he replied.

"Badly?"

"I'm afraid so." Riddell's face was grave.

"Get him fixed up," May directed, "and I'll fly him back to Aklavik!"

While Riddell was getting Hersey ready, May walked to where the posse was gathered, staring at the dead man. Verville turned to the bush pilot. "Just look at his face," he said. "Did you ever see anything like that?"

". . . As I stooped over and saw him I got the worst shock I'd ever had," May said. "Johnson's lips were curled back from his teeth in the most terrible sneer I'd ever seen on a man's face. The parchment-like skin over his cheek bones was distorted by it, and his teeth glistened like an animal's through his bristle of beard. It was the most awful grimace of hate I've ever seen—the hard-boiled, bitter hate of a man who knows he's trapped at last and has determined to take as many with him down that trail he knows he's going to hit. After that sneer I couldn't feel sorry for this man who lay dead in front of me. Instead, I was glad he was dead. The world seemed a better and cleaner place without him."

May hurried back to the plane, where Hersey had been laid on the cabin floor. Bowen got aboard, closed the door, and the graceful monoplane skimmed off the frozen Eagle and pointed toward Aklavik. "We covered the hundred and thirty miles in an hour and forty minutes from the time he was hit," May recalled, ". . . fifty minutes' flying time. We nearly went *through* the mountains on that trip. There was fog and snow and I don't know how we got through. A quarter of an hour later and he'd have bled to death."

Today, Hersey remembers that dash vividly. "I never lost consciousness at any time after I was struck," he relates. "Oddly enough, it was the pain in my left knee that was most severe and Bowen did his best to help me bear the discomfort. I remember the entire flight—and the look of my friend Dr. Urquhart when he saw my white, bloodless face and cut away my parka."

The doctor saw the bullet had pierced both lungs. He found the spent slug just under the skin of the Sergeant's back. "He's in serious condition," Urquhart told May and Bowen, "but we may pull him through." He did.

It was all over. Albert Johnson had crossed the divide over its highest peak, more than eight thousand feet. The trek was truly a tortuous agony every step of the way, for once above the Richardson Mountains timberline, he had no firewood to kindle a campfire to warm himself. He could not thaw his frozen food or melt snow for drinking water. Still he slogged on, pushing into the teeth of the storms that raged on the heights and tore at his ragged clothing.

On the frozen river the bone-weary men searched the grimacing corpse. One of the first telling bullets fired by the posse struck a pack of ammunition in his hip pocket. It had exploded and torn a gaping wound in his hip. There were several wounds in his legs, back, and shoulders, but the bullet that passed through the small of his back and severed his spine put him out of the fight.

His physical condition was unbelievably poor. Thin, emaciated, with his feet, legs, and hands nearly frozen, somehow his determination to escape—and survive—kept him going. Inside his pack was his total food ration—a small packet of tea and two squirrels.

Johnson was a walking arsenal with a .30-.30 rifle, an Iver Johnson 16-gauge sawed-off shotgun, a .22 Winchester rifle, and a good supply of ammunition. The two automatic pistols were never found. Inside his pack were also some pearls, $2410 in U.S. and Canadian banknotes, a small leather pouch of gold dust, a razor, an axe, and two gold dental bridges—neither of which fit Johnson. Oddly, not a scrap of written matter was found on the trapper's body, nor had any been found at his cabin or camps. There was absolutely nothing to give a positive identification to the man, nor is it certain, despite exhaustive investigation by the Mounted Police, that his real name was Albert Johnson. Did he come north to escape the law? His secrecy, the large sum of money, his strange actions seem to point to this. For what other reason would a man harbor such an unreasonable hatred of the Mounties, build a fortress stronghold, and doggedly try to escape the police until he was nearly dead from exhaustion and exposure? Paradoxically, Major Hersey offers this comment today, thirty-seven years after Johnson cut him down that frigid day on the Eagle River: "In my opinion Albert

Johnson was not a vicious man or a vicious criminal. The Yukon-Northwest Territories boundary line was two hundred yards northwest of Johnson's cabin. The boundary is not marked. He could have hunted, trapped, and built his cabin in the Yukon without a license and the so-called Mad Trapper episode would not have happened."

Major Riddell's still-vivid recollections contrast somewhat with those of his friend. "I think Johnson was a very tough and hardened criminal and that he was running from previous crimes. The main thing that stands out is that it was necessary to kill him . . ."

Whatever the speculation, it was an airplane that turned the tide of the chase in favor of the law. Without the continuous delivery of vital supplies by air, the Mounties would have been unable to press the chase, and Albert Johnson would likely have reached the safety of the Alaskan wilderness.

When Inspector Eames collected all available information for his report, he could do little more than speculate on the trapper's identity. He wrote:

> It is not unlikely he was identical with a man who spent some time in the vicinity of Nation, near Alaska, near the Yukon boundary, living alone, occasionally burning down the cabins of persons and disabling trap lines, and establishing a character for moroseness and violence. He disappeared from Alaska about the time that Johnson made his appearance in the Northwest Territories.

Wop May flew the trapper's frozen body back to Aklavik. Fingerprints which were taken from his corpse and sent to Ottawa and Washington were never linked with a criminal record in either country. The body was not claimed, and finally, with the aid of an Indian, Inspector Eames buried it at the edge of the graveyard in Aklavik, under a large spruce on which the initials A.J. were carved. The tree, or at least its stump, was still there in the early 1960s, though it's possible it has now disappeared.

Over the years since the bizarre affair, the Royal Canadian Mounted Police has received many inquiries from persons worldwide who claim to be his relatives. In each case the police have carefully checked descriptions and photos, and have been obliged to reply: ". . . we find that . . . is not identical with the man known as Albert Johnson."

And there the case stands, with no more known of the true identity of the Mad Trapper of Rat River than was known the day Spike Millen questioned him at Fort McPherson.

13

War Flying for the Films

THE air combat film, produced today in glorious sound and vibrant color, continues to entertain millions of war movie fans. Its dashing heroes and sinister villains sit in mock-up cockpits, while a cloud background moves lazily behind them on a giant process screen. Radio-controlled model planes explode or crash and splinter to reveal fleetingly their wood and cardboard frames to the quick eye. Fleets of scale models in mass formations, suspended by fine wires and superimposed against a sky-blue background, give the impression of a mass armada of oncoming bombers. The special effects men produced some realistic scenes for *The Blue Max, The War Lover* and *Battle of Britain*.

But strangely, the nostalgia for the old black and white celluloid air war films, *Dawn Patrol, Wings, Lilac Time, Hell's Angels*—even *Twelve O'Clock High*—remains strong today. The pilots who flew for these epics went all out for realism, too, often at the price of death from crashes and collisions that were not in the scripts. Their adventures were as bizarre as any seen on the Western front or over the flak-filled skies of Europe.

The first great air picture was *Wings,* a silent film of 1926 that clearly reflected the two million dollars it cost. Ex-Lafayette Flying Corps warbird William Wellman was director, and the stars were Buddy Rogers and Richard Arlen. Splendid photography and breathtaking flying scenes—all real —offset the mediocre plot. Paramount's executives got Wellman the use of Kelly and Brooks Fields at San Antonio, plus most of the Army pilots in the country, with their planes. Thomas-Morse Scouts, DH-4s, and Martin MB-2 bombers converged on the Texas location. On five square miles of land near old Camp Stanley, Second Infantry Division engineers from Fort Sam Houston used six hundred laborers to build a facsimile of the St. Mihiel battlefield, complete with shell holes, barbed wire, and winding trenchworks. Then five thousand men from the same division re-enacted the famous offensive. Rehearsals were minimum; the Second had participated in the real battle during World War I. Every plane was airborne for the epic scene and atop a special hundred-foot tower Wellman directed the scrap with twenty-one cameras on the ground and in the air. Strafing planes skimmed low over the scarred ground and hundreds of infantrymen were "cut down" by their flickering machine guns while tanks lumbered over the maze of trenches.

In the midst of this was to be a shattering, splintering crash of a Spad 7 by Dick Grace. He was to fly it squarely into the pock-marked no-man's-land and smash on a twenty-five-foot stretch of battleground especially reserved for the crack-up.

With cameras grinding, two Curtiss P-1's disguised as German fighters got on Grace's tail and forced him lower and lower, their machine guns blazing. At the proper ground signal he let the Germans finish him off, shoved the stick forward and tore toward the nine square yards of marked, churned battleground.

At 95 mph Grace struck the earth with the Spad in a slight left slip. The lower left wing slammed into the mud and crumpled. As the pre-weakened landing gear collapsed the fighter flipped over on its back, debris flying, and stopped seventeen feet from the nearest camera. A cedar post penetrated the cockpit eleven inches from Grace's head and ripped the back of his leather jacket. He crawled out and rolled into a shell hole until the scene was ended.

Grace gained fame during the 1920s and 1930s because of his fantastic ability to reduce planes to rubble and survive. In one film he dropped his handkerchief on the ground to mark the crash spot, took off, smashed down and nosed the plane over on its back. When the dust cleared, he hung suspended upside down in the open cockpit, his head a few inches from the dirt. He reached down and picked up his handkerchief.

An ex-World War One Navy flier, he turned to barnstorming and somersaulting into nets from tall buildings for a living. Richard Arlen and Dick Grace had met years earlier in Wisconsin and later roomed together when both were struggling for acceptance in their respective fields.

The flying double was a believer in the calculated risk and learned early how certain safety measures stacked the survival odds in his favor. He reinforced each condemned plane's cockpit with heavy steel tubing so it would not collapse and crush him. A harness belt held him in. Of his own design, it predated by forty years the type now used by Indianapolis race drivers. Grace knew how and where to weaken wings and landing gears. He got the precise crash effect safely by splitting the impact into its component forces. Because he had a deep dread of fire, he flew with just enough gasoline in the tanks to do the job.

Wellman scheduled a Fokker D-7 crash, but the weather refused to cooperate. For two weeks, as the crews awaited a background of billowing clouds, Grace grew edgier by the day. He lost sleep. He sweated, and the strain of delay weakened him. Finally the clouds appeared and the call came.

The shot called for him to crash on takeoff, from seventy-five feet in the air. It was to be nose first at 115 mph with another plane "strafing" him in the background. He climbed aboard, strapped himself in, and checked the instruments. The gear, fuselage, and wing spars had been partially sawed through, and everyone was ready. Grace was still uneasy. He looked over his shoulder. The "British" fighter was coming in on its strafing run. Wellman signaled and Grace pushed the throttle forward. The old Mercedes engine burst forth and the lightened Fokker was airborne in seconds.

Grace glanced back to see the white-orange flashes from the machine guns of the strafing plane—the signal that coordinated their action. The crash marker was coming up and the timing perfect, thus far. He pushed the D-7's nose down and angled the plane toward the weakened fuselage. Speed, 110 mph. He knew it was too fast, but as the ground came nearer he didn't have the time or distance to abort the scene.

The lower left wingtip dug into the earth and sprayed dirt. The N strut, aileron, and lower wing crumpled. The propeller shattered into a thousand flying splinters. Grace sensed, for a fleeting moment, that the impact and velocity was being distributed as he planned. But something missed cue.

Then one of those things happened, apparently inconsequential in itself, but of vital importance in the overall scheme of things. The steel-tubed landing gear which had been weakened failed to give, as did the solid beams. With my speed little diminished, the injured wing lifted from the ground. The crosswind caught the ship and I was in the air. My ailerons were broken—useless. Impossible to dig the wing in. If the ship traveled much farther, the shot would be no good. It must be a nose in—a nose in at a bad angle of attack meant that the full impact would be transferred on almost a reverse line from the forward and downward approach—transferred to the cockpit and to me. My chest was against the belts so there would be no snap when I hit. The stick was forward.

I felt the jolt quite distinctly and knew that my chest belts had broken. Something in my brain snapped as my head hit the instrument panel and broke through it.

I thought of fire—of how once before I had been so burned. If I lost consciousness, I'd not be able to help them get me clear. I could not be pinned in. I'd help them get me out. It took less time for these details to travel through my brain than for sound over a radio wave. Even so, they were blotted out as the curtain was drawn and I was in total darkness.

When Grace recovered consciousness he found himself on the ground, surrounded by the rescue squad. When they tried to lift him, a blinding pain shot through his back and neck. He had no recollection of leaving the plane and later discovered his subconscious dread of fire had such a grip on him that, semiconscious, he had crawled back into the seat, then tumbled over the side.

He refused to go to the hospital and asked to be taken back to his hotel, where he spent a highly uncomfortable night. By morning his swollen back and neck had locked in a rigid vise-like grip. He could barely walk, and a few hours later passed out. At the Fort Sam Houston Hospital doctors found he had a broken neck—four crushed vertebrae and a dislocation. Only one thing saved him—his spinal cord was miraculously undamaged. He spent sixteen weeks in a cast, immobile.

In 1928 Grace was put in charge of the aviation sequences for *Lilac Time,* which starred Colleen Moore and newcomer Gary Cooper. Airplanes were converted and pilots hired to form one of Hollywood's first "thrill squadrons." (Grace nicknamed them the Buzzards.) They flew formation, made squadron landings, and swirled about in furious dogfights. Grace did the crash scenes.

One smash-up was unusually challenging. It was to be a total washout without allowing the plane to flip on its back or roll on the fuselage. As yet, Grace had not solved this technical problem. He knew when he struck down with speed and power, dipped a wing and plowed the nose in, the tail would automatically rise vertically and the plane would flip on its back. Simply weakening the gear and wings would not keep it down. The problem then was somehow to make sure it never started up.

In the machine shop he had the heavy anvil unbolted from the floor and installed inside the plane's fuselage just forward of the tailskid. He knew he would have to crash with one wing low; to hit the ground head on, level, would be to catapult the anvil the length of the fuselage and squarely into his back.

A brief test flight convinced Grace the director would get the smash-up he wanted so he asked for final instructions. He was shocked to learn at the last minute that a girl would be on the field when he hit—not anywhere on the field, but at the side of the plane at his exact moment of impact. She was Opal Boswell, a courageous stunt girl. Grace had watched her brave explosions while swimming moats, and she had withstood detonations that ripped the sides from movie sets and shattered bricks at her feet. Through it all she never flinched. But Grace realized, even though she did not, that to stand still while an airplane slams down out of control a few feet away, was something else. It was impossible to get out of the way. Would she lose her nerve and dart directly to the spot where he would crash? The scene called for her to break from the sidelines and rush toward the plane, but would she pass the chalk line on the ground before Grace could dig the nose in and shatter the propeller? If she did, she could be crushed, or injured with flying debris.

Grace took off for a dry run rehearsal. When he passed the crash marker, she was on the line. He signaled "ready for the take" and circled carefully, for the heavy anvil in the tail unbalanced the plane and made it unwieldy.

On the final approach Grace saw the cameras, the rescue crews, Opal waiting for her cue. It came as he slanted down. As she rushed from the sidelines, he braced for the shattering plunge.

At the critical moment two things happened in quick succession. Grace saw the girl overstep the line, then he lost sight of her under the lower wing. He was crashing blind. If he overshot the cameras and crashed beyond them, all the work would be lost. The sluggish, tail-heavy machine might not clear the restraining area and would crash into the crowd. The idea of stalling in and ruddering over flashed through his mind, but if the girl had run to the left, he would hit her. Whatever happened, in the next few seconds he *had* to see the girl as well as the crash spot.

Quickly he raised the nose of the old plane until he was at a hundred feet, then he kicked it into a steep vertical sideslip. The area below opened, and there, a few feet from the chalk line, stood Opal. Grace leaned over the cockpit rim and watched the ground loom up. He had never washed out a plane this way before—in a sideslip—and it seemed unnatural. The left side impact would transfer the shock to his heart and stomach. He didn't like the idea, but there was the yellow marker and he zeroed in on it.

Accordion-like, the lower wing folded into the fuselage. Then the nose struck and the plane did a strange thing. It stood almost vertical, made a complete spin with its engine as the pivot, then slid fifty feet backwards! Grace remembered it this way:

> The sensation I had when I saw the ground approaching was but a beginning to the thrill I got when that airplane went into reverse. I had no idea that an airplane could be made to do such

a thing, but at that time my thoughts were on things of greater importance. Would the motor break through and roll back on me? Was I going to stop near that circle of dust? I was sure of *one* thing. The anvil in back was holding down the tail.

Another ship had passed into limbo. The rear of the fuselage received as much damage as the motor and propeller. In the short flight backward it had taken a lot of punishment.

The wreck was not in the yellow ring, but it was only feet from it. I had crashed away from the girl. She was unharmed. The shot was a complete success.

Grace did not escape as easily as Opal Boswell. He had slammed hard against the belts on impact. His chest was sore and he had difficulty in breathing. His neck had taken a severe jolt. In his quarters he stripped to the waist and prodded his chest. Two ribs were broken.

Lilac Time was completed without mishap to the members of Grace's squadron, but the pilots did not survive to gain the recognition they deserved. Within a few months the squadron was all but wiped out. Clem K. Phillips died of a broken neck flying in Hollywood's next air war film. Ross Cooke and Hal Rhouse died in a midair collision. Stunt man Spencer crashed into a tree. Frank Baker stalled during a low barrel roll and spun in. Hay flew into the Appalachians. A student froze at the controls with Baxter, and Crosson had a serious accident in Imperial Valley. Only Charlie Stoffer and Dick Grace remained and Grace decided not to reorganize or replace them. But for him there were crashes and more crashes.

In 1927 the twenty-year-old heir to a burgeoning industrial empire set out to make the most spectacular air war film to that time. He succeeded, and Howard Hughes' *Hell's Angels* remains for many the all-time great flying picture. Hughes borrowed Ben Lyon from Warner Brothers and James Hall from Paramount. He signed up a young Norwegian actress,

Greta Nissen. In three months the dramatic scenes were completed, but not one frame of flying footage had been made. His associates anxiously suggested the $400,000 spent thus far was somewhat steep and perhaps they had better slow down. The boy genius never was a man to waste words. "It's my money," he replied. And it was. Unlike most producers he didn't have to beg at banks. He didn't know the meaning of fear or failure. He was a sincere aviation enthusiast who kept his goal clearly in sight—a realistic, authentic aerial motion picture.

To make sure he'd get it, he set out to locate the genuine articles—Fokker D-7s, Sopwith Camels, S.E.5s and Spads. At Inglewood, Hughes built a flying field on the site of the present Los Angeles International Airport. He built machine and repair shops and staffed them with technicians.

Unlike Wellman, who used Army Air Service pilots, Hughes assembled the wildest assortment of ex-barnstormers and stunt pilots ever to appear in a Hollywood film. At the controls of the vintage war machines were such daredevils as Ira Reed, Frank Tomick, Al Wilson, and Roscoe Turner. Master stunt man Frank Clarke was chief pilot. A handsome debonair type, with a pencil-thin mustache and a fondness for Irish whiskey, Clarke could pass for a cinema star on any lot. His liking for pretty girls added to his allure. He was fun-loving and relaxed, one of the coolest pilots to fly the skies over Hollywood.

Aside from Inglewood, Hughes reserved seven other fields around Los Angeles to film the aerial scenes and chase the most dramatic cloud formations. He wanted soft, billowing cumulus pile-ups for the stunning backgrounds that would convey the effect of speed and motion to the diving, twisting fighter planes.

Hell's Angels almost didn't get off the ground when Hughes decided, early in the filming, to take a short hop over

Hollywood in a rotary-powered Thomas-Morse Scout. He roared off the field and, when he reached a scant four hundred feet, decided to roll into a climbing right-hand turn, a dangerous act with any rotary engine airplane. The overpowering gyroscopic torque of the spinning engine flipped him into a deadly flat spin to the right and with a splintering crunch the Scout was rolled into a tangled heap of wire, wood, and shredded fabric. A horrified Frank Clarke dashed to the wreckage as Hughes slowly extricated himself from the remains. "Are you all right, Howard?" Clarke gasped.

Hughes dusted himself off. "I think so."

Clarke sighed and smiled. "Thank God! I thought for a minute we'd all lost our meal ticket!"

The film had the finest, jam-packed air fighting sequences ever made, and also a high fatality rate. For the big dogfight scenes the sky was filled with almost fifty airplanes swirling about in a spinning, diving, whirling melee as exciting as any watched from the trenches of Flanders. One mistake, one error, one slow move in mid-air maneuvering and the lives of two men could be snuffed out. But surprisingly, while death lurked in the sky and was never more than a split-second away, mid-air collisions were rare. The accidents started small, and grew. Al Johnson narrowly missed death when his wing raked the ground in a tight, too-low turn. Ross Cooke made a forced landing and wiped out an S.E.5 at Santa Paula when he came in too hot and plowed into a tall board fence. George Cooper narrowly missed skidding into a hangar.

Johnson was the first to die. He took off from Glendale in another hard-to-replace S.E.5, struck high-tension wires, and the plane exploded and burned. A few people muttered that the film was jinxed.

One overcast day Al Wilson flew a Fokker D-7 over the heart of downtown Hollywood when, without warning, the propeller sailed off and tumbled crazily to earth. The plane began to lose altitude in the milky mists and Wilson lost no time in scrambling blindly over the side and hitting the silk. He landed safely on a rooftop near Hollywood Boulevard. The propeller narrowly missed several pedestrians and the Fokker crashed into the back yard of movie magnate Joe Schenck. It was two blocks from Grauman's Chinese Theatre, where, strangely enough, the film was previewed several months later.

Then C. K. Phillips took off for location in an S.E.5. He opened the throttle and the ground dropped away as the plane rose on the warm air currents, climbing steeply. A few moments later the engine coughed intermittently, then cut out to solid silence. With only five hundred feet of altitude and one small field available, Phillips decided to land deadstick. He dropped the nose fast and the sighing wind in the wires rose to a shrill pitch as the field grew larger. He flared out, rolled his wheels on the turf, and slowed to a stop. A few minutes later mechanics had remedied the engine's trouble, or so they thought. The propeller was swung, caught, and the engine settled into an even roar. Phillips gave a nod to the men and sped down the field again. At a hundred feet the engine coughed twice and quit. Phillips was desperately low, but he turned the trim English Scout on the axis of its stubby wing and banked back toward the postage-stamp field. He came in fast, struck at an awkward angle, and in a skidding, slithering crescendo of splintering wood and twanging metal the S.E.5 was destroyed.

The mechanics rushed up as the dust settled, to find the cockpit intact. Phillips slumped limply with only a small cut on his forehead. But as they lifted him from the plane they saw his head was loose on his neck. There was no heartbeat. The jinx had caught up with another flying double.

Several of the German warplanes were original Fokker

D-7s. Their solid, coffin-shaped fuselages against the clouds gave just the ominous effect Hughes wanted, but more were needed. Under the skilled technical artistry of J. B. Alexander, Travelaire 4000s were cleverly modified into "Wichita Fokkers" that made veteran pilots look twice to distinguish them from the genuine article. The sky fleet was seriously depleted when three of the original D-7s were completely scrapped due to forced landings.

Clarke had his problems in trying to herd the German and Allied squadrons together for the proper effects. The lack of cloud backgrounds delayed the filming four months. Fighters drifted out of camera range and camera mechanisms jammed. All-too-realistic engine failures frequently dropped four to six pilots at a time from the mock battles.

Clarke watched as two fighters collided and spun away out of control. They were flown by Ira Reed and Stuart Murphy. One pilot hurled himself from the S.E.5's cockpit, tumbled downward in a delayed drop to clear the falling wreckage, and popped his chute open below the battle. It was Murphy. Reed, in the fractured Fokker, limped off in erratic maneuvers and disappeared.

Back on the ground Clarke met Reed trudging home. He had flown his tattered biplane forty miles before all the fabric peeled from a wing panel to expose two sheared spars.

"Hey, Spooks!" he shouted to Clarke. "I won't get fired, will I? I set her down O.K."

"Not a chance," Clarke laughed. "You looked great on film."

An unusual and highly realistic effect was born when someone decided to cast the actual pilots in important roles. Frank Clarke and Roy Wilson had cameras attached to their planes fore and aft of the cockpits. They could operate them remotely and the result was an awesome, vicarious ride by the audience as pursuer and pursued flung themselves dizzily about the sky. Not a single frame of trick photography was used in the entire fight sequence.

The script called for the two American pilots to fly a captured Gotha on a sneak bombing mission behind the German lines. But even Howard Hughes could not find a Gotha—they no longer existed. So Hughes settled for an old Sikorsky S-29, which he bought from dashing Colonel Roscoe Turner with the understanding the mustachioed flier would pilot the big twin-engine monster to Hollywood and fly it in the bombing takes.

The stars earned their pay in this segment of the picture. Ben Lyon and James Hall were clearly visible in the air-to-air shots as Roscoe Turner, out of sight inside the fuselage, flew the bomber. No mock-ups; it was the real thing. Held in with two slender straps connected to a wide leather belt around his waist, Lyon stood up boldly in the observer's well. Because he was willing to fly in this precarious position, the false, simulated process shots were unnecessary and the ultimate daring realism was captured on celluloid. Such hazardous exposure of current movie idols is unthinkable in present-day Hollywood.

In one scene the "Gotha" was to fall into a spin, and it was understood by all that getting it out would be virtually impossible. Turner had contracted only for the bomber scenes, so someone else had to be hired for this sequence. Jimmy Angel turned down the offer and Dick Grace was queried about the job for $250. He made no bones about his thoughts on the matter. To Frank Clarke he replied: "If I spin it and get it out, you pay me ten thousand. If I don't and ride her down, you collect the ten thousand from my estate."

Clarke shook his head. "No, thanks."

It happened that Clarke's friendly rival, Roy Wilson, agreed to do the job. With mechanic Phil Jones in the tail of the S-29 to work the smoke pots, Wilson leveled the rumbling giant at seventy-five hundred feet and throttled the engines. He signaled the camera planes and Jones lit the first smoke pot.

Wilson stalled the plane, felt it shudder, and kicked the rudder. Down and around it went, vibrating and creaking. At the predetermined altitude Wilson tried to recover. Nothing happened; the wild rotation simply got tighter. He shouted backward through the fuselage, "*Get out Jones.* . . . *Jump!*" then he slipped over the side and opened his chute. He looked for Jones' chute, but there was nothing.

Clarke, in a camera plane, followed the spinning bomber down. He saw the smoke stop, then start again. Clarke realized then that Jones was so busily engaged in the tail, lighting the second pot, he was unaware of the danger. Jones rode the doomed plane to his death as it smashed into an orange grove and exploded.

Jim Barton was twenty-four when he flew in *Wings* with Dick Grace. Later he was a pilot and mechanic for *Hell's Angels*. Retired today in Westwood, California, he remembers the filming episodes well.

In late December, before the big bomber scene in *Hell's Angels*, I was flying in the ship with Ned Schram. My chute was accidently opened in the cabin. Ned grabbed my pilot chute and saved me from being pulled out of the plane at nine thousand feet. A couple of days later Phil Jones took my place to earn a hundred dollars and ride with Wilson, and was killed when the bomber crashed in the San Fernando Valley.

I was kept pretty busy looking after Frank Clarke's Fokker D-7. I changed the rear cylinder and spark plugs on it almost daily. We had to remove the gas tank once and shake all the loose solder from the inside of it; Frank had a forced landing when it cut off his gas.

Frank flew over four hundred hours in that D-7 and in those days four hundred hours was a lot of time for a pilot—in one airplane. During World War One the German aces averaged a little over three hundred flying hours in several types of planes. At the 1936 National Air Races in Los Angeles, while Ernst Udet admired Frank's stunt flying, someone told the German how much time Clarke had in the D-7. Udet was astonished.

It was a great life and lots of fun for many years. They were very happy days.

Sixteen months after the first dramatic scene was shot, the film that would make cinematic—and aviation—history was practically "in the can."

Then, almost overnight, the silent film era died as talkies came into being. The only one unperturbed by the innovation of sound to motion pictures was Hughes. With so much already invested, he considered it ridiculous to release *Hell's Angels* as a silent production. He passed the word. Dub the sound into the flying footage; engines, machine guns, and crashes. Scrap the silent dramatic sequences and start over. Greta Nissen's heavy accent was objectionable, however; her film role was that of an English canteen girl. Hughes paid her off and found a replacement—a platinum blond bit player named Harleen Carpenter, whose name he changed to Jean Harlow—and once again *Hell's Angels* was in production. The final scene, with seventeen hundred ex-American doughboys, was shot December 7, 1929—two years, one month, and seven days after the film was begun.

Hell's Angels cost well over four million dollars. More than two million feet of film was exposed by thirty-five camera men and thirty-seven camera ships, to record the flying scenes of nearly ninety airplanes. The film used 137 pilots and a similar number of mechanics. In the mock air battles a total of 227,000 miles were flown and over twenty thousand extras were used in the picture. Three men died in bringing to the screen the undisputed champion of all air-war films.

* * *

Dawn Patrol was an epic of the early 1930s with Richard Barthelmess and Douglas Fairbanks. Late in 1938 it was remade with Errol Flynn and David Niven in the leading roles. For stunt pilot Earl Robinson it was very nearly the last film in which he appeared.

Robinson was one of two Allied fighter pilots bombing a German airfield. After a long strafing run at low altitude they were to swoop low over a row of enemy machines lined up on the ground. As Robinson, who would be trailing, passed over the last plane at less than fifty feet, a demolitions man would set off sixty sticks of dynamite in one of the parked aircraft. Precise timing was essential; for the effect of a dropped bomb the explosion must not be too early or too late.

The flier had never worked with this demolitions man before and was unsure of what to expect. He looked capable, but . . . sixty sticks of dynamite?

The day of shooting arrived and Robinson could not shake his apprehension. The cameras were set up and waiting and there was no rehearsal; the first time was the take. Robinson sat in the cockpit of his scout as the engine warmed. The man who would push the button stood silently beside the cockpit. Robinson thought he looked edgy, but pulling his goggles over his eyes, he turned and shouted over the engine: "Just wait until I get over the last plane and then let her go!" The man nodded.

Chocks were flicked away from the snub-nosed fighter's wheels and Robinson rolled into the wind behind his partner. They circled the field twice.

The *Dawn Patrol* planes were equipped with short-wave receivers over which the pilots received their instructions. The order came for the attack run and with the lead machine ahead, Robinson pushed the stick forward at two thousand feet. From the outboard wing struts the red silk streamers tautened in the descent. The wires began to sing and the deafening engine pounded in his ears. Slowly, at four hundred feet, Robinson began to ease out of the screaming dive. His partner was three hundred feet dead ahead—and so was the line of planes. He let his fighter roll on unchecked; his altitude was one hundred feet and he was still diving. As the engineers and cameramen came into distinct focus his view was momentarily cut off as he skimmed a hangar roof. At fifteen feet he swept over the first of the German machines at 160 miles an hour. It was going to be a great shot.

The lead planes cleared the row. Robinson swallowed as he closed in on the dynamite-loaded plane. He cringed inwardly and gritted his teeth. He was over it, and sure enough it happened.

A mushroom of black dirt and flying debris reached upward into Robinson's propeller. The entire upper wing of the disintegrating plane rose upward on the crest of the explosion and was knocked down by the scout's landing gear.

All he could recall of the mishap was the pressure shock and the sound of the terrific explosion that almost ruptured his eardrums, the choking dust and smoke, and the shower of earth and debris. He was blown seventy-five feet upward.

The plane staggered to fifteen hundred feet and leveled off, its engine vibrating so violently it threatened to tear loose from its mountings. Robinson idled it. All four of his wing panels had gaping holes and streamed tattered fabric. For an instant Robinson considered bailing out but decided against it. With the plane barely holding together, he landed carefully and killed the engine in front of the hangars. The directors and crew rushed to the perforated plane, expecting the worst. The explosives technician was among them, pale and trembling. When he saw Robinson was unscathed, he staggered behind a hangar and was violently sick.

This was one of the few new flying scenes in the new *Dawn Patrol*. When Warner Brothers executives reviewed the original version they declared the scenes so realistic they decided to use them in the 1938 remake.

"Mister, stay out of airplanes or you'll break your neck!" The scene was March Field, California, and these were the final words of an Air Service lieutenant to the young cadet he had just washed out of flying school. The young man didn't follow his instructor's advice; instead, Albert Paul Mantz carved out a flying career that was unmatched for sheer versatility and excitement.

As the early Hollywood pilots go, Paul Mantz was a late comer—if you call 1938 late. Of earlier *Test Pilot* fame, Mantz was technical director for William Wellman's *Men With Wings* starring Ray Milland and Fred MacMurray. The film boasted another "first" in Hollywood's history. It was the first air combat picture to be shot entirely in Technicolor. Blue skies filled with huge white-coated cloudbanks. No old stock shots from former war films here.

Mantz was faced with a herculean task from the beginning, for the earlier air war films had all but depleted the supply of authentic and original airplanes. Few remained flyable; their comrades of the war years were gone—burned, crashed, rotting, or sitting stiffly in museums. After ten months Mantz located them in obscure places and fifty mechanics worked to get the condemned and obsolete birds flying again. They brought them back to life to fly once more, many for the last time, and groomed them for another film epic of the air. Several old planes used in *Hell's Angels* flew again, including the "Wichita Fokkers"—the modified Travelaires. In no other film was there such a variety of flying equipment, everything from early pusher biplanes, Pfalz D-12s, Bristol Fighters, Spads, S.E.5s, Fokkers, and Nieuport 28s. And it was Mantz's job to check them out.

It was while testing one of the rebuilt biplanes before the

filming was begun that Mantz almost "bought it." He opened the throttle to take off and as he began to lift, the engine choked and thick black smoke swept back from the exhaust. Mantz cut the engine. As the plane lost forward speed, it caught fire. The fire engine and rescue crew extinguished the flames quickly as Mantz jumped from the still-rolling plane.

In one flying sequence with Dick Clarke, Mantz in an S.E.5 and Clarke in a Fokker had a wingtip to wingtip collision and each nearly lost control.

Men With Wings had several near-fatalities. "Chubby" Gordon took up a Nieuport 28 to make sound track recording of its unique 165-horsepower Gnome rotary engine. He flew the plane over the field several times for distance recordings, then dove it at the field for wide-open engine recordings. Finally, he prepared to make landings.

As planes equipped with rotary engines approach the field, they alternately cut out and open the engine with a coupé button, a small, spring-loaded switch on top of the control stick. There is no throttle to reduce the engine speed to idle; the engine is fully on or fully off and the pilot relies on the windmilling propeller to "catch" the engine when he needs power.

Gordon swept over the edge of the field and cut the engine while still several hundred feet from the sound crew. As he neared the cluster of men he released the button, expecting the Gnome to burst into its blattering roar. Instead, there was only the wind whistling through the brace wires. The engine refused to catch and squarely in front of his flicking propeller were the startled faces of the technicians, frozen in surprise. Gordon sweated, and barely skimmed their heads as they scattered. The Nieuport touched down just beyond them. In a few minutes a mechanic cleared the difficulty—a clogged fuel line.

The fire ship of the film was a pseudo-Fokker, an old

OX-5 Travelaire, that carried special—and heavy—equipment to produce one of the most realistic fire scenes ever put on film. While other "burning" planes trailed black billowing smoke, this one spouted "flames" as well. A tank of CO_2 extinguisher gas, in which was suspended orange tetra-ethyl, forced the contents under pressure into a long pipe under the Travelaire's fuselage. It entered the air appearing as a long stream of orange fire. A second pipe released a burning chemical for the black smoke effect.

The weight of the special equipment very nearly made the plane a genuine fire ship. Dick Rinaldi was flying it back from a dogfight with eight other German planes when its engine sputtered and cut out over Santa Ana. Burdened by the heavy fire scene apparatus, Rinaldi lost altitude fast. He selected a long, dark green field. Too late, he realized it was an asparagus field, and that he had committed himself. He touched down fast and his wheels rumbled through the vegetation. They hit a small gulley and over went the plane on its back. Rinaldi was unhurt. After a new wing and tail, Mantz, Rinaldi, and others were shot down eight times in it before they created the effect director Wellman wanted.

Mantz saw that money, adventure, and fun went hand in glove in this lusty new industry and decided to become Hollywood's aviation caterer. A serious man with a flair for flamboyant clothes and all things dramatic, Mantz flew through open hangar doors in *Air Mail* until the trick almost became his trademark. For *Blaze of Noon* he spun a plane into the ground. For *Twelve O'Clock High* he flew a B-17 solo and bellied it gear up, the only man ever to take a B-17 off alone. But he was quick to point out: "Lots of pilots brought their Fortresses home 'solo' when their crews were shot up."

In *Flying Leatherneck* he made a low pass in a B-25 when ten cases of dynamite exploded prematurely. "That one," he said, "singed my pinfeathers." After flying in more than two hundred and fifty movies, his only injury was a broken collar bone while filming *Central Airport*. He aimed his plane to collide with another on the ground, then leaped out. But his plane turned around and chased him, and caught him!

During World War II, General "Hap" Arnold commissioned Mantz a full colonel and turned the Hal Roach studio and a supporting cast of famous actors over to him. His assignment: Turn out expert aerial photographers and hard-hitting Air Corps training films. He did, even to the extent of piloting a B-17 up the treacherous Greenland fjords to make a film so ferry pilots could learn how to maneuver into Bluie West One and other nightmarish landing fields.

After the war Mantz continued to fly for films and to direct aviation scenes. He won the Bendix air race in his trimmed-down Merlin-powered Mustang three straight years. From the combination pilot-seat and director's chair in his special-equipped B-25, Mantz supervised the aerial filming for *Strategic Air Command, Spirit of St. Louis,* and *The Crowded Sky*. The secret of his durability? "Nine o'clock," he said, "is sack time for me—regardless."

Barnstormers, race pilots, stunt men, and movie pilots—they were all these rolled into one, and few of the old-time Hollywood pilots are living today. In World War II, Dick Grace wrangled his way into combat with the 486th Bomb Group and flew B-17s and B-24s into combat over Germany. He died in 1965. Frank Clarke, with passenger Mark Owen, died on Friday the thirteenth in June 1948, when he put on a low-level air show in a BT-13 for his old flying comrade Frank Tomick. Paul Mantz crashed to his death in the summer of 1965, flying the big scene in Twentieth Century-Fox's *Flight of the Phoenix*.

The breathtaking air war scenes of the past—panoramas of majestic heights and billowing clouds with angry, growling biplanes snarling and stuttering round and round—were made by men who left behind a record on celluloid that still thrills viewers of the late TV show. It was a record not played against a canvas sky, but against the real heavens.

14

Four Weeks in the Air

Every day, thousands of feet above the earth, pilots of supersonic jets nudge their bullet-nose fighters into a refueling hose that trails from an airborne tanker. They are probably unaware that this sophisticated technique was pioneered over thirty-five years ago in the thermal-ridden skies over Meridian, Mississippi, by two air-minded brothers who struggled to hold on to their city's failing airport and their own dreams for aviation's future.

Where these young visionaries made their record-breaking flight in the depression days of 1935, sleek jet airliners and military aircraft whistle in and out of Key Field, named for the pilots who remained aloft for twenty-seven days by continually refueling their Curtiss Robin in midair. Their official record remains unbroken today.

Because Fred Maurice and Algene Earl Key didn't know how to quit, no flight in aviation's history demonstrated more dramatically the reliability of the steadily improving aircraft engine. For almost a month they lived and worked together in a spectacular show of teamwork in midair refueling. Today this is a vital link in America's long-range global air defense. During the Keys' grueling endurance flight the engine in their small monoplane consumed six thousand gallons of gasoline and three hundred gallons of oil. They made 438 perfect air-to-air contacts with their refueling plane, and their 165-horsepower Wright J-6-5 engine turned the propeller 61,217,700 times without a misfire. In their circling and meandering flight they traveled 52,320 miles—equal to nine times around the earth—and really never left home.

The determination to succeed despite one defeat after another had its roots in the boys' childhood and in the training of parents who taught the value of persistence in reaching success. Al and Fred were born in a farm home in Kemper County, about twenty-five miles north of Meridian. Their father was a doctor, and their mother, anxious that her sons become well educated, saw that they had books early in life. After their famous flight she proudly recalled one of their first readings. It went: "The little boy who says 'I'll try,' will climb to the hilltop."

When his formal schooling ended, Al married, and he and his wife worked for two years in a music store. But he was restless; life behind a music counter was not for him. He had a strong liking for airplanes and he wanted to fly. In 1923 he took his first lesson, which opened new horizons. When his restlessness could no longer be contained, he went to Marshall, Missouri.

In the mid-1920s he learned to fly under the instruction of Claude Sterling and Barney Zimmerly of the then famous Nicholas Beazley Flying School. Fred learned to fly a year later and joined Al in their first flying adventure together— an air training school in Sedalia, Missouri. While there, Al flew a student to Meridian in an ancient aircraft that forced them down twenty-two times en route.

These were boom times and, caught up with the novel aviation expansion of the postwar years, the city of Meridian floated a $75,000 bond issue in 1927 to build an airport three miles south of town. Meanwhile Fred had married, and both fliers, thinking of families and stability, returned to Meridian and opened a flying school. But barnstorming, Sunday afternoon rides, and an occasional student were barely enough to meet expenses, for Meridian wasn't as air-minded as some communities. The going was hard. For a while, Al went to work as a patrol pilot for the Alabama Forestry Department. In 1929, right in the teeth of the Depression, he and Fred were appointed managers of the new Meridian Municipal Airport. The brothers stuck to their shoestring operation as unemployment worsened. In the words of one Meridian native: "Just about the only thing people could do in those times was go fishin' or watch a ball game; there wasn't much interest in airplanes."

Somehow the brothers provided for their families with a handful of commercial jobs, more barnstorming, and an occasional student. But matters failed to improve despite their efforts to make the field go. Remembering those dismal times and the many idle hours they spent in the big, cool brick hangar—hours that sparked the quiet desperation that precipitated the record flight—Al Key says: "The future of the airport was endangered. Meridian was a railroad town then, and some people wanted to plow up the field and plant it in corn and cotton. We knew we had to do something to get the public interested, so we decided on an endurance flight. In July 1929, Jackson and O'Brien circled St. Louis for 420 hours. In 1930 the Hunter brothers of Chicago set a new record of 533 hours, and Jackson and O'Brien beat that with a new time of 647 hours. We believed we could top that.

"It wasn't a stunt—we put a lot of planning and hard work into it," Al relates. "If successful, we thought it would be fine training for a nonstop round-the-world flight later on. We talked with Senator Pat Harrison and very nearly had arrangements completed for military assistance at various refueling places around the globe. But he died suddenly and before we could do more, World War Two was on us, so we abandoned that idea."

Photographer-journalist A. G. Weems was a young man at the time. He remembers:

> It was a dream at first, but in the summer of 1932 I did a lot of loafing around that hangar, and I saw their dream grow. Then the summer was gone and so were the hopes of everyone—except Al and Fred. They talked up the idea every chance they got and it was helped along by other pilots who were doing the same thing in other parts of the country.

W. H. Ward, a friend, had a Curtiss Robin which was put at the Keys' disposal and immediately the necessary modification work began.

The Keys were fortunate to have the help of A. D. Hunter, a skilled machinist whose lack of formal training in mechanical engineering was no handicap. He is still in the employ of the Key Flying Service. Hunter's inventive genius and timely innovations kept the Robin airborne. In many ways the attempt was a community effort in which friends, aware of the importance of the endurance flight, freely gave their time and talents. Dave Stevenson, a welder, designed a catwalk of aircraft tubing and fit it along both sides of the engine. Frank Covert custom-designed a hundred-gallon aluminum fuel tank and fit it into the Robin. The front of the tank was shaped into a pilot's seat. The container was as wide as the fuselage and extended five feet behind the pilot. A small space was left between the top of the tank and the ceiling of the fuselage. This allowed the pilots to slide back into the baggage compartment, which was equipped with a light mattress to support the body for a makeshift bed. Their legs had to rest on top of the tank. The filler neck was at one side and a large sliding panel could be moved back to expose the top of the tank. It was agreed that Fred, the smaller and lighter of the two, would handle the refueling and maintenance as well as relieve Al at the controls.

Hunter, having studied the earlier, crude refueling hardware, designed and built a refueling nozzle that would automatically stop the fuel flow when it separated from the fuel tank filler neck. "The refueling line was a one-and-one-quarter-inch rubber hose that came down from the supply tank in the refueling Robin," Hunter explains today. "I weighted the end of it with fifty pounds of lead tapered into a tear-drop shape, and wrapped smooth with tape. We heard rumors that on an earlier air-to-air endurance flight, a hand guard on the end of the hose caused one man to be pulled out. I designed this one so nothing could hang on it. Inside the nozzle I put an inch and a quarter brass check valve that was held closed by the weight of the fuel on top of it. And because we were safety conscious, a grounding arrangement was designed to connect the two airplanes together—before inserting the hose for refueling—to prevent an explosion or fire that could be triggered by static electricity.

"When Fred would insert the nozzle, a small bar inside the tank neck pushed the check valve open and the fuel flowed into the tank by gravity. When the nozzle was lifted out, the check valve closed immediately and the fuel flow stopped. It was the granddaddy of all midair refueling nozzles," the short, tanned machinist said. This ingenious design was modified only slightly for supersonic military jet in-flight refueling by replacing the spring-loaded brass check valve with an electrically operated solenoid for even faster fuel shut-off at separation.

Slowly, as small amounts of money were made available from scattered sources, the plane was readied. Because Al and Fred were licensed amateur radio operators, they got permission to make one station mobile, installed in the aircraft, and use the other as a ground station for two-way communication. The cowling and nacelle covers were removed to allow inflight engine servicing, and an oversize battery and generator were installed to provide the extra current for the added instruments. The pitch of the metal propeller was flattened to provide more engine power. When the plane stood ready, this Curtiss Robin, designed for a useful load of 925 pounds, would have to carry twice this amount in fuel and equipment.

Several persons suggested names for the Robin, and the one selected was *Ole Miss*. The silver plane had a Mississippi flag painted on each side of the fuselage to signify the State of Mississippi and the University of Oxford. On June 21, 1934, Miss Genevieve Lynn, one of the first women to fly in the state, and a student of Al and Fred, christened the plane as ten thousand spectators watched and waited. The national press was sparsely represented but local newspapers covered the event thoroughly. Mr. J. D. Sellers of Jackson, Mississippi, was the official representative for the National Aeronautics Association and certified the flight. He installed a sealed barograph that would continually record the time as well as the plane's altitude, and indicate whether it landed or not. Since the Key flights, no other air-to-air endurance attempts have been made with this instrument installed, and their endurance record remains the official one.

At 6:35 P.M. the *Ole Miss* lifted smoothly into the cooling evening air and began its solitary patrol. There were minor adjustment problems at first, strikingly similar to those encountered in the space flights to follow three decades later. In 1969, astronaut Frank Borman, stopping at Meridian, chatted with Hunter and compared notes on the endurance flight and space travel. Borman noted the similarities and agreed that like the Key flight the first three days were the hardest. After that, things settled into a routine.

For the first week the Robin's battery had to be exchanged

daily with a fully charged one. Al radioed to the ground crew that the propeller of their wind-driven generator, mounted on the left side of the catwalk, wasn't turning fast enough to deliver the current they needed. Hunter got to work immediately and fashioned a new propeller, which was passed down to Fred, who got out on the catwalk and made the change. It performed perfectly.

But this flight was doomed to fail from the start. "We thought we had the best aviation gasoline available," Al Key relates, "but something went wrong. A few nights after our takeoff I noticed flames dancing from around the base of Number 1 cylinder head. By morning the cylinder looked dangerously close to losing its head."

Al explained their problem to the ground crew, and A. D. Hunter put his machinist skills to work again. He fashioned a steel bracket to hold the head in place. It was lowered on the next refueling contact and Fred installed it. But that night another cylinder head loosened and flames were seen coming from its base. The engine was overheating and in the darkness I could see the cylinders glow a dull red. There was no indication of anything wrong according to the cylinder head temperature and oil temperature gauges, but one cylinder in particular looked dangerously close to breaking free. With this type of trouble it was impossible to continue the flight and the brothers made the decision to land. "They came down after 123 hours," Hunter says, "and we soon found the trouble. We had the fuel tested and found it to be only fifty-two octane instead of the eighty octane we required. Because the engine was operating under continuous detonation, we knew that if they had flown on any longer, the engine would have completely failed."

Failure? For the moment, yes. But the Flying Keys knew why they had failed, and the next morning they were at work again. Support for their objective was still alive as the Junior

Chamber of Commerce and the American Legion raised funds. A new engine was installed, and the old radio was augmented with a new, two-way, five-meter band radio for voice transmission. Although this was long before the day of the tiny transistor, Ben Woodruff, an imaginative local radio engineer, designed a small, highly compact set to fit into a small hole where the wing root attached to the fuselage. The base station was in the hangar, manned around the clock. "I can still hear them working," bespectacled Hunter reminisces. "W5UE calling W5ECP . . . W5UE calling W5ECP . . ."

The Keys had learned several other valuable lessons on the first abortive flight. One was not to refuel at a long distance. This set up serious hose oscillations that were dangerous in rough air. They discovered the best formation position was a tight one, where Al nudged the silver propeller arc of the *Ole Miss* under and behind the wheels of the refueling plane. The transfer was steadier as the combined slipstreams of the two planes worked together for a smoother air flow between them. And working close together was a must; that was why they selected James Keeton and W. H. Ward for their refueling team. Today, Keeton, who lives in Mobile, Alabama, is soon to retire as a pilot for United Airlines.

"Knowing the members of your team—air and ground—is all-important," Al Key asserts. "We'd tried a few professional pilots, but they were individualists. We decided on Keeton. He was a serious boy—no foolishness. We'd taught him to fly and each of us knew what the other was going to do. He could fly like an automatic pilot. It worked out fine."

Bolstered with the experiences built of the first attempt, and with new stores of the proper grade of fuel, the two men took off again on July 21. This time only fifteen hundred persons were present for the send-off.

For the first few days the flight went well. Then, on the

night of July 25, great cloud banks built up east of the city. At ten o'clock Al relieved Fred at the controls and skirted the edge of the cloud wall to see how threatening they were. The line of heavy weather was severe, and widespread. They flew first to Forest to escape it, then to Jackson and Vicksburg. Still the ugly squalls and turbulence chased them. The *Ole Miss* headed for Louisiana in the black early morning hours.

It began to look hopeless. They were flying blind and the storm was closing in on them. Their turn and bank indicator had failed three days earlier, and Al worked desperately to keep the Robin right side up with airspeed, inclinometer, and compass. Finally, his only alternative to another landing was to climb above the weather, but the storm at eleven thousand feet was even more violent. Lightning, rain, and heavy pounding gales tossed the *Ole Miss* like a cork and threatened to tear her apart. Al stuck resolutely to the controls in this, the worst weather they were to experience. Fred still bears a light scar from a canvas burn suffered that night when the oil can inside the canvas transfer bag suddenly flew off the fuel tank and brushed across his face. Al recalls their near-fatal encounter with the elements:

> The front was very turbulent and we were on instruments a lot. Night thunderstorms in particular were a problem because the plane was so heavily overloaded. This night we rode in it about two hours, and it got so rough I was thinking we might have to bail out. Fred was sitting back in the baggage compartment behind the tank, and I called back, "Better get your chute on, Fred. I don't think I'll be able to take this one!" He shouted back: "What the hell do you think I've been wearing for the last hour!"

As quickly as the storm had closed in on them, they ran out of it. They picked up their bearings on the Mississippi River south of Vicksburg, found an opening in the boiling clouds, and headed back to Meridian. Meanwhile, in the dim dawn at the airport, their families and the ground crew had amost abandoned hope. Then, as the time drew near when it would be obvious they could no longer remain in the air even if they had escaped the storm's fury, the little Robin came streaking in from the west. When the waiting refueling plane made contact, the *Ole Miss* had little gasoline remaining. The refueling was handled by a long-time friend and employee, a Negro boy by the name of Germany Johnson, who made the remark that he would climb down the hose and give them the fuel in gallon buckets if necessary.

For a short time the brothers were spared further close calls, but then the electrical storms gathered to plague the fliers again. On the night of July 27, harassed by a failing exhaust collector ring and increasingly bad weather they could not handle because of faulty instruments, they realized that they would have to come down again. After 169 hours aloft, the Robin slipped under the three-hundred-foot ceiling and touched down for the second time. "There was just too much to fight," Hunter commented. "The exhaust pipe was about to fall off and, if it did, the exhaust flame would likely have set fire to the oil-soaked belly. They'd have burned up. Al said he wouldn't try again unless he had the proper instruments and a better exhaust system."

A gyro compass and gyro horizon were badly needed. They were expensive and there was no money to spare. But with the help of Roger Hull, President of the Junior Chamber of Commerce, and Major Claire Chennault, they were available when the time arrived for the third try. The instrument experience gained by the Keys proved fortunate later on. A third of their flying time was on instruments. Later they flew a Ford trimotor quite a bit and when World War Two broke out, both were well experienced on instrument and multi-engine flying—precisely the skills the Air Corps needed.

"Before the third attempt," Hunter tells, "we overhauled

the engine, put in new rings, ground the valves, and replaced the exhaust collector ring with individual straight exhaust pipes. We made them of cast aluminum and designed them with fins for cooling and strength. There were several reasons for the straight stacks: first, they reduced back pressure and allowed more power, second, they allowed Fred and Al to get the best fuel-air mixture at night watching by the shape and color of the exhaust flame. Each of the five pipes was cut off and angled level with the pilot's line of sight. The pilot could check each magneto for proper operation, tell which cylinder had a defective spark plug, which one was misfiring, whether they had the proper mixture—in short, it allowed them to have their own engine analyzer."

After the first two attempts, the pilots found that they had difficulty walking after they landed. Even Fred, who moved about on the catwalk frequently, felt the effects of their long inactivity because he had merely braced his legs and had not exercised them. Then—as with today's prolonged space flights—exercise proved to be of paramount importance to the well-being of the crew. Several doctors were interested in the flight and devised a series of simple exercises for the brothers. With the sliding hatch open above the tank, each man took his turn lying on his back on the tank, legs extended in the slipstream, and "bicycling"—pumping his legs in the air—for several minutes at a time.

Interest in the flight had waned noticeably as the time grew near for the third takeoff. Still, the year 1935 was one of aviation—and space—achievements. Already, before the Keys were airborne, other records had been made. In January, Amelia Earhart flew solo from Hawaii to California—the first woman to do so. In March, Dr. Robert Goddard launched the first rocket to be equipped with gyroscopic stabilizing controls. And on April 30, Redpath, Snead, and Tomlinson set a new transcontinental passenger flight record aboard a TWA Douglas, flying from Los Angeles to New York in eleven hours and forty-six minutes.

The third attempt to break the world's air-to-air refueling record began at 12:32 P.M. on June 4, 1935. This time newspapers paid little attention to the two young fliers and their plane that had twice failed. In contrast with the earlier masses of well-wishers, the Meridian *Star* could only report: "A good crowd of about 100 persons was present . . ." A. D. Hunter says: "When they took off they didn't have a dollar—they'd sunk *everything* into that flight—but they believed they could do it."

Al Key's comment on that departure was: "We'd all worked so doggone hard we were exhausted by the intense preparations, the tensions, and the last-minute planning. It was a relief to be through with all that, and for me that takeoff was the most exciting part of the whole flight."

Again, after the first few days, the steady popping drone of the engine became commonplace, but after ten days the news releases grew longer. After the second week, reporters began checking into Meridian's hotels in a steady stream. In Europe curious crowds gathered around bulletin boards outside newspaper offices to await the latest report on the marathon Americans.

Quarters were cramped in the three-place Robin, especially when the pilots changed places for their turn at the controls. The relieving pilot had to slide between the top of the tank and the fuselage ceiling while the pilot being relieved squirmed tightly onto the bed atop the tank for some rest. Sleep for each pilot, in small amounts, averaged four hours a day. No schedule could be followed. They exchanged places when necessary, but as Fred was nearly exhausted when he came in from his maintenance duties on the catwalk, Al's turn at the controls was usually longer by two or three hours to allow Fred to catch up on his rest. Night hours weren't particularly difficult," he remembers, "in fact, for the first two weeks it was unusually cold at night and this kept us alert. The most difficult time for me to keep awake was from about an hour before daylight to a half hour after sunrise."

On June 15 the Hunter brothers sent the Keys a good-luck message that was read to the men over the radio.

The refueling operations continued smoothly and reflected the efficient organization and soundness of their safety planning around the large fuselage tank. "On the average," Al Key explains, "we burned about ten gallons an hour which, with full wing tanks, gave us enough fuel to stretch for almost sixteen hours. There were times when this safety margin saved the day for us."

There were two refueling rendezvous. One was in the early morning about 7 A.M. while the air was still smooth. The hose was lowered from the Robin overhead and poured into the *Ole Miss* at the rate of sixty gallons every six minutes. Then came the oil, lowered by rope in a five-gallon can inside a canvas bag. After that came the food. It too came down by rope in a canvas bag, weighted with thirty pounds of buckshot sewed in the bottom. Inside the bag was a two-gallon ice cream container that held the hot food and lots of orange juice. When the oscillations stopped, the *Ole Miss* slipped under the canvas bag, Fred unhooked it and sent up the empty can.

When the plane was light and low on fuel, Al decreased the power setting and could maintain about 100 mph airspeed. As they took on fuel—and weight—he had to increase the power while the airspeed dropped to 90 mph as they became fully loaded.

The other refueling transfer took place in the evening as soon as the air calmed down. Sometimes the air never calmed when thunderstorms were nearby. During these times the dangling fuel hose built up a heavy charge of static electricity.

Al Key recalls: "I could actually hear the static discharge when Fred grabbed the hose. It was terribly unnerving and painful —and of course he sometimes yelled out a not-so-nice comment when it hit him." After the fuselage tank was filled, the hand-operated wobble pump in the cabin was needed to transfer the fuel to the two twenty-five gallon wing tanks as needed. Moving a half cup of fuel for every stroke required considerable pumping, and both men claimed well-developed right arms at the end of the flight. A crackling electrical storm and severe gusts buffeted the small airplane and the seventy-third refueling contact was successfully completed. On June 22 they broke the Hunter brothers' official record. Next goal: the unofficial record of twenty-three days set by Jackson and O'Brien.

All during their flight Keeton never left the field. He even had his barber come out to the hangar and cut his hair.

On June 24, as the 485th hour passed into the record, a crisis arose when an abscess developed under one of Al's teeth. His father, Dr. E. B. Key, had sent up medical advice for a week, but now, as the trouble became serious, it was aggravated by Al's loss of sleep and threatened to end their third attempt for the record. Dr. Key called in a dentist who, over the radio, told Al how to lance the painful abscess himself. The plucky older brother set to work. "We had some absorbent cotton, also some iodine and a curved surgical needle used to repair tears in the fabric. I wrapped some cotton around the needle, saturated it with iodine, just inserted it in my gum, gave it a yank—and got relief. I think I slept for a full day afterward."

As the flight time mounted, so did the enthusiasm of the townspeople. The engine was the last noise they heard at night and the first sound they recognized before rising in the morning. On June 26, only thirty-nine hours away from the record, tension began to mount noticeably on the ground.

Although much of the flight was routine, it was not without its anxious moments. Fred, because of his hazardous outside work, had a few minor scrapes. One time he was stunned when the heavy hose end slipped from his grasp and struck his face.

At three-thirteen on June 27 the Jackson and O'Brien record was broken as thousands streamed onto the airport. A band played "Praise God From Whom All Blessings Flow," after which Al radioed: "We're going to stay up until the Fourth of July—if we can." It was all downhill now.

One night Jimmy Haizlip, the pilot of a Shell Oil Company plane, whom the Keys knew well, decided to give the boys a thrill. With all lights off he flew directly toward them in the darkness and as the space between the onrushing planes narrowed to a few hundred feet, the Shell pilot snapped on his bright landing lights squarely in front of the *Ole Miss*. Al smiles about it today. "It's a wonder we didn't pull the wings off, I dived so fast. You can't imagine how it looks to suddenly see someone heading right for you with his landing lights on. We'd just finished laying out our dinner on the gasoline tank and you know where it went! I think we both could have killed him right there if we could have got our hands on him. He sure had a laugh on us."

But there were humorous moments, too. One town resident had the ground crew radio this message to the Keys:

Please fly over my house every morning at five o'clock. My wife is worried and won't let me sleep mornings until she's sure you fellows are still up there.

Or the joke that made the rounds about Mary Louise contemplating suing Fred for divorce, charging desertion.

On the ground, the maintenance men had their fun as well. A. D. Hunter, a smile on his weathered, friendly face that is like rich, tanned leather, recalls: "There were about a dozen outside reporters and newsreel cameramen here, all waiting for something to happen. Every time it rained hard one of us would spread the word: 'They're going to come down!' And this one cameraman in particular would scramble outside and set up his equipment in the downpour. After he got drenched a few times he got wise."

The *Ole Miss* flew on at a steady 90 to 100 mph, keeping a loose circuit around the town except when bad weather forced the men to detour. When they had to fly on top of the cloud cover at night, the radio was of little help so they took a sighting on the North Star and flew a timed course. On this flight the barograph recorded their highest altitude for the flight—twelve thousand feet.

"I think we ate better during the endurance flight than before or since," Al says. "People were very generous with food and a famous restaurant here in Meridian, Henry Weideman's, kept us well supplied. Then, our wives, Mary Louise and Evelyn, still worried that we might not be eating too well, decided to stay at the field and prepare home-cooked meals to send aloft. I lost twenty pounds during the flight; Fred lost seventeen. But it certainly wasn't for lack of food."

Fred, twenty-six at the time, was the smaller and lighter of the two. In early 1970 the sharp-featured, gray-eyed younger brother tapped an active memory in relating his activities on the catwalk. "I wore a helmet and goggles. For safety I had an ordinary lineman's harness around my middle with two straps that could be clipped to the catwalk railing at various places. Once on the catwalk I hooked my toes under the tubing to brace myself. Long hours in the cabin were confining and pretty hard on a fellow," Fred explained, "so it was something of a change to get outside where I could move around.

"It wasn't too difficult working in the slipstream—especially directly behind the propeller and engine where the air was turbulent and boiling. Oil and Marfax grease were everywhere. On one occasion I was leaving the cabin and moving onto the catwalk. I'd just fastened one of the hooks when we hit rough air. Before I could get a good hold it bounced me into the air and for a few seconds I was hanging on one strap. Al said later the sight shook him. Of course we had parachutes but I couldn't wear one out there; they were stored in the back.

"I went out twice a day to grease the rocker arms, change oil, and lubricate the magneto cams. At one time I had to repair an oil leak. The BG spark plugs were never changed. Another time I was faced with the problem of grease that had splashed onto the magneto points and might have shorted the plugs. I used some carbon tetrachloride in our fire extinguisher to dissolve it."

On one of his routine inspections, Fred discovered the right tire had deflated. When the word got out, a New York stunt parachutist offered to transfer in midair from the refueling plane onto the *Ole Miss,* exchange the wheel, then parachute to earth. The proposal was radioed to Al. His reply: "I'm more afraid of the stunt man than of the flat tire."

On the twenty-ninth, Chennault and his acrobatic team known as The Men on the Flying Trapeze performed for Victory Day at the field. Unknown to the Keys the airport had been renamed Key Field in their honor. Fred sent down word that the engine was "smiling all over now."

There was a close call and plenty of excitement on the morning of June 30. James Keeton took a newsreel cameraman up just after daylight to "catch them sleeping" and to get some novel film footage. Keeton flew above them, then slowly descended to narrow the gap so the photographer could get a closeup of Fred asleep on top of the tank. As yet Al, at the controls, was unaware of their proximity. Keeton nudged closer, keeping a sharp eye on Al. Near Al's feet was an oil can with a flexible metal spout used in changing the engine oil. Suddenly Al looked up quickly and saw the other Robin. In that instant, startled, and thinking the plane was likely to collide with them, he acted instinctively. In one movement he dived and slid away from the other plane. The movement was so sudden it lifted the oil can from the floor and the metal neck hit the electrical bus bar, shorted out the radio wires—and the insulation caught fire.

In the other machine the cameraman saw the smoke and shouted to Keeton: "Stay with 'em . . . Stay with 'em! They're burning!" as he continued to grind away with his newsreel camera. Hunter recalled the incident and grins, "I think the newsreel man was disappointed. Al cut the battery switch immediately and put out the fire with the extinguisher."

The *Ole Miss* lost some altitude in the emergency, and dropped to within two hundred feet of the ground. Wire was sent up; they repaired the burned connections and flew on.

Their biggest worry turned out to be the left stabilizer brace on the tail section. "The boys could have gone on," Hunter asserts, "if it wasn't for the risk of losing the plane's tail. On the catwalk, Fred noticed the left side of the stabilizer brace was loose underneath the tail. The bolt had a quarter of an inch slack and moved back and forth in rough air. Fred watched it but of course couldn't get to it. I went up in another plane and got under the Robin as close as possible to have a look but couldn't get to it either. There was no way to tell how dangerous the situation was or how long it would hold. That's when Al and Fred decided to end the flight—and it was the only deciding factor."

On the morning of July 1, Al told the ground crew they would end the flight that evening. As the time neared, cars and thirty thousand spectators converged on the airport, resulting in a traffic jam that wasn't unsnarled until 2 A.M. the next day.

"I was just a lad of seven then," J. B. Skewes, editor of the

Meridian *Star* remembers, "and went out to see them land. The *Star* had pledged a hundred dollars a day for each day aloft after they broke the record."

"Landing with the flat tire was not of great concern to them," Hunter says, "but the newsmen just *knew* they were going to tear it up when they landed. It was another disappointment for them."

At 6:06 P.M. the weary brothers who wouldn't quit glided down and their plane settled onto the field amid a roaring ovation. After three years of planning and two abortive flights, their dream had come true. The Keys' impression of that moment was: "It was tremendous."

Mrs. Fred Key recalled the reunion this way: "They had heavy beards and were covered with oil. It had soaked into their skin. We finally decided to take them to the state mental hospital to soak in steam baths for a few hours." Fred added: "For a while, we thought they might leave us there—some folks were sure anyone who'd stay up in an airplane for twenty-seven days had to be crazy!"

In 1939, when war threatened in Europe, military aviation took on new meaning in America. Al and Fred had trained enough pilots in Meridian to man the Air National Guard squadron that Al and Major Allison Hollifield organized there. Both brothers entered the Army Air Corps before America was in the hostilities. They were ferrying bombers to Newfoundland for submarine patrol when the Japanese bombed Pearl Harbor. Soon afterward Fred, a lieutenant, and Al, a captain, were ordered to Java with a group of B-17Es. Fred's bomber was named *Ole Miss II* and Al's was *Ole Miss III*. The E model of the B-17 was the first equipped with tail guns to reach the combat zone. Prior to this, American B-17 aircrew casualties had been high as the Japanese Zeroes swarmed in on the unprotected bomber tails. On their first mission, the two *Ole Misses* changed the odds drastically.

Again the Zeroes zoomed in, unaware of the deadly stingers in each bomber's tail. Before the startled enemy pilots could collect their senses, several of the fighters literally disintegrated from the impact of the twin fifties. Fred flew his B-17 for 750 hours in combat. When he left it after a year to return to the States, it was renamed *The Guinea Pig* and flown another 750 hours before it was put into retirement.

Al went to Europe for heavy bombardment raids on Hitler's European fortress and for three years was "in the thick of things." Fred taught instrument flying in Nebraska. When a class was graduated he led it across the North Atlantic to England, where the brothers occasionally met. At the end of the war both men were heavily decorated. Their awards included the Distinguished Flying Cross, Distinguished Service Cross, British D.F.C., Legion of Merit, Air Medals, and citations for valor. Fred returned to Meridian after the war to manage Key Field again. Al remained in the Air Force and was assigned to the All Weather Flying Center as director of operations. He flew many research projects, among them: Automatic flight, Cosmic Ray Research, All Weather Airline (twenty-eight months of operations from Clinton County to Andrews Air Force Base, Washington, on a plus or minus thirty-second schedule throughout the period). There was a thunderstorm project that called for skilled pilots to fly directly into hurricanes and thunderstorms. "Of all my flying experiences," Al recalls, "these were by far the most rewarding. We learned a lot that was passed on to less experienced pilots about flying in severe weather." After his retirement from the Air Force, Colonel Key returned to Meridian and is now in his second term as mayor of Mississippi's *Queen City*.

And what of the original *Ole Miss?* From 1935 until World War II, the Robin remained in Meridian. During the war it was stored in Newton, Mississippi. From 1948 until 1955 it was dismantled and stored again at Meridian. Then it was requested for the Smithsonian. "We had no ideas about rebuilding it," Hunter recalls, "much less fly it to the Smithsonian. And we had only from January to July to do it. The engine was in the worst shape. It had rusted in the rain. We sandblasted it, put in new rings and rebuilt the plane. It made its test flight one hour before it was scheduled to leave for Washington. Fred flew it up; Al was still in the Air Force."

The *Ole Miss* is now enshrined with other airplanes that have made aviation history. It keeps company with Lindbergh's *Spirit of St. Louis,* Wiley Post's *Winnie Mae,* and another plane flown by two brothers—Wilbur and Orville Wright.

The famous team was broken in September of 1971 when Fred Key died at sixty-two.

Neither Al nor Fred ever dwelled on aviation's past. Al's sights, like those of his late brother, are always on tomorrow. In his City Hall office, the elder of the Key brothers voiced definite ideas on aviation's future. At sixty-five, he is balding-gray, but his sharp, light-blue eyes reflect his inner stamina of yesteryear through horn-rimmed glasses. "I'm not a skeptic," he says, "not on aviation. To me, it's just a beginning—and it looks better all the time. When the jet airliners first appeared, people said they weren't practical; too hard to fly; they'd never show a profit. It turned out they're much easier to fly than the old conventional airplanes, much more practical, much more reliable. I feel the same optimism about the coming SST—Supersonic Transport. It's going to be as far ahead of the present jet as the present jet is ahead of the old propeller plane. Even at my age, I am confident I'll live to see the day when a passenger can fly anywhere on this globe in two hours, and I'm looking forward a few more years to see this wonderful progress in air transportation—progress which is so essential to our national security."

Thirty-five years ago the Flying Keys gave their generation

an insight into how safe and reliable the airplane of the future would be. They were saying there were great things ahead for aviation. And although their record remains unbroken, Al Key knows a new generation of air adventurers could outfly their revolutionary feat today. Looking back, he reflects:

"The human being is pretty adaptable. He can adjust to most anything—more so than he realizes. Some people think in those cramped quarters we would have continuous arguments, but we were so busy keeping the *Ole Miss* flying and trying to outsmart the weather, we didn't have time for disagreements. That, I believe, was the key to winning—each had goals and kept working toward them. Our undertaking was most successful. It accomplished its primary purpose to save the airport. It put people on the spot; they realized if this was the aviation center they had to do something about it.

"The men who helped us set our record donated their time and services. All were dedicated to our objective and were just as proud of the accomplishment as we. And we did it for a lot of reasons, I suppose; not only to save the airport, but for aviation, for friendship, to prove it could be done. But as A. D. Hunter says, we did it mainly for the love of it!"

15

The Man on Devils Tower

IN Norwalk, California, a wiry, fifty-eight-year-old engineer leaves his wife and children each morning and goes to work for a high-rise construction firm. Except for a slight graying at his temples and a few wrinkles around his blue eyes, he appears much as he did on October 1, 1941, when he parachuted onto the top of a famous windswept pinnacle of rock in Wyoming.

A solitary volcanic plug that rises sharp and vivid above the flatlands of northeastern Wyoming, Devils Tower is the most isolated of America's national monuments. The Belle Fourche River meanders near its base and to the east stretch the Dakota Badlands and the Black Hills. A cataclysmic underground upheaval millions of years ago pushed this lone, freakish rock pillar 1280 feet from the river bed and into the brilliant western sky. The early Indians called it "The Bad God's Tower," and with modification it became *Devils Tower*.

By 1941 men had reached the one-and-a-half acre summit only three times. In 1893 a local rancher climbed it by building a crude ladder over many months. The first alpine-type ascent was made in 1937, and two years later a second mountaineering climb was successful. The near-vertical sides of the imposing monolith challenged the best of mountaineers and only a skilled climber could cling to its perpendicular surface. The technique demanded precarious toe and finger holds and complicated body braces. Shoulders and elbows had to be forced into every available crevice. There is an abundance of crevices on the mass of vertical, polygonal columns, but they all run the wrong direction—and that's what made climbs slow and dangerous.

George Hopkins is the only man who reached the top by a different method. On a crisp clear morning the twenty-nine-year-old, 115-pound daredevil tumbled from a light plane and aimed himself at the summit. It was a publicity stunt with a thousand-to-one chance of success, but Hopkins was accustomed to taking chances, and winning.

The parachutist was no beginner at hitting the silk. He held the U.S. records for total jumps: 2347; for jumping from the greatest height, 26,400 feet; and the world's record for the longest delayed jump, 20,800 feet. And Hopkins had started early in the game. He tells it this way:

> When I was a kid in Oregon, two barnstormers kept their planes in a hayfield near our house. I was there every minute I could get away from home and on summer nights I slept under the wings. The pilots let me help around the planes, clean them and polish the struts with cedar oil. I never asked for anything in return; I was too happy just to be working on the machines. Perhaps one day they'd offer me a ride.
>
> The men were impressed with my interest. I told them I wanted to be a pilot and a parachute jumper some day and they talked with me about the chances. They were joking of course and I must have missed the knowing grins that surely passed between them.
>
> For almost two summers I worked with them and each thought the other was giving me an occasional short hop as payment. It

was this misunderstanding that brought about my first flight *and* my first parachute jump—on the same occasion.

In 1924 they bought a "new" plane, a war surplus Jenny. I thought it was a beauty and finally worked up the courage to ask for a ride in it.

The boss asked, "What's so special about the JN-4, kid?" I stammered, "Nothing, it's just that I've never been up." He looked at me and frowned, and began asking questions. That's when he discovered each one thought the other was paying me in rides. He turned to me. "All right, George . . . you want to be a parachute jumper? I'll take you up this afternoon and throw you out!" He walked away chuckling. I didn't see anything funny about it; I swallowed it all.

I went home to lunch so keyed up with what was in store I couldn't eat. I didn't tell my parents. Early in the afternoon I got the parachute from the storage shack and put it on. It was one of the first free-fall-type chutes, manually operated. An old Smith back pack made about 1919. I got into the front seat and the boss grinned when he saw me wearing the old parachute. We took off and he treated me to some loops and a spin. I loved the air from the very beginning and wasn't at all frightened when the earth and sky went crazy, or of what I knew was supposed to happen. I only knew if I backed out now I'd never get another ride.

The boss leveled off and looked over the side and down, then he leaned forward, tapped me on the shoulder and pointed to the ground. *This was it—time to jump!* He looked down again and fixed his attention on the ground. I unfastened my seat belt and stood up in the cockpit. He tapped me again—more insistently this time—and again pointed down. Then he turned his head and peered straight over the side. He told me later that when he saw me rise in the cockpit he thought I was kneeling on the front seat (I was twelve and small for my age) to get a better look where he was pointing.

With his attention on the scenery below, I grasped the center section strut and swung out onto the left wing, into the propeller blast. He looked up and saw me there. I'll never forget the expression on his face—even behind his goggles. My sudden appearance on the wing took him completely by surprise. For a split-second he gaped—then lunged for me. I thought he was going to push me off and, determined to prove I had nerve enough to jump of my own accord, I let go. His clutching fingers brushed me as I swept past and down. Everything tumbled. I heard the plane's engine droning on above me and caught a few blurred glimpses of its oil-streaked belly.

I'd heard them talk about counting to ten before pulling the ripcord, but I forgot about it in my total amazement that there was no sensation of falling. Then I yanked the metal ring. The chute opened, snapped me suddenly upright, and everything came into place again. Except for the wind through the shroud lines and the fading drone of the Jenny overhead, it was quiet.

I landed in a remote area. When the boss finally reached me I learned that neither he nor his partner were ever really serious about me jumping. He explained that when he had prodded me and pointed down, it was to draw my attention to a burning barn directly below us.

The word got around about my jump and people didn't believe it, so I did it again—and again. Here was the realization of an ambition I'd had since I was five, and none of the crazy stunts I'd done earlier could match this kind of thrill. I started wing-walking and parachuting to pay for my flying lessons.

My parents were concerned, but they realized how much it meant to me. They thought, at worst, I'd get a good scare and the whole idea of barnstorming would become a passing fancy. But it didn't. I continued to work with airshows, took the hazards in stride and enjoyed the near-brushes with death.

In the early thirties the "bat wing" jump became popular in airshow circles and Hopkins made dozens until, in 1936, Hollywood beckoned with steady employment and better pay. He crashed planes, jumped, and flew acrobatics through *Ceiling Zero, Here Comes the Navy, Parachute Jumper, Hell Divers,* and *Murder in the Clouds.* "The studio I worked for sublet us out to other studios for stunt work," Hopkins recalls, "and the film not used in the picture was canned for stock shots. Motion picture pilots were under contract, so our studio had to make money on us one way or another. They managed to come up with some wild ideas for sensational crash scenes."

Nineteen months before Claire Chennault organized the American volunteer group—the Flying Tigers—Hopkins was in China instructing pilots for Chiang Kai-shek's air corps and training his airborne soldiers in combat jumping. Then, in 1939, he became involved in the European war. At that time an American who joined a foreign army automatically lost his citizenship, but the R.A.F. arranged for him to become a civilian instructor with an officer's rating. When he flew with the R.A.F. in jump instruction, he was an officer on active duty; if enemy aircraft were encountered, he was a civilian instructor.

In 1940 every available seaplane and ship was called to evacuate the trapped armies at Dunkerque. Hopkins was there, shuttling a four-engine Sunderland flying boat across the Channel to airlift French and British troops from the beleaguered beaches.

George returned to the States and resumed parachuting for airshows. At that time the world's record for the number of consecutive jumps in one day was thirty; it was held by Herbert Stark. Hopkins got the urge to break it and selected the Black Hills of South Dakota as the most advantageous site. He liked the altitude and atmospheric conditions there. In Rapid City he met enterprising Earl Brockelsby who was to become his lifelong friend. Brockelsby's early interest in reptiles led to his establishment of the Black Hills Reptile Gardens five years earlier. Brockelsby recalls how the episode of Devils Tower began.

At the time of George's jump Brockelsby was twenty-five.

in the fall of 1941 George was in Rapid City making plans to set a new parachuting record. One day in mid-September Robert Dean, who owned radio station KOTA in Rapid City, Boyd Leedom, George, and Brockelsby had lunch together. They speculated on various publicity stunts that would attract attention to George's forthcoming record try. Brockelsby can't remember that any one of them had the exact idea for George to jump onto the Tower, although when the thought began to materialize it became as much George's idea as anyone's. He did much of the planning.

They knew that to hold the record attempt at Rapid City airport they would need a large organization to handle the crowds and ticket sales, so Brockelsby approached the Junior Chamber of Commerce. They decided to back the show, with their share of the profits to go toward new hospital construction for Rapid City. Leedom had considerable misgivings about their financial security to back George on the Tower jump. He felt it would be too dangerous. But Robert Dean and Brockelsby let their enthusiasm carry them on.

George and Brockelsby selected what they believed would be the necessary equipment for his descent from the Tower. This was a Ford axle sharpened at one end, a sledge hammer, a hundred feet of rope, and an ordinary single-reel hayloft pulley. Another thousand feet of rope would be used for the actual descent. All of this would be air-dropped after he landed. The plan called for George to drive the axle into the rocks, attach one end of the hundred-foot rope to it and connect the other end to the pulley. Then he would put the end of the thousand-foot rope through the pulley, tie it around his waist, and, by paying out the other side of the rope loop, lower himself over the most vertical sections of the rock. When he reached a point several hundred feet from the ground he would lower himself hand over hand to the base.

Brockelsby can't overemphasize how eagerly George wanted

to make this attempt to drop onto Devils Tower. He had looked forward to the thrill he would experience when he touched down on the rock. Brockelsby had considerable fear for his safety but George assured him he could bring the jump off with as little danger as Brockelsby experienced in milking poisonous snakes. As it turned out, Earl's worries about the jump were overemphasized, and his concern about George's descent from the Tower, which all thought would be routine, was underemphasized.

One other detail remained. The pilot. Brockelsby knew a young amateur flier, Joe Quinn, whose regular job was delivering milk in Rapid City. They approached him about dropping Hopkins on the Tower and he readily agreed. Hopkins figured because Quinn was a novice pilot, he would fly Hopkins exactly as he was told and not as he thought he should fly. Several days before the jump Hopkins looked the Tower over carefully, both from the ground and from the air. He ran several tests to make sure of drift factors. The jump meant everything to him; he simply could not afford to fail.

Experienced pilots on sightseeing flights around the Tower avoided the swirling, treacherous winds and blasting updrafts that made an air approach to the summit perilous enough, but a parachutist trying to land on it—! If Hopkins should misjudge, he would be flung against the side of the shaft with little chance of survival. Brockelsby worried more as the time drew near.

The men set Sunday morning, September 28, for the attempt. A dozen of them gathered in a hayfield a few miles from the Tower to watch. This was their base of operations. When the small plane landed, however, it tipped over on its nose and broke the propeller. By the time they got a new one from Rapid City, the wind had grown so strong they decided that, despite George's exceptional skill and willingness, it was too risky for him to jump that day. They called it off reluctantly and drove in silence back to Rapid City.

Another date was set, this time for Wednesday, October 1. Hopkins recalls the jump preparations this way:

> The Rapid City airport is about eighty-five miles east of the Tower. Joe Quinn and I left early in the morning in a 65-horsepower Aeronca Chief and about ninety minutes later landed in the hayfield. The day was clear and sunny with the wind velocity about thirty-five miles an hour on the ground. I'd decided on a morning jump because there was usually less wind then. I knew it was probably stronger at the summit but I didn't have any special worries—other than to hope and pray I was right in my calculations. Although the weather was quite cold at that time of year, I was dressed in a pair of white coveralls to give my 115 pounds lots of freedom for the rope descent. After all, I would be back on the ground by late afternoon—or so I thought.
>
> I used only one chute for the jump, a 1929 Irvin seat pack with a twenty-four-foot canopy made of pongee silk. An emergency chute might tangle with the main chute. If the Irvin fouled when opening, I would be better off working to get the lines of one chute free—than two.
>
> Joe leveled the Aeronca off two thousand feet above the ground. I had him fly the drop pattern once for practice, exactly as I wanted him to fly it when I jumped. It went perfectly and when we came around again I got ready to go. As I watched the top of the Tower move under us, I signaled Quinn and he throttled back and raised the nose slightly to slow the plane. That plot of rubble seemed very small.
>
> I left the plane twelve hundred feet above the top of the shaft and about fifteen hundred feet south of it. I delayed opening the chute for a short fall—probably not more than two hundred feet. It opened normally and I turned the chute to face the oncoming rock.
>
> From my low flights over the monument I knew very well what to expect if I misjudged the air currents and wind velocity. Bluntly, it meant I'd be a dead duck. Although the top covered

little more than an acre, I knew I couldn't use it all for landing. I had to land on a strip of ground about sixty feet wide and eighty feet long because almost in the center of the top a huge rock, six feet wide, was fused into the formation. I had to maneuver my approach so as to touch down on the windward side of this rock. My chute would drag me up against it and stop me. The success of the entire venture depended on this and with a stiff wind to handle, I knew if I overshot I'd be dragged over the edge to sure death.

As the Tower loomed upward I realized I was going to overshoot my landing point, so to check my drift I partially collapsed my chute as my last—and only—resort. This resulted in an even more rapid descent and I landed hard. I put one foot forward to keep from overshooting the raised rock and skinned my ankle. But I landed in almost the exact center of the spot I'd aimed for. The chute was easily collapsed; it was on one side of the big rock and I was tight against the opposite side.

As soon as I bundled the canopy together and weighed it down, I went to the edge and waved to those on the ground to let them know I was safe. Joe Quinn circled and I waved to him as he turned toward the hayfield to pick up the rope and axle.

The Brockelsbys arrived at the base of the Tower a few minutes later and were told George had landed safely on top. Earl grinned and drew a welcome sigh. He remembers: "Ned Perrigoue had just finished taking motion pictures for Pathé News. He assured me the pictures were good and that George was safe. As Bob Dean got into his car for the drive back to Rapid City he cautioned me, 'Be sure to keep him up there until this afternoon, Earl. It'll take me that long to get back to Rapid City. I'll put the news out by wire as soon as I get there.'"

Complications in the form of an agitated park custodian set in almost immediately. Brockelsby tells that he and his wife were the only two at the Tower when Newell Joyner, the head ranger for the monument, came running up to them and demanded to know whether he was responsible for the man who parachuted onto the Tower. Brockelsby admitted he was. Joyner was more than a little unhappy and demanded to know what Earl intended to do about getting the man down. Brockelsby explained the plan but Joyner was unimpressed and remained upset.

Atop the windblown summit, Hopkins braced himself against the stiff gusts and explored his privileged perch.

My first impression was that the top was far more rugged than it appeared from the plane and the base. It was almost totally strewn with rock and the pillarlike formations could be seen even from the top. The only vegetation was a little sage and cactus that grew from between the rock crevices where dust and dirt, carried by the winds over the centuries, had been trapped. The height of the Tower was no greater than I thought it would appear and I didn't have—at that moment—one foreboding thought about escaping; I was too elated about having brought the jump off successfully.

In a half hour Quinn returned and flew low overhead. The sledge, axle, and pulley were dropped all right, but when the bundle of rope landed it bounced into the air a few times and disappeared over the side. I inched over carefully and saw it snagged on a bush growing out of the rocks fifty feet below me. The walls of the shaft on that side were almost perpendicular and it was impossible for me to reach it. Meanwhile Quinn was rapidly moving out of sight toward Rapid City.

By shouts and signals I made the ground party understand the rope was lost. I knew they'd soon drop another coil so I got ready for my descent. On the side we'd selected, at a spot about ten feet from the edge, I pounded the sharpened axle well into the rocky surface. Then I sat down to wait. Although I didn't have a watch I thought it was taking a long time.

Unknown to Hopkins, Earl Brockelsby was having a difficult time. He had two problems: arranging for another rope drop and calming Newell Joyner. He telephoned the Rapid

City airport to tell Quinn to pick up another thousand feet of rope and drop it as quickly as possible. But the airport manager told Brockelsby that Quinn had already landed and left the field. After several frustrating attempts to locate the pilot, Brockelsby put a call through to Clyde Ice. The veteran pilot was surprised—and relieved—to learn Hopkins was safely atop the rock and he readily agreed to do whatever he could to help.

"As the day wore on," Brockelsby said, "Joyner became more upset. He told me my publicity stunt had backfired and forecast dire results for George and myself because of the jump. Meanwhile, Bob Dean released the news of the successful jump to the wire services. In a short time the Associated Press had the story and almost immediately it attracted nationwide attention.

Meanwhile, George sat on the edge of the Tower and wondered what was delaying Joe Quinn. "Finally," he recalls, "about two hours before sundown, an Aeronca glided low overhead and a bundle of rope was thrown out. It was coiled loosely so it would 'splash' when it hit, and not bounce off as the first one had done, but it landed in such a tangled heap there was no chance of untangling it."

With a pencil stub, Hopkins wrote a note on some scraps of paper to tell Earl what had happened. He unraveled some strands from the heavy rope, tied the note to a rock and heaved it over the side. Brockelsby and the ground party were not pleased with the news; clearly, George would have to spend the night on the Tower.

With barely an hour of daylight remaining, Brockelsby knew what had to be done. "Clyde Ice had remained on the scene after he dropped the second soil of rope," Brockelsby relates, "and he volunteered to drop food, a tarpaulin, blankets and cigarettes and a flying suit to keep George warm. Included in the drop was a reassuring note in which I told

George to 'hold on' and not to worry, that everything possible would be done to get him off the next morning."

Ice made the supply drop just before sunset and when he touched down at the hayfield in the semidarkness it was with the news that a blasting wind was driving sleet and freezing rain onto the top of the unprotected Tower. As the ground party watched in the gathering gloom, the storm swept in and the top of the rock shaft disappeared from sight.

George tried to make a bed with the blankets, using large stones to hold the edges down.

The novelty of complete success in the jump hadn't worn off as yet and the realization that I'd have to spend the night up there didn't worry me. I'd proved my point; I did what I said I'd do, and I got comfort from the thought that I'd escaped serious injury in bringing it off. Tomorrow I'd tackle the problem of getting down; right then I was too happy to think about anything else. My ego bolstered my spirits.

The clouds closed in solid below me and cut off my view of the ground. It started to rain, and the howling air currents along the Tower blew the rain *up* on me instead of down. The blankets helped, and despite the wet and cold, I managed to get a little sleep. Due to my youth the discomfort didn't bother me; today I'd be mighty uncomfortable.

The tarpaulin blew away during the night. When the storm came sweeping in, powerful winds threatened to send the blankets over the side as well. Hopkins struggled against the chill blasts and was forced to roll up in a tight ball inside them. He shivered through most of the long night before he finally dozed off toward dawn.

Stiff and chilled to the bone, George arose the next morning to a sea of clouds that covered the valleys and obscured the base of the Tower.

About nine o'clock the next morning the fog layer drifted away and I waved to Earl and the others to let them know I was all right. I'd been thinking about how to get down and halfway decided to use my chute to blow me off. I reasoned that because there was always a strong wind on top of the Tower it would balloon my chute out enough to drag me off. At first it would act like a sail, but as soon as it pulled me clear, my weight would swing under it and the canopy would fill with air above me.

It seemed like such a good idea that I wrote a note and told the ground party what I had in mind. I put it in one of the cardboard food boxes with some rocks and threw it down. By their frantic signaling and gestures I gathered they didn't want me to try it and in taking a second look over the sides and base of the rock I realized there wasn't enough side clearance. Some of the boulders that jutted out were as large as houses. The parachute try would likely have been suicide.

Joyner had become thoroughly upset with the news that George planned to let himself be blown off the Tower and into the vertical air currents. When the head ranger from Yellowstone Park arrived, he absolutely forbade any try by George to descend by means of the rope and pulley as well. "The rope will be cut to ribbons on the rocks," he said flatly, "and I don't want the life of this man on my hands!" A call was put through to Rocky Mountain National Park in Colorado, and Superintendent Canfield made arrangements for park ranger Ernest K. Field, the most experienced mountaineer in the Service, and Warren Gorrell, Jr., a climbing guide, to leave at once with full rescue gear on the 450-mile drive to Devils Tower.

Meanwhile, another twelve hundred feet of rope appeared at the airstrip. "It was tied up in a solid ball like binder twine, to uncoil from the center," Ice says, "and when I dropped it, it bounced and rolled off the west side of the Tower." Ice returned to drop more food, dry blankets, a weatherproof flying suit, and a personal present—a thick, rare steak. With it went a note telling George not to try to descend by rope, and not—definitely *not*—to try being blown off with his parachute. It informed him that he would be brought down by mountain climbers.

The food and water parcels dropped to me hadn't been wrapped for protection against breakage, so the packages that didn't break open and scatter their contents bounced over the sides. The water containers burst on hitting the rocks, so for water I was obliged—like the chipmunks—to drink the rainwater or melted frost where it collected in the rock crevices.

Rodents appeared from everywhere. None of them was troublesome or aggressive, in fact the rats, chipmunks—even the birds—were quite tame. A little startled at first, but highly curious about me. As time wore on they brought their families and friends, none of whom paid any attention to me. I think they regarded me as some sort of oversized creature who's struck it rich and they spent all their time going after my food.

News of the daring parachutist stranded on Devils Tower in the bleak Badlands spread swiftly. At the nearby airstrip light planes appeared with regularity to drop off reporters, feature writers, and radio newsmen. Over a thousand cars were parked at the base of the Tower by late afternoon; hotels and motels in nearby Sundance were crowded with the influx of sightseers.

Brockelsby, watching and waiting helplessly through the second day, was deeply concerned about what would happen if the latest rescue plan failed. He didn't want to take any chances in case the climbers couldn't get him down and especially feared for George's life in case a sudden blizzard should hit eastern Wyoming. After driving to Rapid City he spent the entire evening trying to locate Igor Sikorsky, who built the only helicopters at that time, but he was unsuccessful.

On the Tower the temperature fell, but unlike the previous night there was no rain. George was somewhat more comfortable, although his skinned ankle was becoming infected.

At 3 A.M. Phil Potter, editor of the Rapid City *Journal,* drove Brockelsby to Devils Tower. At daybreak Field and Gorrell joined them. The climbers were cheerful and full of energy despite their all-night drive. They sensed Brockelsby's anxiety because each gave him a friendly pat on the shoulder and told him not to worry. "We'll have your buddy down in no time," they assured him.

Shortly before noon on the third day the climbers, Field and Gorrell, started up, but their progress was slow. As the afternoon wore on, one of the men slipped and fell far enough to be injured, though not seriously. They stopped their ascent at a hundred and fifty feet, assessed the situation, and decided to abandon the climb for the balance of the day. Back on the ground the first thing Gorrell told them was that the job was beyond their experience. "It takes acrobatic technique," he said. "Better call Jack Durrance." Brockelsby got busy and telephoned Dartmouth College in Hanover, New Hampshire, where Durrance was a medical student. The founder and president of the Dartmouth Mountaineering Club, he had climbed Devils Tower two years earlier after figuring out the exact route to the top. Durrance asked to bring his own climbing partner, Merrill McLane. Brockelsby agreed and told him he would pay all expenses. Durrance arranged to meet two other assistants in Cheyenne, Henry Coulter and Chappel Cranmer. Then Brockelsby experienced a surprising twist in events.

In the late afternoon Joyner received a call from the Area Park Supervisor at Omaha. The Omaha *World Herald* had arranged to send the Goodyear blimp *Reliance* to rescue Hopkins with a special pick-up basket. He advised Joyner to keep the parachutist on the Tower until the blimp arrived; the Park Department liked the publicity angle. Until now, there had been nothing but thinly veiled threats that Hopkins and I would be arrested as soon as George was safely down. I'd also been presented with a form I was instructed to sign; it stipulated I was to pay all expenses incurred by the government as a result of the increased traffic caused by George being marooned. As soon as Joyner put down the phone he turned to me and, in a completely different mood, said cheerfully, "Come on, Earl, let's get our shoes shined and our pictures taken; the Park Department is happy. We just want to be sure George stays up there until the blimp arrives!"

I was shocked and surprised by Joyner's complete turnabout. I couldn't stop Durrance and McLane who were already en route and I told Joyner flatly, "We'll just have to hope the blimp reaches here first." The blimp had departed from Chicago but storms and strong headwinds prevented it from reaching the Black Hills. It ended its flight in Omaha.

George was unaware of the frustrating situation on the ground. Air traffic around the Tower increased considerably and many planes buzzed the top. When Field and Gorrell failed to make headway up the side it didn't bother him; he had confidence that somehow, someone would solve the problem. "I spent most of my time joking with the people below and praying," he recalls, "and trying to figure different ways a person might get off that big rock." Empty cardboard food boxes made good message containers. He put notes inside with rocks as weights, but there were a few times when the strong updrafts threw them back at him.

He spent an uneventful third night inside the blankets. "I remember looking forward to the next day," he said, "when I would likely have a lot more company down below. I'd begun to look forward to the mornings and, to be honest, I think it was because I enjoyed the attention. I can truthfully say I wasn't disheartened or worried, nor did I think I wouldn't survive. I was absolutely certain the Lord would not let me accomplish this wish of mine only to have me perish."

From Jackson Hole, Wyoming, Paul Petzoldt, a professional alpinist, experienced in acrobatic climbing, telephoned Joyner and offered to help. Petzoldt, a climbing instructor in Grand Teton National Park, had climbed the Tetons with Durrance and once had attempted Mount Godwin-Austen (K-2) in the Himalayas. That night, he and his wife, Patricia, with mountaineer and park ranger Harold Rapp, left in the teeth of a howling blizzard and deep snow for the five-hundred-mile drive over the Continental Divide and through Togwotee Pass.

Jack Durrance was evidently delayed. He was to have telephoned from Cheyenne but there was no word. Joyner paced impatiently. Then a wire arrived, not from Cheyenne, but from Chicago. The storm had canceled all westbound flights and after a long wait, Durrance and Merrill McLane were now aboard the Burlington Zephyr on the way to Denver. They would fly to Cheyenne and land about 10 A.M. the next morning.

The fifth day dawned—a Sunday. Sightseers continued to swarm around the rock. In the late morning the Petzoldts and Harold Rapp drew up in a snow-covered car after an all-night drive through the blinding snowstorm. Patricia later recalled: "The day was bitter cold and misting. As we neared the Tower we were astonished to see thousands of people gathered near the base."

At noon radio station KLZ in Denver called to report that Durrance, McLane, and Cranmer, who had been flying from Denver to Cheyenne, would be delayed. Cheyenne was weathered in. The climbers had returned and were circling over Denver waiting for the storm to pass so they could land. More delays.

Gorrell and Field, working on the Tower, came down again with bad news. The shaft was icing badly. Petzoldt and Rapp held a quick conference and decided any further delay in rescuing George would be flirting with disaster. A tense situation flared. Press and radio promoters of the blimp rescue were angered. The *Reliance* was en route, they countered, and it was the only safe way to get the parachutist down. If the Tower was icing, the newsmen argued, the climb and descent might well mean the deaths of several men, regardless of their skill. It was finally agreed that all of the climbers would pool their skills to prevent an accident. Petzoldt and Rap joined Field and Gorrell in preparations against the arrival of the Dartmouth men who were expected by late evening.

Ice again dropped George supplies, dry blankets, and the latest news. Protection of the supplies against impact remained a problem. "I made the drops from six to fifteen feet above the Tower top," Ice recalls. "They included sandwiches and canned goods. We packed the food in straw and put the water in cans also packed in straw. But the lids came off on impact and George didn't get much to drink while he was up there.

"A lumber company in Gillette built a little house—like a doghouse—and I dropped it in sections along with some fuel oil and coal. The oil can burst on contact."

Before sunset, Hopkins dropped a note to say he was all right and asked the climbers not to take chances if the conditions weren't safe.

Shortly before midnight, amid howling sirens and screeching brakes, the long-delayed mountaineers arrived at the base of the Tower with police escort. All eight climbers held an immediate conference and agreed to begin the ascent early in the morning.

At 7:30 A.M. on the sixth day of Hopkins' isolation—a Monday—the climbers started up the sheer rock columns. Durrance led the men over his 1938 route on a slow, grueling, and exasperating ascent. The sides were spotted with ice; erratic gusts of wind threatened to pluck them off. Below, crowds of milling spectators watched as they inched upward.

Wings of Adventure

At 3:45 that afternoon, Durrance at last came into George Hopkins' view.

I heard the climbers making their way slowly up the sides but I wasn't able to see them until they were within seventy-five feet of me. Durrance was in the lead and lower, Petzoldt. Durrance smiled and slowly made his way up. He stopped several feet below me, out of my reach, and waited. He visited with me for several minutes and I knew he was looking me over carefully, trying to decide whether I was going to lose my head at the thought of being rescued and do something drastic when he came within reach. When he was satisfied I was completely rational, he came over the top.

That was the greatest moment! I knew for the first time in a week I was really safe.

The others followed one by one until finally the largest assembly of men—nine in all—were gathered on the top of Devils Tower.

Daylight was going fast. While the climbers rested, I told them I was sure I could go down with them as one of their party rather than as a dead weight, if they'd just show me what to do. They were glad of this and demonstrated the rappel, a simple technique of running the line through the crotch and over a shoulder. By carefully adjusting its friction against my body I could walk backwards down the vertical surface, my body out in space at a right angle.

Because of his strength and experience in teaching beginners, Paul Petzoldt was selected to belay me down. He tied a stout rope around me in case of a slip, and we started over the side at 4:35. Progress was slow because he took every precaution. He snubbed the descent rope around a rock or piton, and his own body, then payed it out slowly. We repeated this in short relays all the way down. There was little trouble in the descent and I wasn't worried about the seriousness of it. I still had my strength and was apparently unaffected by the six days of raw exposure.

Dusk came at 6:00 and from the ground Newell Joyner called up to ask Petzoldt about the hazards of continuing the descent in the darkness. Petzoldt told him not to worry and to get some light around the base of the Tower. One of the radio sound trucks had a large floodlight and some smaller spotlights. It pulled in close and directed them on the area just below us. The last two hundred feet were made in darkness and while I had no idea what thoughts were going through Durrance and Petzoldt's minds, their instructions to me remained calm and reassuring. At 8:20 we were all down, to be greeted by a wild ovation from the crowd.

No one was more delighted to see George than Earl Brockelsby. With mingled emotions he stood before the weary, disheveled man and grasped his hands. George grinned and Earl realized the ordeal was over at last.

A week later, George Hopkins made his record-breaking try for consecutive jumps at the Rapid City airport. Through circumstances beyond his control, it soon developed into a heartbreaking failure. George recalls:

I started early in the morning with a large crowd already on hand. Two thousand feet was my jump altitude and instead of using a twenty-eight-foot chute I used a twenty-four-foot seat pack similar to the one for the Tower jump. On my third fall the chute streamed but didn't open. I pulled the ripcord on my reserve chute and as it strung out it tangled with the main chute. I climbed my lines and managed to get them about one-third open. My descent was eighteen to twenty feet per second and the stiff wind gave me a forward speed of around thirty miles an hour. I hit hard. When I got to my feet I was bruised and bloody.

Earl watched as his friend struggled frantically to free the fouled parachute. "The rigger who had been hired to pack his chutes didn't arrive," he explained, "so George would parachute to the ground, literally wad the canopy and lines into the pack, run to the waiting plane, climb in and take off to jump again. One of the chutes he had stuffed too hastily opened as a stringer. His emergency chute opened too late and at such an angle that he landed with terrific impact on the runway apron. Doctor Don Bailey examined George, found him badly bruised, and ordered him to rest for an hour. In the afternoon George started jumping again. He was so weak from the beating he was taking he would hit the ground like a sack of flour and bounce and drag along the airfield because he didn't have enough strength to pull the bottom shroud lines and collapse the chute. George asked Earl to promise that no matter in what condition he appeared later in the day, Brockelsby was to see he was dumped back in the plane after each jump. "He grinned at me through the bruises and scratches," Brockelsby recalls. " 'Don't worry, Earl,' he said. 'Once I'm up there I can always come down again.'

"After George's twelfth jump Doctor Bailey told me: 'He won't survive another; he's too badly bruised and beaten—and he's completely exhausted. Stop him now. You won't have another chance.' We did."

George recalls: "I tried to keep right on going but they moved in and stopped me. It was bitterly disappointing. I tried to get another pilot to fly me after mine refused to go up again. I made some bitter comments, but they were all firm. Some of the anguish went out of my failure when I realized the spectators didn't want me to continue either. They cheered the announcement that I wouldn't jump again—and no one asked for their money back."

While telegrams and phone calls poured in from all over the country, Hopkins made a speedy recovery from his second punishing ordeal in two weeks. There were radio shows and personal appearances. After several appearances the U. S. Army asked Hopkins not to commercialize on the jump but to use it instead as an inducement for young men to join the paratroops.

For the young parachutist, the emphasis placed on his rescue from the Tower puzzled him. "What amazed me," he said, "was that my jump, which proved that a parachute could be manipulated over a tricky peak like Devils Tower in the face of those awful wind currents, wasn't really the big news at all. It was the fact that I couldn't get down that made the headlines."

During World War Two, Hopkins served with the OSS and was involved with the cloak and dagger action that was part of it: sabotage, espionage, and demolition. He experimented with new methods of dropping men and equipment behind enemy lines. After the war he started a small airport but lost it all in a hailstorm. He flew in airshows across the country and eventually took a position flying for the Mexican Federal Police. In October 1958 he flew for the last time—and made his last parachute jump as well.

In contrasting the fine art of parachuting today with that of his own time, he says:

Today's sport of sky-diving is vastly different—and much safer —than the parachute-jumping era in which I grew up. The chutes are better and the students are well trained. When we old-timers jumped, every free-fall was something of an experiment. Today the jump has been perfected to a science and sky divers do with ease things that in my day would have been spectacular. Still, sky-diving lacks some of the thrill, the excitement, the tense uncertainty that was so much a part of the early days. Speaking from a personal standpoint, it's taken much of the fun out of jumping.

And that's the reason I decided to quit; the thrills of the barnstorming days were gone. Too, I knew I'd reached my peak and felt it was better to quit while I was still on top.

In a sense we early daredevils are pretty egotistical. We like to believe—honestly believe—it was through our love of flying, wingwalking, and parachuting that we had a hand in bringing aviation to its present state.

Index

Angel, James Crawford, 54-70, 304
  Auyántepuí and, 58 ff
  death, 68, 69
  marriage, 62
  Nicaraguan revolution and, 62
  payroll pilot, 63
  personality, 54, 56
Angel, Jimmie Jr., 62, 69
Angel, Marie, 54, 62, 65
Angel, Rolan, 62, 69
Angel Falls, 55, 64 f, 69 f
Auyántepuí, 54, 58 f, 59, 63 ff, 67 ff
  See also Devil Mountain
Ayers Rock, 84, 86 ff, 90, 96, 92 f

Bailey, John, 71, 75, 84
Barton, Jim, 305
Bernard, Joe, 269 f
Black, Campbell, 152, 259
Blakely, Fred, 75, 82 f
Blakiston-Houston, Captain, 76, 78
Bleier, Ingelein, 159 ff
Boswell, Opal, 297 ff
Bowen, Jack, 280 f, 284, 286 ff
Bowman, Isaiah, 22, 28
Briggs, Edgar, 241 f, 261

Brockelsby, Earl, 340 ff, 344 ff, 350 f, 355 f
Brown, A.R., 264
Buck, Bob, 94 f

Cardona, Felix, 66 ff
Carlin, Robert E., 58 ff
Carter, W.S., 280 ff, 284, 287
Central Australian Gold Expedition Company, Limited, 75, 77 f, 80, 85, 92
Chennault, Claire, 323, 330, 340
Clarke, Frank, 300 f, 303 ff, 310, 312
Cooke, Ross, 299, 301
Colson, Fred, 76 ff
Colwell, Charles H., 167 f, 167 f, 176
Coote, Errol, 72, 75, 77 ff, 80, 82 ff, 91
  Ayers Rock and, 87 ff
  crash at Aiai Creek, 81
  flight to Alice Springs, 76
  rescued, 90
Cramer, Parker "Shorty," 32, 44, 47
  forced down at sea, 40
  trek to Søndre Strømfjord, 41
Curry, engineer, 63 f

Index

Dahlmann, Hermann, 162
Daniel, old, 156 ff
Dawn Patrol, 307 f
Dawson, Peter, 242 f, 245, 252
Dean, Robert, 341, 344, 346
Delgado, Miguel Angel, 66
Dennison, Lee R., 65
Devil Mountain, 65
  See also Auyántepuí
Devils Tower, 336 ff, 342, 349, 354
Durrance, Jack, 350 ff, 354

Eames, A.M., 267, 272 ff, 279 ff, 287, 290
Egan, John, 167
Eielson, Carl Ben, 3-31
  Antarctic flight, 29
  awards presented to, 28 f
  crashes, 4, 8 f, 12, 30
  death, 30
  first Alaska air mail flown by, 6 f
  forced landings, 15 ff, 26
  injury, 20
  joins Wilkins, 10
  Nenana flight, 5 f
  personality, 4 f, 22, 25
  trek to Barrow, 19 f
Eielson, Ole, 4
Einsiedel, Margot von, 143
England-to-Australia flights
  Douglas-Ross, 240
  Howell-Fraser, 240
  Poulet-Benoist, 240 f
  Smith;Vickers-Vimy, 240 f, 243, 259 f
  Wilkins, 240 f
Etes, Elmer, 45

Fancke, Arnold, 144, 156
Field, Ernest K., 348, 350 ff
Firth, John, 266 f
Foster, Mrs. 4, 6
Frederick IX, 46, 50
Frederick, L.H. (Ky), 36, 39 f

Garlund, Karl, 272, 274 f, 277 ff
George V, 126
Goering, Hermann, 140, 159 f, 160 ff, 195, 199, 211
Golden Quest, 76, 82
Golden Quest II, 82, 86
Gordon, "Chubby," 310
Gorrell, Warren, Jr., 348, 350 ff
Grabe, Herr, 155
Grace, Dick, 293-299, 304-305, 312
Gragg, Robert, 217, 225, 227, 234
Grant, Lewis, 126
Greater Rockford (NX54083), 35 f, 39 f, 51 f, 52 f
Greim, Ritter von, 197, 210 f
Guynemer, Georges, 132 ff

Hassell, Bert, 32-53
  forced down on ice cap, 40
  interview with Knud Rasmussen, 42 f
  military service, 33, 47 f
  professional services, 47 f
  reunion with *Greater Rockford*, 52 f
  Rockford-Stockholm attempts, 36
  shipwrecked, 46
  trek to Søndre Strømfjord, 41
Hassell, Vic, 52 f
Hall, James, 300, 304
Hall, Pat, 82 ff
Harding, surveyor, 73 ff
Hazzard, 221 f
Hell's Angels, 55, 173, 299 f, 304 ff, 309
Heny, Gustavo, 66 f
Hersey, Earl Franklyn, 263, 275 f, 279, 282 ff, 287 ff
Hitler, Adolf, 192, 195, 199 f, 211
Hobbs, William H., 35, 37 ff, 44 f
Hoover, Herbert, 29, 46, 75
Hopkins, George, 336-357
  childhood, 337
  Hollywood stunt work, 339 f

record jumping attempt, 355 f
rescue attempts, 348 ff
Horner, Vic, 265
Howard, George, 215, 235
Hughes, Howard, 299 ff, 303 f, 306
Hughes, William Morris, 239
Humberstone, Frank, 179, 182
Hunter, A.D., 317 f, 320 f, 323, 325, 328 f, 331, 335
Hummell, Hosie, 9
Hutchinson, Palmer, 11 f
Huyliger, Belgian, 111 ff, 115 f

Ice, Clyde, 346, 353

Jacobsen, Ben J., 34 f
Jagger, Jock, 179, 182
Jenkins, John, 72
Johannsen, prospector, 92 f
Johns, Paul, 82, 86, 91, 93 f
 argument with Lassetter, 92
Johnson, Albert, 267-291
 burial, 290 f
 death, 286
 flight toward Alaska, 275 ff
 Hersey wounded by, 285
 King wounded by, 271
 Millin killed by, 279
 provisions, 276, 289
 trapped, 285 ff
 weapons, 289
Jones, Phil, 304 f
Joyner, Newell, 344 ff, 348 f, 350, 354

Keeton, James, 321, 327, 330 f
Kent, Rockwell, 156 f
Key, Algene Earl, 314-335
 war service, 332 ff
Key, Dr. E.B., 327
Key, Fred Maurice, 314-335
 death, 334
 war service, 332 f
Kimball, Melvin, 164 f, 171 f, 176
King, Alfred W., 266, 269 ff

Klier, Chester P., 213-236
 aircrew training, 214 f
 Boulogne raid, 222
 decorations, 214
 fighter tactics described by, 221, 225
 missions:
  first, 215 ff
  fifth, 218 f
  thirteenth, 223 ff
  twenty-sixth, 228 f
  thirty-ninth, 230
  fifty-sixth, 233 f
 postwar activity, 236
 trapped in turret, 233 f
 wounds, 226 f

Lang, Knud, 272 ff
Langen, Frau von, 162
Langhorn, Gordon, 49 f
Lanphier, Major, 11 f
Lascelles, Lt., 127
Lassetter, Lewis Harold Bell, 71-96
 background, 75
 death, 93 ff
 expedition with Harding, 1900, 73 f
 finds reef, 72 f
 letter to wife, 94
 personality, 77 ff, 83 ff, 91 f, 94 ff
 rescued by Harding, 73
 survey flight, 83
Lassetter's Reef, 71
 description, 72, 83 f
 expeditions, 74 f, 95
 value, 74
Lilac Time, 296, 299
Lowenhardt, Erich, 140
Lyon, Ben, 299, 304

Mad Trapper of Rat River, *see* Johnson, Albert
Maitland, Lester J., 215
Mantz, Albert Paul, 309 ff

Index

Marauder (B-26)
  flying characteristics, 213
  record, 213
Massdorp, C.R., 135
May, Sydney W., 282 ff
May, Wilfred Reid "Wop," 262-291
McCrackin, Rob, 56 f, 61, 66
McDowell, Constable, 270 ff, 275
McGarry, Thomas P., 178-190
  Berlin "spoof," 179 ff
  fall, 182 f
  hospitalization, 187 ff
  imprisonment, 187 ff
  in custody, 185 f
  injuries, 183 f
  liberation, 189
  RAF service, 178
McIntosh, John Crowe, 241 f
  death, 259
  personality, 256
  skirmish with Arabs, 251
  war service, 242
McKay Aerial Survey Expedition, 77, 94
McLane, Merrill, 350 ff
Meservey, R.R., 235
Men With Wings, 309 f
Messerschmitt, Willi, 161, 195
Millen, Edgar "Spike," 265-279, 291
Milche, Erhard, 160 f, 199

Nanuck, 29 f
Nissen, Greta, 300, 306
No Foxes Seen, 28

O'Brien, Jack, 127
O'Brien, Patrick Alva, 99-128
  actor, 127
  determination to escape, 99, 103, 111, 120 ff
  escape into Holland, 125
  hardships, 105 ff
  house searched, 119 f
  Huyliger defied by, 117
  joins R.F.C., 99
  jumps from train, 103 f
  marriage, 127
  mystery of death, 128
  missions, 99 f
  prisoner of war, 102 f
  return to England, 126
  shot down, 100 f
  trans-Atlantic flight plans, 127
  wounded, 101
  victories, 99 ff
O'Kane, Robert, 217, 225 ff, 234 ff
Ole Miss, 319, 321 ff, 326, 329 ff
  record attempts:
    first, 319 f
    second, 321 ff
    third, 324 ff
  restored, 334 f

Parer, Raymond, 241-261
  personality, 241, 256
  postwar air pioneering, 259 f
  skirmish with Arabs, 251
"P.D.," 243, 250, 261
  crashes, 243, 253, 255
  departure, 243
  description, 257 f
  forced landings, 244 f, 247, 251, 253 f, 258
Perrigoue, Ned, 344
Petzoldt, Paul, 351 ff
Phelps, William, 65
Pittendrigh, Leslie, 92 f
Popovici, Anthony, 217, 224, 229, 234, 236
Port of Brunswick, 58
Preston, Robert, 235

Quinn, Joe, 342 ff

Raney, Paul, 100, 102
Rapp, Harold, 352 f
Rasmussen, Knud, 42 f, 46
Redfern, Paul, 58
Reed, Ira, 300, 303

Index

"Reichenberg," 201, 210
Reinhard, Oblt., 140
Reitsch, Hanna, 191-212
   decorations, 194 ff
   suicide pilot plan, 197 ff
   test pilot:
      Me-163, 195 f
      Me-328, 199 ff
      V-1, 204 ff
   postwar flying, 211 f
Richthofen, Manfred von, 135 f, 140, 264
Rickenbacker, E.V., 153 f
Riddell, Robert F., 265, 268, 275, 277 ff, 283, 285, 287, 290
Rinaldi, Dick, 310
Rio Caroni, El, 66
Robinson, Earl, 307 f
Rolfe, missionary, 83, 86, 90

Sanders, Homer, 168
Schneeberger, cameraman, 145 ff, 156
Sholto-Douglas, Wing Commander, 152
Siedentopf, "papa," 145 ff
Sittichiulis, Lazarus, 270 ff, 275, 279
Skewes, J.B., 331 f
Skorzeny, Otto, 201, 203 f
Smedley, Don, 179, 182, 186
Smith, Emerson A.L.F., 128
Solbakken, Knut, 51 f
S.O.S. Iceberg, 156 f
Stefansson, Vilhjalmur, 10
Stinson, Eddie, 33 ff
Suchocky, pilot, 145 ff
Sussky, Ira N., 168 f, 169 ff, 172
   Air Force service, 176 f
   decorations, 176
   rescue of Kimball, 171 ff
Sutherland, Ernst, 272, 275
Sutherland, George, 75, 79, 82

Taylor, Philip, 75 f, 78 f, 82, 84 ff, 90, 94

Terry, Michael, 93
Thompson, Wrong Font, 6
Thornton, Charles V. 220, 232
Tomick, Frank, 300, 312
Tucker, Paddy, 84, 86, 90
Turner, Roscoe, 142 ff, 300, 304

Udet, Ernst, 129-162, 195, 306
   at Chicago convention, 154 f
   at Cleveland National Air Races, 152 f, 159
   crashes, 130, 160
   death, 162
   decorated, 130
   divorce, 143
   fight with Guynemer, 132 f
   in Africa, 144 ff
   in Greenland, 156 ff
   Luftwaffe duties, 159 ff
   marriage, 143
   personality, 129 f, 134 ff, 155, 160 f
   postwar flying, 143 f
   war flying, 130 ff
Urquhart, J.A., 272, 281, 288

V-1; *Vergeltungswaffe eins*, 199, 201 ff, 210, 229, 232 f
   description, 232 f
   development, 201 f
   effectiveness, 210, 233
   launch sites, 208
V-2, 235
Verville, Noel, 274 f, 277 ff, 285
Vincent, Don, 217, 227, 235 f
Vincent, Leon, 22 f

Wanamaker, Walter, 141, 154
Ward, W.H., 317, 321
Weems, A.G., 317
Wellman, William, 293 ff, 300, 309
Wilkie, James, 217, 236
Wilkins, Sir George Hubert, 3, 12
   Antarctic flight, 29
   Arctic Expedition, 20 ff

Wilkins, Sir George Hubert (*Cont.*)
  awards, 28 f
  death, 30
  London-to-Australia flight, 10
  selects Eielson, 10
  Shackelton Antarctic Expedition, 11
  trek to Barrow, 19 f

Wilson, Al, 300 ff
Wings, 293 f, 305
Wood, Dick, 5 f
Wright, Howard, 167 f

Zink, Lolo, 136, 140